THE OTHER SIDE

Also by Jennifer Higgie

Non-fiction
The Mirror and the Palette
The Artist's Joke (editor)

Fiction
Bedlam

Children's Fiction
There's Not One

THE OTHER SIDE

A Journey into Women,
Art and the Spirit World

JENNIFER HIGGIE

WEIDENFELD & NICOLSON

First published in Great Britain in 2023 by Weidenfeld & Nicolson
an imprint of The Orion Publishing Group Ltd
Carmelite House, 50 Victoria Embankment
London EC4Y 0DZ

An Hachette UK Company

1 3 5 7 9 10 8 6 4 2

A CIP catalogue record for this book is
available from the British Library.

ISBN (Hardback) 978 1 4746 2332 2
ISBN (Export Trade Paperback) 978 1 4746 2333 9
ISBN (eBook) 978 1 4746 2335 3
ISBN (Audio) 978 1 4746 2336 0

Typeset by Input Data Services Ltd, Somerset

Printed and Bound in Great Britain by Clays Ltd, Elcograf S.p.A.

FSC
www.fsc.org

MIX
Paper from
responsible sources
FSC® C104740

www.weidenfeldandnicolson.co.uk
www.orionbooks.co.uk

To my sister, Suzie Higgie, magic musician

Contents

Prologue

'I thought: I cannot bear this world a moment longer. Then, child, make another.'

Madeline Miller, Circe (2018)

In 1996, I went to a Greek island to write a novel about a nineteenth-century fairy painter. Twenty-five years later, I returned to write about women artists and the spirit world.

In Greece, the idea of magical women is nothing new. For more than twelve centuries, the High Priestess at the Temple of Apollo - also known as the Oracle of Delphi - counselled mortals, and even today, each mention of Athens invokes the goddess of wisdom and war. Recitations of Ancient Greek poetry always begin with an entreaty to the nine female Muses - the source of all inspiration. Their mother, Mnemosyne, is the goddess of memory.

Both periods in my life were times of great transition. In 1996, I was a painter working as a waitress who was becoming a writer; little did I suspect that on my return to London, I would become an editor at a contemporary art magazine, something I had never imagined or planned. Two decades later, I left my job at *frieze* to write full time. Everything felt hopeful and precarious; to make such a leap involves levels of self-confidence I wasn't entirely sure I possessed. But something needed to change. The relentlessness of it all had worn me out: the juggling involved in trying to write alongside a full-time job, the endless daily decisions, the keeping abreast of every twist and turn of the contemporary art world, and

Marble statue of Athena from east pediment of Temple
of Athena Polis, 520 BCE

the constant demand to have an opinion. In the late summer of 2021, I, like everyone else, was rocked by the interminable pandemic, but the enforced solitude made something very clear. I wanted to return to a place of speculation, to open myself up to new ways of inhabiting the world. I wanted to embrace doubt, nurture curiosity, write with no conclusion. The precariousness of it all - financial, emotional, intellectual - scared me. What I longed for was a kind of re-enchantment - something that art is very good at.

In the Aegean, transience is normal. Islands appear and disappear in the heat; the edges of things - land, buildings, thoughts - feel tremulous in the dazzling light. I arrived on Amorgos in late August

2021 bone-tired with insomnia, the pandemic, the sodden grey London skies. But summer in Greece has a way of lifting even the most doom-laden of spirits. For the first time in a long while, waking up was a joy. Each day was mine to do with as I pleased; in my bolder moments I felt that the future would take care of itself. I'd wander barefoot onto the sunny terrace, looking out to sea, drinking coffee to the sound of cicadas and the distant boom of the ferries. Occasionally, I'd paint a watercolour, unconcerned as to whether or not it was good. My friends and I drove across the island, exploring ancient sites and empty coves and climbed the 300 steps to the spectacular Monastery of Hozoviotissa, that was somehow built on a precipice in 1017. In the Aegean, unlike the Pacific, the ocean I grew up with, sea creatures can't kill you. In the midday heat, we swam in water so clear and blue it was like floating in warm air. The immensity of the natural world dwarfed us; all that surrounded us was water and, in the distance, cliffs and a few small rocky beaches. We might have been alone on Earth. I liked to think it was the same view a swimmer might have experienced a thousand years ago; somehow, it was reassuring to be reminded that I was insignificant in the grand scheme of things. In the heat of the afternoon, we retreated into the cool of our rooms to write, where I time-travelled to the worlds of remarkable women for whom being an artist was less a career than a calling; women who found solace in the spiritual realm because the physical one was too hostile to their seemingly limitless talents. The things that I and many of my friends worry about - how to live a creative life and pay the bills - meant little to these artists, even the ones who struggled financially. They knew that our time on this planet is brief, and they responded to it, in the main, with joy and energy. Long dead, they still blaze with life.

STRANGE THINGS
AMONG US

SUMMER EXHIBITION & EVENTS

5 JUNE – 6 AUGUST 2021

Open Tuesday to Sunday: 11.00 – 17.00
collegeofpsychicstudies.co.uk 🐦 📷 📘

THE COLLEGE OF
PSYCHIC STUDIES
EST. LONDON 1884

Drowsing in the heat, I kept thinking about an exhibition that I had visited on a rainy afternoon in July 2021, just as lockdown momentarily lifted in London. Titled 'Strange Things Among Us', it was staged at the College of Psychic Studies, founded in 1884 and housed in a grand Victorian townhouse in South Kensington.

Four floors of rooms were filled with spirit photography, psychic drawings and paintings, Ouija boards, planchettes and more. Faces emerged from the ether; flowers bloomed from chalky ground; minds clicked like cameras. The exhibition was enthralling, not least in the way it cast a new light on a famously censorious era: the nineteenth century. The curator, Vivienne Roberts, showed me around. She explained that by focusing on various preternatural energies - auras, souls, visions, spirits, ghosts - she wanted to explore how 'the strange things among us' have the power not to terrify but 'to evoke awe and wonder in our lives'. In one of the strangest years in recent times, I drank it up.

To trust in art is to trust in mystery. The suggestion that no serious artist would attempt to communicate with, or about, the dead or other realms falls apart with the most perfunctory scrutiny. Across the globe, the spirit world has shaped culture for millennia. In the West, the Bible was the source of most pre-modern art - and it's full of magic, the supernatural and non-human agents. Where would the Renaissance be without its saints, angels and devils, its visions of humans manipulated by powers beyond their comprehension? Or Ancient Greece without its gods and goddesses, who shape-shifted at the drop of a hat? Or, for that matter, the many riches of First Nations art? But then art itself is a form of alchemy - the transformation of one thing (an idea, a material) into another. It is in its nature to be allusive rather than literal, to deal in association, symbol and encryption, to honour intuition and imagination over reason - all of this chimes with much magical practice. It's as unconcerned as a prophet with accuracy.

Physicists tell us that our reading of time is crude, but artists have always known this; they constantly mine the past even as they're imagining possible futures. How can change - be it new machines or new ideas - be visualised if it can't first be imagined? And who would ever assume that imaginations run along straight lines? Most artists are, in some shape or form, time-travellers and ghost-whisperers. They have myriad ways of accessing the dead: via the tangible proof of their thinking - books or paintings or music, say - or through more esoteric means: mediumship, intuition, ritual, dreams, call it what you will. Although numerous nineteenth- and early twentieth-century artists created their pictures via spirit communication, the more I discovered about them, the less I cared about the veracity of their claims about connecting with the dead. The creative act is often mystifying; to pin it down and dissect it is possibly the least interesting - and possibly most futile - thing you can do with it.

I'm fascinated by the ways in which arcane beliefs have influenced the course of art over the past 150 years or so and, in particular, the drawings, paintings and sculptures made by women. For too long, these works were seen either as fascinating curios or sidelined or omitted from Western art history, despite the clear and documented reality of their existence. Even in art, reason, order and ambition were considered to be masculine traits; men were active and intellectual, whereas women were assumed to be passive, fragile and emotional. Many of the explorations and innovations of artists who happened to be women were seen as eccentric - although in the early days of modernism they often drank from the same spiritual well as their male contemporaries, many of whom were lauded. However, it's not only the omission of female artists from art history that is significant: in the nineteenth century, some of them were also vocal about women's rights. It's hard not to see a correlation between their criticism of patriarchal power structures and their absence from the male-shaped canon. Sometimes, the best way to shut someone up is to ignore them.

It's worth reiterating that finding inspiration from the deep past does not mean avoiding the present. The falsehoods we have been told about women's contributions to the artistic life, for one, dissolve in the face of historical fact. Despite being taught for too long that culture was, in the main, shaped by men, there are well-documented accounts of mythic and historic women who exerted their influence across all spheres. But of course, it's only very recently that women's contribution to art (and everything else) has been acknowledged. Gender exclusion, including that of queer, trans or non-binary artists, is just one of numerous omissions. First Nations artists, artists of colour, those who weren't professionally trained or who are differently abled, all were - and in many cases, still are - sidelined or ignored. A true story of art should reflect the fact that humans make art, and that what it means to be human is infinitely variable. What is clear is that at a time when women didn't have the vote and were barred, in the main, from training as professional artists - and had to acquiesce to masculine authority on just about everything - Spiritualism allowed not only a creative and personal freedom but a sense of community free of male control and criticism.

Today, the words 'spiritual' and 'soul' have become kitsch approximations of immateriality that imply a vague yet sincere search for something inexpressible and communicated from a higher plane. But still the question lingers: What *is* a spirit? God's prophetic voice? Someone who has died but refuses to rest? An ancestor? An immaterial energy? A sense? An agent of good or evil? A belief in a god or goddess is an equally complicated business; even the meaning of the word 'god' is open-ended. Is it an energy or a being? Male, female or gender nonconforming? A human in spirit form or something or someone beyond our comprehension? Each artist who has grappled with these questions has come up with a different answer.

It wasn't so long ago that Spiritualism - the belief that the living could communicate with the dead - was a fresh idea, a subject loaded with potential, and it had an immense influence on the trajectory of modern art. And yet, the esoteric impulses of many avant-garde artists from the mid-nineteenth century to the present

- including those expressed by successful male artists, such as Paul Klee, Piet Mondrian and Wassily Kandinsky - were, for decades, all but brushed aside. As the art historian Charlene Spretnak observes: 'One cannot grasp the complexity and depth of modern and contemporary art if the spiritual dimension is ignored, denied, downplayed or dismissed.'

Across millennia, innumerable painters, sculptors and filmmakers have used various forms of enchantment as a springboard to explore the recesses of their minds and the symbolic possibilities of their lived experiences. In recent years, more and more exhibitions have focused on the creative endeavours of mediums, mystics and channellers - many of them women. The originality and power of much of the art created by these artists is astonishing. When watercolours by the little-known nineteenth-century English spirit channeller Georgiana Houghton (1814-1884) were exhibited in London in 2016, critics raved: the *Sunday Times* declared that 'we are learning something crucial here [. . .] about the origins of all art, and the insistent templates for it that survive in the collective unconscious'. In 2018, the Serpentine Gallery in London held the first UK solo exhibition of the Swiss researcher, healer, naturopath and artist Emma Kunz (1892-1963); it included forty or so of her geometric 'energy-field' drawings, which she used to heal patients and which were never shown in her lifetime. In the same year, 'Paintings for the Future' - an exhibition of works by the Swedish visionary artist Hilma af Klint (1862-1944) - opened at the Guggenheim in New York. It attracted more than 600,000 visitors, making it the most popular exhibition in the institution's sixty-year history. The Tate recently acquired more than 5,000 sketches, drawings and paintings by the British Surrealist and occultist Ithell Colquhoun (1906-1988); and London's Drawing Room and the Hayward Gallery Touring staged 'Not Without My Ghosts: The Artist as Medium', an exhibition of artists from the past and present whose work was, or is, inspired by mediumistic methodologies. In

2019, the Whitney Museum in New York held the first retrospective of the German-born American 'desert transcendentalist' Agnes Pelton (1881-1961), whose work was inspired by various strands of mysticism. The critic Ben Davis described it as part of 'a vogue that is currently rewriting how museums approach the history of modern art'. In late 2021, 'Witch Hunt' opened in the Hammer Museum and the Institute of Contemporary Art, Los Angeles: it included sixteen mid-career women from thirteen countries who are pushing back against the patriarchy via explorations of the body, mysticism, new ecologies, myriad forms of protest and symbolism. Around the same time, 'New Time: Art and Feminisms in the 21st Century' - 140 works by seventy-six artists - opened at the Berkeley Art Museum and Pacific Film Archive. Aspara DiQuinzio, the show's co-curator, declared that 'there has never been a more relevant time to think about a new path forward for society than now'. Her exhibition devoted a section to 'Gender Alchemy', which one reviewer described as 'something magical: artists transcending the strict male-female binary through fluid or hybrid imagery'. Across 2021 and 2022, the exhibition 'Supernatural America: The Paranormal in American Art' toured to three museums. Alongside contemporary art, it included 220 objects - from First Nations artefacts to documentation of the Salem Witch Trials, to art made in the name of Afrofuturism - a movement that spans media, sci-fi, fantasy, history and myth to reconnect a Black diaspora with their African ancestry. In the introduction to the enormous catalogue, Katherine Luber, director of the Minneapolis Institute of Art, declared: 'Instead of treating spirit artists or mediums as specimens of outliers, weird or "making it up" 'Supernatural America' takes their accounts seriously and asserts that what they sense is real.' In April 2022, the main exhibition of the 59th Venice Biennale opened; it included 213 artists from fifty-eight countries - and for the first time in its 127-year history, it showcased a majority of female artists. Curated by artistic director Cecilia Alemani, it was titled 'The

Milk of Dreams' after a book of illustrated children's stories by the Surrealist artist Leonora Carrington which describes a world filled with magical energies, where life is shaped through the prism of the imagination. Cecilia explained that four questions shaped her thinking: 'How is the definition of the human changing? What constitutes life, and what differentiates plant and animal, human and non-human? What are our responsibilities towards the planet, other people, and other life forms? And what would life look like without us?' Around the same time that 'The Milk of Dreams' opened, 'Surrealism and Magic: Enchanted Modernity' opened at the Peggy Guggenheim Collection on the Grand Canal in Venice – the first large-scale exhibition to examine Surrealism's interest in magic and the occult. Gražina Subelyte, one of the show's co-curators, writes in the catalogue that: 'During a time of unprecedented global conflict, the Surrealists embraced magic and the occult primarily as metaphors of change, using them as symbolic discourses with which to map their faith in a time of healing after the war.' It could be a description of many artists working today.

It's clear that the spirits are back in favour. There's a groundswell of interest in ways of understanding the world, and our place in it that, at best, honours the complexities of the past as it accommodates natural, even cosmic, rhythms. I, and many of my friends, find solace in the hazy promise of words that thrive on their intermingling: magic, myth, mystery, Spiritualism, spirituality. They're the things - feelings, ideas, instincts - we can't always put our fingers on but often (and often secretly) hunger for when we're confronted by the thought: Is this all there is? Many of us search for something intangible that, we hope, might heal us - of our grief, our fears, our longings, our all too fallible bodies, our materialism. Perhaps what we really crave is to become magical ourselves; transcendent creatures not ground down by bills, work, family; the stress and strains of the physical realm. Yoga and meditation have never been more popular in the West, while magic, meditation and naturopathy have become big business. The *New Yorker* recently reported that almost 'a third of Americans say they have communicated with someone who has died, and they collectively spend more than two billion dollars a year for psychic services on platforms old and new [. . .].' In 2021, Netflix broadcast a serious six-part documentary titled *Surviving Death* which, via case studies, argued persuasively about the possibility of life after death. The director, Ricki Stern, told the *Guardian*: 'I would call myself a sort of non-believer, but someone who was open to it.'

There are currently more than a hundred Spiritualist churches in the United States, more than three hundred in the United Kingdom, and hundreds of others in more than thirty countries around the world. The hashtag 'witch' has over 18 million posts on Instagram and more than 5 billion people have watched #witchtok videos. Feminist witch parties are popular with millennials and astrology and tarot are booming. Aspects of esotericism have also become popular with the LGBTIQ+ community, some of whom have embraced the occult as a space that has long pushed back against binary definitions. Tomás Prower, the author of *Queer Magic: LGBT+ Spirituality and Culture from Around the World*, explains that his book is a response to the fact that in most religious, spiritual and magical traditions non-heteronormative individuals have, at some point, 'been variously recognized for their innate power' – a power emerging from an approach to life that embraces a fluidity to which esoteric beliefs have always been attuned.

It's important, though, to remember that despite the current swell of interest in all things magic, these beliefs are not new – far from it. As Jamie Sutcliffe asks in his introduction to his recent Reader on magic, which is co-published by London's Whitechapel Gallery: 'What would it mean for us to accept the mysterious currents of magical intrigue that animate human cultures with the spirit of speculation as an unceasing continuum? What if we had never really been disenchanted?' It's apt that the origins of the word 'occult' lie in the Latin *occullere*, meaning to conceal or hide: generally speaking, it embodies the search for knowledge - about ourselves, the planet - that has been hidden from us, often in plain sight. And what is art if not a revealing of hidden truths?

Within this renewal of interest in all things magical lies something sincere and grounded in historical fact: the desire to respond to the unknown or the unseen not with terror but with curiosity; to see mystery as a signifier of possibility, as something to thrill at, to explore, to dig into; as a way of thinking that counters the so-called rationalism that has resulted in our sickened planet, our seemingly infinite capacity for cruelty and inequality, and the rampant disrespect humans display towards nature and non-human species.

While artist mediums - whose popularity surged in the nineteenth century - believe that the dead, or spirits, can be contacted, how they express their knowledge has been tremendously varied and culturally specific. Some create abstract or diagrammatic paintings and drawings or compose pictures that, however obliquely, reference both physical and psychic spaces. Some channel spirit guides, while others are receptive to dreams, origin myths, occult knowledge, alchemical symbolism and philosophical systems such as Theosophy - a synthesis of religions, science, colour theory and philosophy co-founded by the enigmatic and controversial Russian émigré Helena Blavatsky in 1875 (more on her later). Other artist mediums are aligned with art movements such as Surrealism that celebrate the unconscious or are inspired by a mêlée of esoteric ideas without identifying with any particular belief system. More and more, I hear artists describe themselves as 'spiritual' but when pressed to explain what they mean, they often struggle for words. Generally speaking, it would seem to indicate a strong feeling - or hope - that there is more to existence than meets the eye.

It's important to remember that art, unlike science, is not reducible to a formula. Perhaps this is why the spirit world (a loose term) and art have co-existed for so long: both summon something from nothing, are preoccupied, to varying degrees, with a hunger for change and a reliance on authorities that - and often, who - cannot be verified. Even the most fluent art critics and experts are guided by their own tastes, prejudices, preconceptions and belief systems.

This book is, in no way, conclusive; rather, it's a collection of reflections and memories exploring this particular historical moment from a personal perspective. It grew from my fascination with the connections between women and spirit worlds in both the art of the past and that of the present, and how they intertwine with healing and nature - literally and symbolically - and what they might be able to teach us about new ways of shaping the future. But it's important to stress that while the artists who interest me are linked by their openness to different realms, the similarity ends there: each has her own story to tell. As do I.

A Season in the Life of a Thought

'To see a World in a Grain of Sand
And a Heaven in a Wild Flower
Hold Infinity in the palm of your hand
And Eternity in an hour'

William Blake, 'Auguries of Innocence' (1863)

Time drifts in the heat. Long-buried memories float to the surface. One, in particular: a painting I made when I was sixteen in the late 1970s: a study in green and yellow I titled *A Season in the Life of a Thought*. I painted it after reading William Blake's poem 'Auguries of Innocence'.

A Season in the Life of a Thought

All those decades ago, I lay on the ground and observed, as closely as I could, a blade of grass. I zoomed right in and infinite patterns, shifts in tone and colour became apparent. Around me, the hot Australian summer pulsated to the sound of cicadas. The blue sky stretched into infinity. The earth was dry; it crackled softly when I walked on it. But Blake - who claimed to see a fairy funeral at the bottom of his garden, angels in the trees and the spirit of the poet John Milton as a star who fell on his foot - was right: there was a world in there. It was remarkable how much was going on in a space smaller than my fingernail. I translated my findings and my feelings into oil paint as faithfully as my limited skills would allow, and my portentously titled painting was born: a mess of smudged greens and browns, flashes of yellows held together by blurred black lines. That the result didn't look much like anything in the so-called real world was, I felt, par for the course: nature - or, indeed, life - was far more mysterious than the sum of its very complicated parts.

I created my painting soon after my high-school art teacher taught us about abstraction. Between 1910 and 1914, we learned, the Russian-French artist Wassily Kandinsky painted seven Compositions, in which he explored how to transform feeling into form. In 1911, *Composition V* came into being, a work that was, for many years, widely credited as the first abstract oil painting in Western art, a claim that - without detracting from the artist's talent - has now been widely debunked. Our teacher declared Kandinsky a genius who had changed the course of art, along with a group of other men including Robert Delaunay, Paul Klee, František Kupka, Kazimir Malevich, Franz Marc and Piet Mondrian, all of whom, to varying degrees, achieved fame in their lifetimes by apparently creating the first non-figurative pictures in the European tradition. In a heartbeat, I was in love: the pictures swirled, pulsated, expressed life as something vivid, explosive, unstable. They were as restless as I was.

Kandinsky's tastes were eclectic. A gifted musician, he had trained as a lawyer and only turned to art at thirty. He practised meditation and visualisation and had a library filled with occult texts. Like so many of his avant-garde friends, he was in thrall to Theosophy. He was also a follower of the artist, educator and founder of Anthroposophy Rudolf Steiner, who claimed to be clairvoyant, and who believed that Kandinsky had mediumistic powers too. Kandinsky held that a new, more spiritual era was coming - and that art, freed of the rusty chains of representation, could herald its arrival in an explosion of colour and form. Questions hovered: What should this new artform look like? How to picture an aura or a soul? How best to visualise modernity's exciting disorientations?

Technological developments and discoveries - X-rays, electricity, the atom - intrigued not only Kandinsky but numerous avant-garde artists because, for the first time, invisible energies could be visualised. Kandinsky came to believe that conventional figuration - objects and people painted as they appear - fell short of conveying the complexities of an interior life, which he felt we all have access to but often struggle to articulate or acknowledge. He felt that art is born in a 'mysterious and secret' way and he wanted painting to aspire to the condition of music, developing his concept of 'synaesthesia', or the translation of sound or music into form. He claimed to see music and hear paintings: 'In music a light blue is like a flute, a darker blue a cello; a still darker a thunderous double bass; and the darkest blue of all - an organ.' In 1911, a concert of Arnold Schoenberg's atonal compositions inspired one of Kandinsky's earliest abstract canvases.

In the same year, Kandinsky published the essay that was to have an enormous impact on the development of modern art: 'Towards the Spiritual in Art'. In it, he posits the idea that in order to express abstract truths, art need not be representational. 'Colour,' he wrote, 'is the keyboard, the eyes are the hammers, the soul is the piano with many strings. The artist is the hand which plays, touching one key or another, to cause vibrations in the soul.' Believing that 'the measure of freedom of each age must be constantly enlarged', he approvingly quotes Madame Blavatsky: 'The earth will be a heaven in the twenty-first century in comparison with what it is now'. His essay is full of questions about the potential of art to express an inner reality, but ultimately, it's a rally cry: 'There is no "must" in art,' he writes, 'because art is free.' He felt that enigma was the lifeblood of art: without it, an image – an idea – is too easily reduced. The act of looking should be one of boundless discovery. 'It is the conviction,' he wrote, 'that nothing mysterious can ever happen in our everyday life that has destroyed the joy of abstract thought.'

Looking at Kandinsky's pictures in reproduction filled me with the same sense of anarchic possibility I felt listening to the post-punk bands so popular among the youthful cognoscenti of Canberra. Kandinsky refused to believe that what we could see was all there was, proposing nothing less than the dissolving of external reality to express a profound truth about the nature of being. Abstraction did not mean absence of meaning: quite the opposite. It meant allowing new meanings in. Along with his fellow travellers, Kandinsky blasted light, colour and movement into the hushed galleries of Europe's museums. He allowed paint to sing an atonal song and forged a new language from myriad old ones. He pushed hard against the conventions that inhibited him. But not all of them – even though many creative women were part of his circle, among the many composers and artists whom Kandinsky cites, none are female.

Although I saw something of myself in the maelstrom of Kandinsky's pictures, as a young woman I was excluded from his world view – not that I took any notice; I was used to muscling myself into the story. But as teenage me tried to believe in what Kandinsky and my teacher called abstraction, the more I pushed

against it: however hard I tried to embrace the transcendent intentions of *Composition V*, objects came crashing in: amid its cyclonic
composition, I saw red-tipped paintbrushes and frothing clouds,
a white horse and smudges of flowers; the profiles of thin men, a
dust storm, a vicious wound, a blue satin hat.

I couldn't imagine looking at something and not seeing something else. If I studied a flower, I recalled the sun; if I gazed at a
wash of blue paint, I saw the sea. Also, in Australia, abstraction
is a complicated concept: at a distance of four decades or so, I'm
astonished that my teacher didn't highlight the spiritual dimensions of First Nations art, created equally by men and women. The
uninitiated describe these hypnotically beautiful paintings as abstract, when in fact they're codified maps of the land and culturally
specific representations of knowledge: ancestral stories embodied
in pigment, form, colour and line – a language that has existed for
for tens of thousands of years.

Gabriele Münter, Kallmünz Bridge, Germany, 1903

As far as I recall, my teacher didn't mention any women artists, either: the assumption lingered that, historically speaking, they didn't exist. We weren't taught that Kandinsky was in a long-term relationship with the German expressionist artist Gabriele Münter (1877-1962) or that Robert Delaunay was married to the Ukrainian-born French artist and designer Sonia Terk (Sonia Delaunay; 1885-1979), and that they were exploring the possibilities of a new kind of art *together*. Why not? Because it was the late 1970s and, despite the number of vociferous feminist art historians battling the canon, in my high school their voices were muted. The idea of art being an inclusive discipline was still a radical concept.

After *Composition V* was rejected for an exhibition staged by the Munich New Association of Artists in 1911, Kandinsky - along with fellow artists August Macke, Franz Marc, Gabriele Münter, Alexej von Jawlensky, Marianne von Werefkin and others - co-founded the avant-garde group Der Blaue Reiter (The Blue Rider) to explore the possibility of expressing, by a variety of means and forms, the inner life of the artist.

The origins of the group's name are vague. A Kandinsky painting from 1903 has the same title but in 1930 Kandinsky asserted that he and Franz Marc had come up with the name because they both loved the colour blue, horses and riders; Marc often employed animals as symbols of rebirth. The group's first exhibition ran from 18 December 1911 to 1 January 1912 in the Moderne Galerie Heinrich Thannhauser in Munich. It comprised forty-three artworks by fourteen artists, including three women: von Werefkin, Münter and Natalia Goncharova (1881-1962). In February 1912, a second exhibition took place at Galerie Goltz, also in Munich: 315 works on paper by more than thirty artists, including Pablo Picasso and Paul Klee. For the next three years, works by Der Blaue Reiter artists toured Germany, Hungary, Norway, Finland and Sweden, creating controversy and interest wherever they went, but the First World War effectively put an end to this: both

Macke and Marc were killed on the battlefields, in 1914 and 1916 respectively.

But despite their originality, these radical European artists were far from the first to make waves with their declarations around art and the ineffable. Decades earlier in England, the artist Georgiana Houghton had created a slew of deliriously complex and beautiful paintings and drawings, many of which contain elements of so-called abstraction. In Sweden, Hilma af Klint was pursuing a line of inquiry not dissimilar to that of Kandinsky – and interestingly, they both had work exhibited in the 1914 Baltic Exhibition in Malmö, although the women's paintings were banished to two small back rooms near a stairwell and an emergency exit. Whereas Kandinsky was bold in his declarations of modernity, for Hilma, art was a method of investigation, a research tool, a salve for a broken world. She kept much of her radical artistic research under wraps (more on this later) and in the exhibition she was represented by her more conventional, figurative work. There's no record of Kandinsky and af Klint ever meeting. What has become clear over the years, though, is that Houghton and af Klint weren't alone. Far from it. Both of them were part of rich artistic communities.

For all Kandinsky's brilliance, the suggestion that a European man 'discovered' abstract art at a precise date is plain silly. Yet, he was happy to perpetuate the untruth, writing to his New York gallerist in 1935 about a now lost 1911 work, baldly stating that: 'Indeed, it's the world's first ever abstract picture, because back then, not one single painter was painting in an abstract style. A "historic" painting, in other words.' When, in 1911, Kandinsky published 'Concerning the Spiritual in Art', it was a good five years after af Klint had begun *The Paintings of the Temple* and decades after other artists, such as Georgiana Houghton, had created their 'spirit drawings'. But it is wrong to think that female creative achievement is isolated or rare. Over space and time, countless women artists have employed various forms of abstraction as a conduit to connect with, or respond to, non-physical realms. How they did this was wildly varied: art evolves in waves, in fits and starts, in bolts from the blue, in singular minds and collectively.

I wonder how I might have reacted all those years ago if my art teacher had shown me the paintings of Georgiana Houghton, Hilma af Klint and Gabriele Münter alongside those of Kandinsky, Mondrian and Klee. Or if she had taught us that while male artists forging new languages also had to battle prejudice, they had a massive advantage: by the simple fact of being men, they were challenging structures from a position that was far more secure and powerful - both legally and culturally - than their female equivalents.

I've written about this before, but I think it's briefly worth repeating: even though there is clear documentation of women working professionally across Europe from the sixteenth century onwards, and First Nations women across the planet have been central to cultural expression for millennia, in the first editions of the most popular art-historical textbooks of the twentieth century, E.H. Gombrich's *Story of Art* (1950) and H.W. Janson's *History of Art* (1962) - the ones I studied in high school - the only women mentioned are those *painted* by men, and even their names are rare. Similarly, in the renowned art historian Kenneth Clark's *The Nude: A Study in Ideal Form* - which was first published in 1956 and covers art from Ancient Greece to the 1930s - not a single female artist is cited. Women have always made art, but their journey to professionalism was, for centuries, hindered in countless ways - they had no political agency, were barred from life-drawing classes and public art schools, rendered unseen by most history books and dependent on men for financial support. Once she had a baby, the pressures a woman faced to stop making art were enormous; it's extraordinary that so many managed to forge artistic careers against such heavy odds. But our ongoing exclusion isn't simply the preserve of the past. In 2019, for example, the art critic Hettie Judah conducted fifty interviews with artist mothers in the UK and reported that:

> . . . the impact of motherhood can be felt as soon as an artist knows she is pregnant. Already, there may be a shift in the behaviour of curators, gallerists and commissioning bodies. One pregnant artist had performances cancelled without consultation. Another experienced tension with a gallerist who did not approve of her decision to start a family. Others report work drying up, and diminishing communication from institutions, galleries and funding bodies.

And this, in a developed country in the twenty-first century. It's hard to imagine how tough it must have been in earlier times. Although the situation has dramatically improved for women, statistics don't lie. In America, the work of female artists constitutes only 13 per cent of the collections of eighteen major art museums put together. In Britain, it's worse: female artists make up only 7 per cent of the art in the collections of top public museums.

If I, and my fellow students, had been exposed to the work of radical women artists and taught basic sociology, instead of the assumption that innovation was the preserve of powerful men, and the vitality of *Composition V* the achievement of a lone genius, I would have discovered that the evolution of any artistic language is complex, organic and unpredictable; part of a meandering, often heated, conversation that spans gender, race, borders, communities, belief systems and centuries and that, even now, hasn't reached a conclusion. I might have understood that the liberation promised by new artistic languages applies to everyone – and that language is malleable. Would Kandinsky have created the work he became famous for without his spirited debates with Münter and other artists around 1910? It's clear he was open to a new, more inclusive art history - one that embraced liminal states. As he wrote in 'Concerning the Spiritual in Art': 'the measure of freedom of each age must be constantly enlarged'.

When you're sixteen, nothing feels logical; you long for new languages to express your place in the world as the old ones seem so inadequate, so irrelevant, so indifferent. At night, my brain projected baffling dreams, and by day, my body was a riot of hormones and inarticulate longings. Although I was hungry to learn, I wasn't sure what shape or direction it should take. Art, music, cinema and animals were my helpmates. Dazzled, I watched Derek Jarman's *The Tempest* at Electric Shadows, our local arthouse cinema. A queer artist who considered film to be a kind of alchemy, Jarman's world view - around the malleability of gender, language and art, be it film, painting or gardening - was joyously, startlingly liberating. *The Tempest* opens with an image of a sleeping woman who glitters, as if her very dreams have the power to dazzle her skin. Miranda is played by Toyah Wilcox, a popstar, among the most magical creatures of all. 'Make thyself like a nymph of the sea!' she is ordered. Could any command be more wondrous?

Despite my longing for a glimpse of somewhere else - a feeling which I hazily understood to indicate something beyond both mortal comprehension and homework - my family's Presbyterianism didn't cut it: the minister was kind, but his teachings felt stolid, even as he invoked the rule of supernatural beings. When I rode my horse into the hills around Canberra and told him about my trials and tribulations, his listening, twitching ears indicated near-mystical powers of empathy; he was a far more sensitive friend than many of the humans I knew.

Teenage me on my horse, Jason

I volunteered at Amnesty International and went on marches about the environment and witnessed the cruelty of our species – to each other, to the land, to non-humans – on a daily basis. Even at our local shops, the genial butcher horrified me; his walls were painted with images of happy animals, although he daily traded in their carcasses.

I gave up eating meat and remained alert, suspicious of the old orthodoxies, open to new energies. Terrible things happened. One friend died in a car accident, another of a drug overdose. A few years later, I lost two friends to suicide. Like so many people in mourning, I could not – cannot – wrap my head around the idea of their non-existence.

I look at my painting *A Season in the Life of a Thought* and now see it for what it is: as an oblique map of my teenage mind, a mess of suggestion, smudged lines and half-baked ideas struggling to-wards a conclusion it could never reach. But I have held onto it: battered and slightly faded, it's on my sister's wall at her home in a small country town in Australia. It's something of a talisman: the first picture I ever made that meant something real to me; an image that embodied the struggle of trying to express something about a world that seemed inexplicable.

Enter the Fairies

'Still there are seeds to be gathered, and room in the bag of stars.'
Ursula K. Le Guin, *The Carrier Bag Theory of Fiction* (1986)

After high school, I was accepted into the painting department at the Canberra School of Art. For the first time in my life, I felt that I had found my people.

One summer, three friends and I spent weeks searching for a house to rent. We were young and broke, and the possibilities were gloomy and rundown. We were despairing when, out of the blue, one of us heard that a professor was going on sabbatical and looking for someone to house-sit. On a sunny Saturday morning, we arrived for our interview. The professor's 1920s home had white floorboards covered in Afghan carpets and French windows that opened onto a garden full of native wildflowers; there were desert paintings on the walls and spacious bedrooms and a kitchen that gleamed with polished tiles. Weirdly, it was quite cheap, as the professor needed whoever moved in to be caretakers of his worldly goods. We offered ourselves up immediately. The professor professed himself equally delighted with us but just before we shook on it, he paused. 'I feel you should know something,' he said. We looked at him expectantly.

'My home,' he stated, 'is haunted.'

It stunned us into silence. He was a man of wealth and authority, a professor, no less. We were taught to trust people like him. He went on: 'The architect who designed this house died in the end room in the 1920s. He was obviously of a mischievous bent. Nothing malicious, but he likes playing tricks.' He laughed. The sunlight danced across the floor. The cockatoos screeched in the garden. As one, we reassured him it didn't matter; we were fine with ghosts. He handed over the keys and we moved in.

At first, we dismissed the professor's warnings as the words of an eccentric. But strange things started happening. Heavy footsteps in an empty corridor in the middle of the day; bedsprings squeaking for no apparent reason; and, most disturbingly, a bulky bookshelf that moved across a room overnight – a room in which two friends were asleep. (Their rage in the morning that we had somehow played a trick on them negated any possibility that they were faking it.) I was spending a lot of time drawing in nature and felt a heightened relationship to the rhythms and energies of the bush, but after a while everything felt amplified, not just nature: there was an energy in that house. Looking back, it's hard to know how precisely it affected me, but the pictures I painted at the time certainly flirt with other dimensions: spectral horses flying through vague landscapes; sleeping dogs floating above their beds; a self-portrait hovering above trees; a woman drowning in a bath, which I titled *Angst*. The professor's words may have unconsciously influenced me, but the spooky occurrences were too frequent, too tangible, too inexplicable to dismiss. Handing back the keys on the professor's return was something of a relief, but by then, I was attuned to the possibility of other realms.

Over the years, across decades and continents, frequent unexpected happenings have reinforced my belief that time and space are more complex than we assume. In my early twenties, I lived with my family in Rome, and apparently rational friends of my parents who lived in an ancient apartment which backed onto the library of a Catholic seminary were baffled by a series of unexplained happenings. My younger brother Andrew was babysitting for them and was startled to discover that during the course of the evening postcards had fallen off the fridge, glasses were rearranged, and cups and plates had been moved to the floor. When the parents returned, they lightly asked him if the kitchen had behaved. What he remembers, though, isn't fear; rather, he was curious. The seminary caught wind of what was happening and ordered an exorcism, which took place behind closed doors; overnight, their home returned to normal. At the time, I was friends with a group of young men who were training to become priests and they, of course, took it in their stride. In Sydney, Andrew saw the ghost of a woman in nineteenth-century dress at the end of his bed and in Belgrade, he glimpsed a soldier from the Second World War in an attic. At art school, I became close friends with a fellow student I didn't know because of a dream I had that contained knowledge about him I had no access to. When one of my nieces was three, she had an invisible friend called Topia, who, she informed us, was a gardener. She was too young to know the horticultural connection between 'topiary' and her friend's name, but she spoke quietly with her for years. During a winter break, I lived by a lake in a caravan and witnessed two friends saved by a sense of dread; they refused to enter their caravan and moments later, it was flattened by a collapsed wall. Another friend, fully awake, felt the breath of her dead father sleeping beside her.

Perhaps they heard the shift in earth, and felt the wind come up. Perhaps my brother was dreaming, even though he insists he was wide awake. Perhaps I had overheard something about my friend-to-be. Perhaps my housemates moved the bookshelf in their sleep. Perhaps the ghosts were simply tricks of the mind and eye. Perhaps. But there are so many stories. I have yet to meet someone who hasn't been baffled by a coincidence, a premonition, a dream.

Acknowledging that there are ways of living that are not always constrained by reason is not necessarily a call to be apolitical or divorced from the very real problems the planet is facing - rather, it's about embracing fresh, more nuanced ways of governing that are sensitive to difference; about seeing alternatives to tired or outdated structures and of finding other ways to reconnect with and heal ourselves and the environment. Positive change demands imaginative solutions. Listening to your unconscious can reveal something unprecedented, both about yourself and where you live. At best, magical thinking is fluid; it can expand the ways we perceive our bodies, our societies, nature; it's about possibility - about looking forward. About making new images from the old ones.

Which is exactly what happened in the nineteenth century.

Much like the present moment, the nineteenth century was a time of rapid social and technological change and political turmoil. In England, the first railroads began crossing the country in 1830, which opened the floodgates to individual mobility and mass industrialisation. The revolutions of 1848 that swept across Europe challenged absolute monarchies and capitalism; protesters demanded everything from freedom of the press to women's suffrage, workers' rights and political reform. In 1859, the publication of Charles Darwin's *On the Origin of Species* questioned long-held beliefs in divine creation; the discovery of electromagnetic waves in 1886, the invention of the X-ray in 1895 - what was invisible could now be seen - and radioactivity in 1896 proved that the physical world was as mutable as alchemists had always believed. A flurry of artistic movements came into being, testing the limits of art's perceptual relationship to the spiritual and physical realms. Romanticism - full of moody lakes and brooding mountains, with men gazing into infinity and women embodying everything from virtue to sin - valorised subjectivity over eighteenth-century rationalism and paved the way for Surrealism, with its embracing of unreason and journeys into the recesses of the mind. In Paris's *belle époque*, Symbolism offered an escape from the hardships of every-day life via waking dreams and mysticism. Inspired by movements such as Rosicrucianism – the seventeenth-century Brotherhood of the Rosy Cross – a dizzying amount of Spiritualist groups gained a foothold in the imaginations of artists and writers. Two of them in particular were to have an impact on modern art: Theosophy, and London's Hermetic Order of the Golden Dawn, a late nineteenth-century secret, ceremonial magic order devoted to the study of the occult, metaphysics and the paranormal.

In the mid-1990s, I was granted a fellowship from my art school in Melbourne to travel to London to paint. A few months after I arrived, I visited the Royal Academy to see an exhibition of work by the so-called Young British Artists – Damien Hirst, Sarah Lucas and others. I was in a conundrum: I felt I had to return to Australia, but I wanted to stay in London. I was looking for something but what it was, I couldn't say. I knew it wasn't the work of the Young British Artists; much of it sizzled with life but was too big and brash for my state of mind; it was like being shouted at in a pub. (It reminded me of the Melbourne art movement in the 1980s, which was called 'Roar'. My friend David and I decided to start a counter-movement called 'Whimper'.) I was worrying about the pictures I was making; the money was running out and I had just begun waitressing in a Soho café called Aurora. (The irony of its celestial name in a city where light pollution had made all but the brightest stars disappear didn't escape me.) Feeling rather dejected, on my way out of the Royal Academy my attention was caught by a sign advertising a side exhibition of Victorian fairy painting.

I entered and felt an immediate kinship: sixty-six hallucinatory paintings and drawings from the golden age of fairy painting, which took place between about 1840 and 1870 – something I knew absolutely nothing about. I was entranced by the near-super-natural powers of observation of Richard Dadd, the wild fancies, translucent beings and benign animals who populated John Anster 'Fairy' Fitzgerald's canvases and the thinly veiled orgies – which masqueraded as meetings of fairy courts – of Noel Paton and Robert Huskisson. Out of the thirty-five artists included in the show, only two were women: the pre-Raphaelite painter, illustrator and women's rights campaigner Eleanor Fortescue-Brickdale, and the Italian-British artist, writer, illustrator and folklorist Estella Canziani. The strange worlds these artists evoked, so teeming with life, chimed with my sense of dislocation. In one fell swoop my inarticulate longing for something that might elevate a waitress's daily grind was assuaged.

Whereas the words 'fairy painting' now imply something saccharine, in the nineteenth century it was a serious business – a convenient loophole in the skewed logic of Victorian censoriousness. Unlike contemporary fairies, who have been relegated to the nursery, their Victorian audience was an adult one and painters competed to come up with visions that were ever more extreme. If a painter put wings on an image of a naked girl, then she was no longer human, and so exempt from the rules of propriety that governed representations of the so-called real world – she could fly half-naked, if the painter so desired. Yet despite the wild scenarios, these artists weren't plucking their visions from the air. The many motivations for wanting to believe in other realms have, over the centuries, been manifold. British culture, like all cultures, is rich with occult references. Many of the esoteric beliefs that were to become so popular in the nineteenth and twentieth centuries grew from myths, which, as the embodiment of the cumulative experience of generations of country-dwellers, changed with each telling. Shakespeare, in particular, made use of folklore, especially in *A Midsummer Night's Dream* and *The Tempest*, plays which understood that life is fleeting, dreams can guide us and the physical realm is often illusory. Fairies were slippery signifiers: stars of the stage, symbolic remnants of a displaced people, fallen angels, heathen dead, the embodiment of a pure soul or the unconscious made flesh.

Shakespeare was just one of the many sources of inspiration for Victorian painters: the fourteenth-century poet and author Geoffrey Chaucer, whose 'elf-queene' features in *The Canterbury Tales*, and William Blake, along with Celtic myths and folk tales, were often referenced. Charles Dickens argued with George Cruickshank - who, in 1823, was the first British illustrator of the *Tales of the Brothers Grimm* - about the latter's tendency to use fairy tales as a way of lecturing on the evils of drink. Dickens believed that fairy tales instilled in children 'forbearance, courtesy, consideration for poor and aged, kind treatment of animals, love of nature, abhorrence of tyranny and brute force', and that 'in a utilitarian age, of all other times, it is a matter of grave importance that fairy tales should be respected . . . A nation without fancy, without some great romance, never did, never can, never will hold a place under the sun.'

Two decades later, Hans Christian Andersen's *Fairy Tales* arrived in England and became a bestseller, translated from the Danish by the poet and activist Mary Howitt, whose husband, the writer William, and daughter, the author and artist Anna Mary (more on her later), were Spiritualists (Mary later converted to Catholicism); the first séance they attended was at the home of the logician and mathematician Augustus de Morgan. In 1862, 'Goblin Market', Christina Rossetti's best-known poem - a sinister story of two young sisters lured by goblins into eating forbidden fruit and so losing their innocence - was published, and in 1863, Charles Kingsley's book *The Water Babies: A Fairy Tale for a Land Baby* - a tale of a chimney sweep escaping his grim life via drowning and becoming a 'water-baby' in a fairy realm - was a hit. In 1865, Lewis Carroll wrote *Alice in Wonderland* - which he originally titled *Alice in Elfland* - imagining a dreamworld more vivid than reality. This constant shift

- from oral folk tales to literary fairy tales to poems and pictures, from culture to culture, language to language - was symptomatic of a wider restlessness, or perhaps unease, at the speed of cultural change. As the country became industrialised, the old ways were deemed increasingly anachronistic. But still, the fairies persisted. They were, it would seem, adaptable.

That so many Victorian fairy paintings verge on the hallucinogenic wasn't simply a response to folklore, urban malaise or swift social change; many artists were imbibing vast amounts of laudanum, the opiate derivative used by painters (and Queen Victoria, who was believed to have attended a séance at her home on the Isle of Wight), to stimulate their imaginations to even higher levels of invention. I read somewhere that fairy painters guarded their visions so closely that they would cross the road if they saw another painter coming. That said, some artists, such as Richard Dadd, had no need of drugs to induce their revelations: in 1842, on a grand tour of Europe and the Middle East, he became a devotee of Osiris, the Egyptian god of the dead and the afterlife. When he returned to England the following year, Dadd murdered his father at the deity's behest and spent the rest of his life in a lunatic asylum creating extraordinarily detailed paintings of the creatures who populated his dreams.

I became so obsessed with his pictures - their robust delicacy and wild, imaginative flights, their microscopic flourishes - that I decided to stop painting for a while and write a novel about the year in Richard Dadd's life when everything went so tragically wrong.

Richard Dadd painting Contradiction: Oberon and Titania, *c.1875*

Islands in the Mist

'Tell us this story, goddess daughter of Zeus, beginning at whatever point you will.'

Homer, *The Odyssey* (c.725-675 BCE)

It was 1996. I was in London, staying at a friend's house, broke, unemployed and doubting my artistic abilities, immersed in Richard Dadd's 1842 journey from the galleries of Piccadilly to the pyramids of Egypt and insanity. It was tragic and inspiring in equal measure. He was a gifted artist and a kind and charming man, but a terrible madness took possession of him. The father he killed was the best, and perhaps most foolish, of men: he refused to have his son hospitalised as he believed that he alone could help him.

A close friend from art school, Martine, arrived in London from Australia. She wanted an adventure. I resisted, she persisted: 'Where would you go if you could go anywhere?' 'Greece,' I replied in a heartbeat. I was sick of England's cold, grey skies. 'But I can't even afford a trip to Margate.' Mid-conversation - Martine trying to persuade me, me fearful of a destitute future - the phone rang. I had sold a painting. It was the first time in years this had happened. I took it as a sign. I called a friend who is the most widely travelled person I know and asked him where we should go. After a few queries about what we were looking for - somewhere hot, cheap, untouristed, interesting - he recommended the island of Amorgos in the Cyclades.

Martine and me in London, en route to Amorgos, 1996

We had never heard of it, but we trusted him and bought our tickets. After a flight to Athens, a sojourn in the dingy Hotel Dionysus and a nine-hour ferry, we arrived. We stepped off the boat, weighed down with music and paintboxes, books and journals, and blinked in the bright light. The small, whitewashed port was the gateway to a place of astonishing beauty: an island that rises from a sea that swells like a mess of smashed sapphires beneath mountains that look as if Ursula Le Guin dreamed them up. The remnants of ancient civilisations are scattered across the island.

We stayed for three months on a budget of £5 a day in a basic room with a terrace overlooking a large hill scarred with an archaeological excavation. We cooked aubergines and tomatoes and onions in every possible combination and tried to sell home-made postcards. We had never-ending conversations about how to be creative when creativity cannot always pay the bills. All the artists, writers and musicians we knew, ourselves included, worked at jobs bereft of joy, a sacrifice undertaken to guard the sacrosanct mental space that is needed to conjure something from nothing. I waitressed on and off for about fifteen years to support myself; it was tiring but at least it didn't mess with my mind in the way a low-level office job would have.

But in Amorgos, we lived like goddesses. The heat warmed our bones; we unfurled; the very air felt luxurious. We did yoga in the morning and dived again and again into the warm blue sea. Each afternoon, we painted and wrote. In the evening we ate on the terrace, beneath a sky thick with stars, and read Homer's *Odyssey* out loud, a story in which ghosts and spirits, gods and goddesses govern the lives and journeys of mortals - whose skin is a thin membrane that can be refigured at whim. I tried to imagine what Richard Dadd was feeling as he made his way across Europe in the company of a pompous former mayor. In one letter, he wrote to a friend: 'I have lain down at night with my imagination so full of vagaries that I have really and truly doubted of my own sanity.' I looked at his paintings and felt his struggle: how hard it is to translate a word, or a feeling, into an image. Some said that Dadd's madness was brought on by sunstroke, which is curious given that Osiris, to whom he devoted his life, was not only the god of the dead and the afterlife but the son of the sun god Ra. Family betrayal is central to the myth of Osiris: he was murdered by his brother Set and resurrected by his sister Isis.

How to reconcile Dadd's acute sensitivity with the murder of his father? I tried to evoke how his paintings embodied the un-speakable nature of what he did: to the end of his days, he believed that the man he killed was an imposter, and the god who he trusted above all had simply pointed this out to him. His pictures make his state of mind clear. Surfaces are unstable, leaves tremble with energy, the sky blazes with portents; a hazelnut is as sinister as a child is malevolent; a game of chess a prelude to violence. Women's bodies are as capable of flight as a bird. I cannot imagine the cacophony that greeted Dadd each time he visited a garden.

One morning, walking to our first swim of the day, we were astonished to see an island appear on the horizon where, in previous days, we were sure had only been water. A heat haze must have veiled its existence. We suddenly understood something of the idea of transformation in the *Odyssey* and in so many of the Greek myths. In such a place, not even the land is solid. The foundations for modernism's dizzying instabilities were laid millennia ago.

To write about Richard Dadd's tragic journey in such a place was apt. How the shift from the sodden landscapes of London into the scorching heat of southern Europe and the Middle East discombobulated him. The way his Anglicanism was supplanted by a long-dead religion which had held cultural sway for 3,000 years and whose remnants, physical and psychical, were everywhere. (How do religions die? At what point do they move from relevance to fiction and madness?) The way he distrusted the surfaces of the world and saw time as something misleading and man-made. The way he bristled at the confines of his culture: the idea that the imagination should be censored. The way his imagination was more real to him than anything else. I titled my novel *Bedlam* after one of the asylums in which he was incarcerated, and, obviously, his state of mind. (And, to some extent, mine.)

When I reluctantly returned to London, I was determined to stop waitressing. Painting was making me anxious - after my deep immersion in Dadd's work, I could see all too clearly my failings - and so I put it on hold and focused on writing. I tried to get *Bedlam* published but no one wanted it. One publisher described it as 'too French', whatever that meant. (It was eventually released by the Berlin arthouse publisher Sternberg in 2007 and sold about ten copies.) I tentatively started pitching ideas to editors of art magazines. I had no idea how to do it; I had never trained as a writer and had scant faith in my ability, but I reasoned that if I made a fool of myself, it wouldn't matter – I was new to England and anonymity grants its freedoms. Astonishingly, months after I had contacted *frieze* magazine and had almost given up all hope, James Roberts, the reviews editor, rang me out of the blue. After we met, he asked me to write about an exhibition of Andy Warhol's 'skull' or 'vanitas' paintings – self-portraits made the year before he died. Warhol seemed to be asking questions that chimed with my own thinking, such as 'how to imagine the paradox of our own death, the impossibility of visualising our own mortality?'

After penning a few reviews, in 1998 the then-editor of *frieze*, Matthew Slotover, commissioned my first-ever 'think' piece: 'Seeing is Believing: How Photography Killed Fairy Painting'. I wrote about how, in the late nineteenth century, developments in photography demanded that fairies relocate from their niche in the imagination of storytellers, folklorists, dramatists and artists, to science's inhospitable laboratory. It was a move that, as it sanitised, de-sexualised and trivialised a rich mythology, revealed the relationship between the physical and psychic realms to be as layered and co-dependent as the pieces of a Russian Doll.

Much of this is now well-worn territory – there have been countless books published on the subject. However, it began to dawn on me that the focus of most exhibitions, including the one I visited at the Royal Academy, was male creativity. The fascination for so many nineteenth-century female artists in other realms, and in particular Modern Spiritualism, was sorely neglected – and it's only in recent years that it's begun to be addressed. The more I learned, the more astounded I became that despite my immersion in Victorian fairy painting, I had read next to nothing about the women involved. The search began.

Mysterious Knockers

'Rap, rap, rap! Rap, rap, rap! Rap, rap, rap!
Lov'd ones are rapping to-night;
Heaven seems not far away . . .'

Emma Rood Tuttle, 'Spirit Rappings' (c.1880)

Only six years after Richard Dadd set off on his doomed Grand
Tour, Modern Spiritualism was born: a movement that erupted, in
the main, from female energy.

Maggie and Kate Fox, 1852

This is what happened: on 31 March 1848, in Hydesville, New York, two sisters, Maggie and Kate Fox, aged fourteen and eleven, claimed to have communicated with the spirit of a peddler called Mr Splitfoot via a series of knocks. He was, he told them, murdered for $500 and buried in the cellar. Their mother was frightened, the neighbours curious; the girls, for now, stuck to their story. Crowds flocked to their home; newspaper journalists tried to catch them out. The attention became too much: Mrs Fox sent her daughters to live with their elder sister Leah who believed the veracity of the claims - or was a good businesswoman, depending on who you trust - and she launched their careers as mediums. Before too long, Leah, too, identified as a Spiritualist, changing her profession in the city's directory from music teacher to 'mysterious knocker'.

The nineteenth century was a time of constant astonishment. Only four years before the girls heard the rapping, Samuel Morse had transmitted the biblical message 'What hath God wrought!' across a 38-mile wire from Capitol Hill in Washington, D.C., to the Mount Clare rail depot in Baltimore. Minds boggled. If thoughts could be transmitted across time and space, then perhaps spirit communication was possible - especially in a town like Hydesville in western New York, which was built on earth soaked in complex spiritual and ancestral belief systems. The traditional owners of the land - the Seneca, Cayuga, Mohawk, Onondaga, Oneida and Tuscarora tribes - had been displaced by settlers, whose religious fervour blazed so fiercely it became known as 'the burned-over' district. Women's suffrage and abolitionism also had strong local support. The first Women's Rights Convention was held in Seneca Falls on 19-20 July 1848, an event that is honoured in the name of the nearby Women's Rights National Historical Park.

The Fox sisters were the match that started an even greater blaze: in every city across the country séances became all the rage and mediums a dime a dozen. Bells rang, lights flashed, tables tipped and furniture flew; musical instruments burst into life, automatic writing transformed the unconscious into words, trances resulted in ectoplasm pouring from human bodies. Some performances were sexually charged; scantily clad young women emerged from the ether, as did various First Nations spirits. But the Fox sisters hadn't appeared from nowhere: they popularised a movement that had been gaining traction across the United States. Followers of the eighteenth-century German physician and healer, Franz Anton Mesmer, toured the country, preaching that all living things are governed by a magnetic field. A sick patient who was put into a 'mesmerised' state could have their 'magnetic field' manipulated in order to restore their good health. Amateur mesmerists - precursors to hypnotists - roamed the country, attracting paying customers, many of whom claimed to have witnessed other dimensions while they were in a trance. The teachings of another eighteenth-century inventor, the Swedish theologian, philosopher and mystic, Emanuel Swedenborg - who claimed, matter-of-factly, to have talked with angels, 'heavenly beings, the dead and spirits' - also became popular. He believed in an afterlife comprising three heavens, three hells and an intermediate world of spirits, in marriage as a union of equals and that intelligent life forms existed on other planets.

The nineteenth-century American seer Andrew Jackson Davis - known as the 'John the Baptist of Modern Spiritualism' - helped to resurrect the popularity of Mesmer and Swedenborg. Claiming to have communicated with Swedenborg's spirit in a trance in 1847, in the pamphlet *The Principles of Nature, Her Divine Revelations, and a Voice to Mankind*, he stated: 'It is a truth that spirits commune with one another while one is in the body and the other in the higher spheres.' When the Fox sisters said they channelled spirits, Davis felt vindicated, writing in his diary: 'About daylight this morning, a warm breathing passed over my face and I heard a voice, tender and strong, saying "Brother, the good work has begun - behold, a living demonstration is born."'

In spite of the mixed messages and the many crooks and char-latans who exploited gullible audiences, Spiritualism flourished. When, from 1861 to 1865, the American Civil War tore the coun-try apart and 2 per cent of the population lost their lives, many of those left behind were desperate to contact their loved ones. It's estimated that between four and eleven million Americans at some time dabbled in Spiritualism - many of them, sincere, intel-ligent people - such as Mary Todd Lincoln, who cherished a spirit photograph of herself with her dead husband, President Abraham Lincoln, taken by William H. Mumler. In 1861, he had inadvertently discovered what became known as 'spirit photography' when he took a self-portrait that supposedly revealed the presence of his dead cousin.

Spurred on by the feverish pace of technological development, many Spiritualists considered themselves to be rational: after all, if science argued that nothing should be taken for granted, then communing with the other side wasn't beyond the realms of the possible. A wonderful summing up was given by R. Laurence Moore, Professor of American Studies at Cornell University: 'The professional medium appeared in America at about the moment Thoreau heard a locomotive whistle penetrate the wood around Walden Pond.'

In the nineteenth century, debates raged about the possibility of contacting the other side: more than a hundred Spiritualist period-icals came into circulation in the United States and a new book on Spiritualism - covering the gamut from sceptical scientific investi-gations to memoirs extolling the veracities of the spirit world - was published once a week for four decades.

Black Spiritualists also flourished and a number of prominent abolitionists - Harriet Beecher Stowe, William Lloyd Garrison, Joshua R. Giddings, Parker Pillsbury and others - believed in spirit voices; even the Fox sisters had rapped 'spiritualism will work miracles in the cause of reform'. In her posthumous autobiography, the Black preacher and founder of a Shaker community, Rebecca Cox Jackson, described how 'she was under the tuition of invisible spirits', and the novelist Harriet E. Wilson was described in one of Boston's Spiritualist newspapers as 'the eloquent and earnest colored trance medium'. But perhaps the best-known nineteenth-century Black Spiritualist was Sojourner Truth, who had been born into slavery and walked to freedom with her daughter Sophia after conversations with God. She became famous for the rousing speech which she delivered at the 1851 Women's Convention in Akron, Ohio, in which she declared: 'I am a woman's rights. I have as much muscle as any man [. . .] The poor men seem to be all in confusion, and don't know what to do.'

Sojourner Truth devoted her life to the abolition of slavery and capital punishment, arguing for racial equality, women's suffrage, property rights and prison reform. In 2009, she was the first African American woman to be memorialised with a statue in the Capitol building.

The Fox sisters spent decades travelling; thousands flocked to their performances, and they were both mocked and revered. This strange new world engrossed Kate Fox in particular: she performed automatic writing, made drawings at the behest of her spirit guides and materialised ectoplasm. But it was too much: their childhood taken from them, their adulthood became a whirlpool of speculation, adoration and scandal. When Maggie's beloved, the Arctic explorer Elisha Kent Kane – who wanted her to renounce Spiritualism – died at the age of thirty-seven, Maggie converted to Catholicism and took to drink; both sisters became alcoholics. On 21 October 1888, everything came to a head: the newspaper *New York World* published an explosive 1,500-word confession written by Maggie declaring that Spiritualism was a hoax. She opened with the lines: 'I do this because I consider it my duty, a sacred thing, a holy mission, to expose it (Spiritualism). I want to see the day when it is entirely done away with. After I expose it I hope Spiritualism will be given a death blow. I was the first in the field and I have a right to expose it.'

At the New York Academy of Music, in front of a sold-out audience of 4,000 people, including her sister Kate, Maggie - now in her mid-fifties - read from a prepared statement, admitting to the expectant crowd that she and her sister had perpetrated 'the fraud of spiritualism on a too-confiding public'. Three doctors joined her on stage and, examining her stockinged foot, confirmed that the cracking of her big toe resulted in the raps. (But even now, I wonder: how is it possible that the sound of a woman cracking her toes could ricochet around a concert hall and convince a large audience?) She ended her performance by shouting: 'Spiritualism is a fraud from beginning to end!'

A year later, at the home of Henry J. Newton, president of the First Society of Spiritualists of New York, Maggie, by now broke and desperate, recanted her confession. Trembling, she told the intimate gathering that everything she had said over the past year had been 'false in every particular' and her spirit guides had advised her that she must 'refute the foul slanders uttered by me against Spiritualism'. She vowed to go on another lecture tour to put the record straight. But by now, Spiritualists and the public alike had grown tired of her ramblings.

Within a few years, the sisters died poor and drunk - Kate in 1892 and Maggie in 1893 - but their legacy lived on. Decades later, in 1927, Spiritualists erected a stone on the site of the Fox family home. They inscribed it with the words: 'There is no death. There are no dead.'

The Cracked People

'Cries are heard on every hand that women are conspiring, that
women are discontented, that women are idle, that women are
overworked, and that women are out of their sphere. God only
knows what is the sphere of any human being.'

Barbara Leigh Smith Bodichon, *Women and Work* (1857)

Going on the evidence of the nineteenth century, spirits are as captivated by art and women as they are by the bereaved. Time and
again, they used a receptive female as a tool to express themselves,
via pencils, planchettes and paint. Although some Spiritualist
groups banned women, in the main they championed stereotyp-
ically feminine instincts and intuition in ways that conventional
society denied them. For too long, art academies had barred
women, they were forbidden to study naked bodies, own property
or vote. When they were given access to art materials, what they
could look at or represent was tightly controlled. Spiritualism gave
them a community.

While the individual work of each artist is unique, the women
involved in Spiritualism shared the same goal: to use art as a conduit to communicate with, and to learn from, other dimensions
– to give voice to their lives and the lives of others. It's not too
much of a stretch to describe what they were doing, in today's par-
lance, as a form of 'socially engaged' art. And yet, even with their
radicality, to be a medium implies a certain passivity: your body,
your voice, is inhabited by another. Were the artists who created

their astonishing works via spirit guides sublimating their own creativity into that of someone or something else? Was it because she was afraid to put her own name to her wild imaginings that a female artist relinquished authorship? Whatever the answer, and for all its dubious practices, it's undeniable that Spiritualism - aptly, a movement started by two girls - encouraged female visibility and supported universal suffrage. It gave women a voice, allowed them to perform in public, to earn a living and to travel; an unusual state of affairs in the nineteenth century.

The story of Victoria Woodhull is a good example.

An impoverished medium, she arrived in New York City in 1868 at the behest of her spirit guide, the Ancient Greek orator and statesman, Demosthenes. His advice was good. Bold and entrepreneurial, she and her clairvoyant-healer sister Tennessee orchestrated a meeting with Cornelius Vanderbilt - one of the richest men in the United States and a supporter of Spiritualism - and before long, they were assisting him with spirit-guided financial advice. Along the way, they made a fortune on the stock market, established the first female brokerage firm on Wall Street, were the first women to launch a weekly newspaper - *Woodhull & Claflin's Weekly* - and the first to publish a translation of *The Communist Manifesto* in the United States.

Audaciously, given that women didn't have the vote, in 1872, Victoria - an advocate of 'free love' who was known as 'the witch of Washington Avenue' - was nominated by the Equal Rights Party as the first female presidential candidate. Frederick Douglass, a formerly enslaved man and abolitionist leader, was declared vice-president, although he never acknowledged the nomination. 'They cannot roll back the rising tide of reform,' proclaimed Victoria. 'The world moves.' Her radical platform included an overhaul of government institutions, the establishment of a people's referendum, a proposal that monopolies be abolished, workers' rights be protected and an end to capital punishment. She also insisted that 'minorities, as well as majorities, should have representation in government'. Yet, despite a fiery and well-publicised campaign, her name wasn't listed as a candidate: not only was she a woman, but at thirty-four she was a year too young to run for the Presidency - but the fact that she had campaigned at all had great symbolic power.

When Cornelius Vanderbilt died, his family, fearful of scandal by association, offered to pay Victoria and Tennessee - who had most likely had an affair with the millionaire - to leave the country. In 1877, they moved to London, where they opened a progressive school. In her later life, however, Victoria's politics became more conservative. Distressingly, she became a supporter of eugenics, even though her son Byron, who she dearly loved and cared for, was severely disabled.

The mania for Spiritualism spread to the United Kingdom, Australia and South Africa - and was not without its very vocal detractors. In 1853 alone, around thirty plays in London's West End mocked the craze and the *Illustrated London News* called it 'a disease'. It's possible that the savaging of Spiritualism had as much to do with its association with female suffrage and liberal and emancipatory politics as it did with scepticism about the possibility of contacting different realms. In 1863, James Burns - future editor of *The Medium and Daybreak*, a weekly journal 'devoted to the History, Phenomena, Philosophy and Teachings of Spiritualism' - opened The Progressive Library and Spiritual Institution on London's Southampton Row, in order to sell not only Spiritualist publications but those focused on social and political reform. Characters abounded, such as the soprano Georgina Weldon, who achieved fame after escaping the lunatic asylum to which her husband had her committed because of her Spiritualist beliefs. She paid her way by performing in musical soirées and, based on her own mistreatment, became a campaigner for legal reform. Spiritualism continued to be both denounced and embraced across the country - but perhaps its lasting legacy was upon women artists, many of whom were, unsurprisingly, very open to new ways of engaging with fresh forms of creativity that side-stepped male control.

Although it was a time of great social change, very few of the women involved with Spiritualism would live to experience female suffrage and, despite a few broad-minded exceptions, the patriarchal art world was hell-bent on excluding them. The experience of the author, artist and illustrator Anna Mary Howitt is telling. She was born in 1824 into a literary family; between them, her parents Mary and William wrote and translated more than 150 books, and they worked together on their short-lived publication, the liberal and reformist *Howitt's Journal*. Her mother was a poet, translator and writer of children's books, and a fervent believer in women's education, the abolition of slavery and the extension of the vote to the middle and working classes. She raised her daughter to be independent and to speak her mind. After leaving the Quaker Society of Friends in 1847, both Mary and William became interested in Spiritualism; in 1863, William published *The History of the Supernatural in all Ages and Nations, and in all Churches, Christian and Pagan, demonstrating a Universal Faith*.

From an early age, her parents encouraged Anna Mary to work. At fifteen, she illustrated their book *Hymns and Fireside Verses*; denied admission to the Royal Academy because of her gender, she studied at the Henry Sass Art School in London - one of the few places that accepted female students - alongside Dante Gabriel Rossetti, who was to become both a friend and a founding member of the Pre-Raphaelite Brotherhood. He sketched Howitt in about 1853 in a few swift lines: she's standing, leaning forward, her face animated, her hands raised, as if to emphasise a point.

Anna Mary Howitt: sketched by Dante Gabriel Rossetti, 1852

The Brotherhood were a loose association of artists who rejected both modernity and Victorian academicism in favour of Italian art before the sixteenth century, art which they believed had a spiritual integrity lacking in much late nineteenth-century art. Their compositions are shot through with references to nature, mysticism and symbolism and although female artists such as Evelyn de Morgan, Marie Spartali Stillman and Maria Zambaco were associated with the movement, gender stereotypes persisted: the men they picture are heroic or tragic, while the women are otherworldly. Nonetheless, in 1850, Howitt was invited to contribute to the brotherhood's journal *The Germ*. She also wrote for the *Athenaeum* and Charles Dickens's magazine *Household Words*. Her friends included George Eliot, Dickens, the artist, poet and muse Elizabeth Siddal and the painter and illustrator Jane Benham. In 1850, Howitt travelled to Munich with Jane to study art; the unchaperoned women shared a flat, a radical act at the time. In contrast to the patriarchal dominance of the art world - which is spelled out in the name of the Pre-Raphaelite Brotherhood - the friends embraced the idea of a 'sisterhood': a familial, broadly religious term that united art and activism. In 1852, Howitt wrote a story, 'The Sisters in Art', which was published in *The Illustrated Exhibitor and Magazine of Art*. The plot revolves around an artist, Alice Law, her two 'sisters in art', and the support she receives from older women: her 'mothers in art'. Inspired by the circle of friends with whom Howitt had studied in Munich, the narrative expresses a feminist demand for education, independence and respect for female labour; the friends refuse offers of marriage and open an art school for women. Howitt also published articles about her life in Germany, which were later collected, along with her illustrations, in *An Art Student in Munich* (1853). The freedom and joy she experienced with her friends leaps off the page: 'What schemes of life have not been worked out whilst we have been together! as though this, our meeting here, were to be the germ of a beautiful sisterhood in Art, of which we have all dreamed long, and by which association we might be enabled to do noble things.'

On 11 May 1854, *An Art Student in Munich* was well-reviewed in *The New York Times*: 'There is a fascination about this book which does not readily admit of an explanation . . . we read only a few pages and are struck with an indefinable charm.' The unnamed writer quotes a reviewer in the *Athenaeum* magazine who described Howitt's painting *Faust's Margaret Returning from the Fountain* in an exhibition at the Portland Gallery as 'like stepping out of the glare and noise of a country theatre into the soft lustre and dewy freshness of a May morning . . . It is tenderly conceived, full of more heart than women usually show to the sorrows of their own sex and painted by a hand with the firm delicacy of a man's execution.'

Howitt's career was going well. *Faust's Margaret* was sold, possibly to the painter John Rogers Herbert, and other paintings were acquired by important collectors, including the philanthropist Angela Burdett-Coutts. Anna Mary's work had been positively reviewed and she was receiving commissions. Most of her pre-Spiritualist paintings, however, like the work of so many pre-modern women artists, are now lost – but hundreds of her spirit drawings survive.

Howitt was close to Barbara Leigh Smith (later Barbara Bodichon), the radical English educationalist and women's rights activist who was a co-founder, with Emily Davies, of Girton College for Women at Cambridge University, and, with the poet Bessie Parkes, the *English Woman's Journal*, which promoted 'the present industrial employments of women, both manual and intellectual'. Leigh Smith was the author of – among other articles – *A Brief Summary in Plain Language of the Most Important Laws concerning Women*. She was a woman of great character and was moderately renowned as an artist. Her ink drawing, *Ye New Generation* (c.1850), gives a sense of her personality: it depicts four young female artists brandishing their brushes like swords at a glowering bull; one waves her notebook. The model for the heroine of George Eliot's novel *Romola*, Barbara refused to wear corsets, shortened her skirts, and wore blue-tinted spectacles. The daughter of parents who never married, she referred to herself as 'one of the cracked people of the world' who like to 'herd with the cracked such as ... queer Americans, democrats, socialists, artists, poor devils or angels'. She described Howitt as 'cracked' too and together they attended séances. Howitt paid homage to her magnificent friend by portraying her as the warrior queen *Boadicea Brooding Over Her Wrongs* (now lost) – a generous gesture that was to have dire consequences.

Howitt's career as a professional artist was crushed when her painting – which depicted a woman who avenged the violence inflicted upon her and the rape of her daughters – was not only rejected by the Royal Academy but widely criticised. The first blow was a review in the *Athenaeum* of 7 June 1856, which described the painting as 'pretentious and affected', derided the 'wearisome green salad of the background – the mincemeat of raw leaves' and concluded: 'What is this but an angry woman, whose wrongs we only know by the Catalogue?' But worse was to come. Anna Mary asked a family friend and the leading art critic of the day, John Ruskin - who had once declared that 'the woman's intellect is not for invention or creation' - for his thoughts. His reply was harsh: 'What do you know of Boadicea?' he asked. 'Leave such subjects alone and paint me a pheasant's wing.' Howitt was devastated; her mother wrote in her autobiography that Ruskin, 'king among critics, so crushed her sensitive nature as to make her yield to her bias for the supernatural'. Her response was extreme, especially given how robust she had been: travelling, writing and exhibiting. She destroyed much of her work, had a nervous breakdown and, in 1859, married Alaric Alfred Watts, a poet, founder of The Ghost Club, and a leading Spiritualist - and devoted the rest of her life to Spiritualism.

Creating extraordinarily elaborate drawings while in a trance, she shifted the weight of authorship to the other side. Her pictures are wild: the heads of babies and Christ emerging from bouquets of flowers, women morphing into snail shells, intertwining spirals and spheres, angels, flames, crosses, orbs and snakes. The writer William Michael Rossetti (Dante Gabriel's brother), who had admired her earlier work, didn't approve: 'If only the spirits had let her alone, she would have drawn and painted very much better than she ever did under their inspiration.' George Eliot wrote to a friend: 'Have you heard that Anna Mary Howitt has, alas!, become a spirit medium?'

In 1857, Howitt, using the pseudonym 'Comfort', illustrated the popular novelist Camilla Dufour Crosland's memoir *Light in the Valley: My Experiences of Spiritualism*. A letter written by Howitt, outlining her experiences as an artist medium, is also included. In it, she expresses frustration at her 'spiritual drawings' not being understood by sceptical friends but describes her delight in the way that 'ideas of most lovely new truths have gradually unfolded themselves and old truths, breathed upon by spirit, were no longer dry bones but clothed in the blooming freshness of immortal life'.

An example of Howitt's automatic writing leaps out: surrounding a drawing of what might be an anchor are wild scribbles that begin with the words 'you must persevere'. They peter into an incoherent scrawl - like a line of waves in a choppy sea. Six reproductions of Comfort's (Howitt's) 'spirit emblems' are grouped together: a radiant eye floating in the sky, above what appears to be an abstracted bird formed of flames, a snake weaving around its body ('Intellect, no longer a source of discord between Man and Woman'); an oval shape formed of two red halves, like red lungs, vibrating with flowers; a crescent moon in an orb, topped by a coiled snake, on a bed of what appears to be hair ('Woman hidden in Man; Intellect crowning creation'). These images were, most likely, the first spirit drawings to be reproduced. They are premonitions of work by twentieth-century artists such as Hilma af Klint and Surrealists such as Leonora Carrington. Critics weren't impressed: the reviewer for *The Spectator* described the book as blasphemous and the messages which accompany the drawings as a 'jargon of silliness in a delirium'.

Despite her originality, Howitt was far from alone: London was home to numerous mediums who painted or drew during séances and many of them created startlingly original pictures. They included Catherine Berry, who was guided by an Egyptian spirit called Semiramide, exhibited 500 watercolours (now all lost) in Brighton, and could apparently throw sitters to the ground with a wave of her hand; Barbara Honywood, who painted lush, swirling celestial plant-worlds inhabited by dreamy young women and floating eyes; Alice Pery, a direct descendant of King Edward III, who drew swirling crowds of floating heads; and Jane Stewart Smith, who created dense, elaborate pictures of ecstatic crowds celebrating the triumph of good over evil. There were many more. But the woman the spirits seemed particularly keen to communicate with was perhaps the most extraordinary artist of them all: a respectable, middle-aged spinster called Georgiana Houghton who painted *The Spiritual Crown of Annie Mary Howitt Watts, 24 April 1867*. A portrait, of sorts, Anna Mary is depicted as abstracted swirls of colour: a light-filled image of a woman transformed into a cosmic garden.

A Dagger in Her Hair

'Everybody is talking about the Spiritual pictures in Old Bond Street. I went there yesterday, and a more surprising collection of 150 paintings I never saw ... beautiful workmanship, warmness, manual application - and the colouring is a new revelation.'

Unattributed newspaper review of Georgiana Houghton's 'Spirit Drawings' (1871)

Georgiana Houghton, 1882

This is the photograph she chose to represent herself.

It is 1882. She's in her late sixties, but she seems older. Slightly stooped, she wears a black dress, or maybe a coat, as the fabric is thick. Its long collar is heavily embroidered with thread that looks, from this distance, like a plaited horse's mane. Her white, high-collared blouse is a design that is popular today. She has two cameos: one at her throat, the other at her waist, but it's impossible to see their details. Her pale hair is thin, pulled back, flattened down. She gazes into the distance, a faint smile on her lips. She looks like so many elderly Victorian ladies - conventional, stout, uncomfortable in her tight clothes - until a detail leaps out. It's unmistakable: her hair seems to be held back by an elaborate dagger.

I send the photograph via WhatsApp to my friend Judith Clark, who is a costume historian. I ask her what Georgiana's dress represents and if wearing a dagger in your hair was popular in the late nineteenth century. She replies that her dress is 'rather stark, though her jacket appears to resist the extreme corseting that was fashionable at the time - she has nevertheless emphasised her waist (and the inverted triangle) with the unusual styling of two cameos'. She adds that she has never seen a dagger used as a hair decoration before.

The details are sketchy. Born to a middle-class family in 1814 in Las Palmas in the Canary Islands, Georgiana was the seventh of twelve children. Her father was a wine and brandy merchant; her mother had her hands full with her enormous brood. The family moved to London when Georgiana was small, but they lost their money. Not much is known about her childhood, apart from the fact that the family experienced genteel poverty. It's clear, though, that Georgiana suffered great losses: her nine-year-old brother Cecil Angelo died when Georgiana was twelve, her elder brother Warrand when she was twenty-seven, her brother Sidney when she was thirty-one, and her especially beloved younger sister Zilla Rosalia when she was thirty-seven.

I suspect we assume that people in previous centuries - given the higher mortality rates - were more accustomed to death than we are. While that might be true, death is still death. To those left behind, it's unfathomable to grasp non-existence: grief can be inarticulate. If there was even a glimmer of possibility, who wouldn't want to try and reach those we love, to know that they were safe and well?

Georgiana trained as an artist - it's not known where - but for some reason she gave it up when Zilla, who was also an artist, died. Georgiana never married. She lived with her family, then her parents, then her mother, and then alone - although the word 'alone' in her case is not one she would have agreed with.

In 1859, still mourning, at the invitation of her cousin, Mrs Pearson, Georgiana attended a séance held by a neighbour, Mrs Marshall. She was not young and impressionable: she was a middle-class woman of forty-five, but she heard and saw things that day that made her believe in the veracity of supernatural communication. Her experience convinced her that death was not the end; it was more like moving into a different room and talking through a wall.

And so, it began. Spiritualism would consume her until the end of her life.

Georgiana discovered that, with persistence, she could train herself to become a medium. She was a Christian, but Christianity doesn't preach communication beyond death. She brushed this aside. She began by sitting with her mother at twilight, discussing spiritual matters. After three months, on 31 December 1859, the table tipped and messages from the other side began to flow. So did the pictures.

In 1861, Houghton saw the spirit drawings created by, or through, a Mrs Wilkinson. Impressed, she began producing her own, first by attaching coloured pencils to her planchette - French for 'little plank', a wooden device on two-wheeled casters that holds a pencil.

After a while, on the advice of her spirit guides, she drew freehand and then graduated to painting, combining watercolour, gouache and ink. In 1863, she began hosting weekly soirées to showcase her pictures. It was around this time that one of her guests, the American Reverend John Murray Spear, admiringly called her the 'Holy Symbolist'.

She had the gift of sight, perfect vision, in all realms. Spirits appeared before her as clearly as the artists and archangels who guided her hand. Images poured from her. Even now, 150 years later, the energy and inventiveness of her work leaps off the page. In gouache, pen and ink, it's as if her dreams are ensnared by a spider web: primary colours whirl and dance beneath a delicate net of white translucent lines. Her pictures pulsate with life and rhythm: they're at once abstract, representational, full of intense, feverish feeling; exultant, dense, replete with possibility. Colours swirl and eddy; fruit, the faces of Houghton's dead sister Zilla Rosalia and Jesus emerge from the maelstrom only to be submerged, once again. She saw flowers as 'the essence of a person's life and character' and they populate her pictures like phantoms. This is art as the expression of life: one in which death is equally vivid, unconstrained, unique. No one was making anything like this in the London art world of the 1860s. No one is making anything like this today.

Georgiana gave her pictures descriptive titles: *Study of Curves, A Little More Design, Still More Design, Cecil's Fruit, Zilla's Flower*. Some of them are grouped into series of flowers, or the names of friends and family members she contacted via her mediumship; her dead siblings and her first guide Henry Lenny, H.R.H. the late Prince Consort, H.R.H. Victoria, Princess Royal of England, and artists including William Blake, Caravaggio, Correggio, Bartolomé Murillo, Titian and seventy archangels. Via her guides, she explored subjects such as The Trinity, God, Spirit, Peace, Wisdom and the Unveiling of the Heavens. Along with self-portraits, she drew some of her fellow mediums and other living people close to her.

She used colours to represent particular states: Yellow for God the Father, Wisdom and Faith; Chinese Orange for unselfishness and Violet Carmine for religion; Cobalt Blue for truth, Crimson Lake for love, and so on. In 1865, some of her works were accepted by the Royal Academy but they were never displayed. There is no record of why, but it's not difficult to imagine. Her pictures would have been as startling as a spaceship landing among the horse-drawn carriages of Piccadilly.

The year 1869 was a terrible one for Georgiana: her mother, younger brother George and her nephew Charlie - Zilla's son - all died. Charlie eventually became one of her spirit guides. He had drowned and his presence was often heralded with a sensation of damp.

In 1871, Georgiana rented The New British Gallery on 39 Old Bond Street to display 155 of her drawings. Titled 'Spirit Drawings in Water Colours', the catalogue accompanying the exhibition was something of a work of art in itself: its pages were tinted a delicate pink, the colour of 'a type of the Love exemplified in all the teaching'; the cover was brown, 'to exemplify that it was given through an earthen vessel' and it was partly covered in cloth, 'because it was not intended as only an ephemeral production, but one that I trusted might still go on doing a work when the Exhibition had become a thing of the past'. She was not modest about what she - or her spirits - had achieved. She sent bound copies to Queen Victoria, the Crown Prince of Germany and the Emperor Louis Napoleon. She never heard back from them.

The evolution of her exhibition is as mysterious as the work itself. In 1882, two years before she died, Georgiana published her memoir: *Evenings at Home in Spiritual Séance*. It's a gift of a book: it is rare to have such access to the thinking of an artist. She outlines in great detail how the exhibition came about. She is visited by an 'artist friend' - a cryptic Mr L - who, impressed by her pictures, asks her: 'Why do you not exhibit?' Georgiana explains that the main reason is that her use of religious symbolism 'would be out of place in a heterogeneous collection', and that her 'Royal Monograms had not been admitted by the Academy'. But Mr L does not mean the Academy and encourages her to have an exhibition of her own. The thought initially bewildered Georgiana: how could she achieve something like this, in her 'lonely life, a weak woman, with none to help me in an undertaking of such magnitude? The very notion of such a thing seemed an utter incongruity, and I could only point out to him that I should not even have an idea how to take the very first step towards such an attempt, or as to what ought to be the first step.' But Mr L is happy to help with the organisation of the show and when Georgiana appealed to her 'counsellors' as to the wisdom of such an undertaking, she was surprised to hear it was to be. Before the exhibition opened, Georgiana sent out a leaflet outlining her intentions:

> Miss Houghton has taken the above Gallery for the purpose of exhibiting the collection of Drawings in Water Colours that have been executed through her mediumship during the last ten years, to offer to others, as well as to Spiritualists, an opportunity of seeing the representations of some of those flowers that may meet their eyes when they enter upon a future existence, and likewise to give some insight into spiritual symbolism in an artistic point of view. To those who do not understand the subject, it may be needful to explain that in the execution of the Drawings, she has been entirely guided by invisible spirits, who could thus delineate what was beyond the human imagination.

When the exhibition opened to the public, the baffled art critic for *The Era* newspaper declared it: 'The most astonishing exhibition in London at the present moment.' The critic for *The Daily News* wrote that the paintings looked like 'tangled threads of coloured wool' and concluded: 'They deserve to be seen as the most extraordinary

and instructive example of artistic aberration.' One writer felt that
the pictures were 'quite unlike anything that is seen in this world'.
The *News of the World* praised 'the brilliancy and harmony of the
tints' and asserted that 'the idea presents itself to the imagination
of a canvas of Turner's, over which troops of fairies have been
meandering, dropping jewels as they went. Miss Houghton, the
lady executant, is a clever and tasteful artist; and furthermore, a
sincere believer in what she says.' Other critics weren't so kind.
One journalist fumed that: 'We should not have called attention
to this exhibition at all, did we not believe that it will disgust all
sober people with the follies which it is intended to advance and
promote.' But as the sympathetic reviewer for *The Queen* observed:
'The water-colour drawings, numbering one hundred and fifty-
five, are so extraordinary in character, and are so entirely opposed
to one's ideas of art, ancient or modern, that criticism in the ordinary manner becomes difficult, not to say impossible.' Georgiana
explains that the exhibition was most popular among the clergy,
of all denominations, and especially artists, who 'revelled in the
glories of colour, the marvellous manipulation, the delicacies of
delineation'. One of them said to her that 'all artists well know . . .
that the more entirely they yield themselves to intuition, subduing
the self-hood, the more perfect becomes their work'.

Georgiana was trusting enough to believe that an audience
would find her work as fascinating as she did – who wouldn't be
amazed by messages formed in colour and line from the other
side? Despite everything being for sale, at the advice of Mr L she
priced the pictures very high; only two sold and she was almost
bankrupted. Just fifty or so of her watercolours are now known to
exist: most are in the collection of the Victorian Spiritualist Union
in Melbourne, and the College of Psychic Studies in London owns
seven. Yet, Georgiana was not one to be brought down by something as earthly as commercial failure. In her memoir she recalled:
'And about my Gallery! my beloved Exhibition! Heavy as was the

loss, never for one moment have I experienced a shadow of regret for having undertaken it.'

Her faith in herself, and her spirit guides, was vindicated in the twenty-first century. When London's Courtauld Institute of Art staged an exhibition of her work in 2016, it was the first time her pictures had been seen in the United Kingdom since her Bond Street show - and they were astonishing. One critic wrote: 'To look at these works, you'd think they were Freudian experiments, made at the height of European Surrealism, or else acid-addled '60s psychedelia.' Personally speaking, they shifted everything for me. Not only were they wildly, surprisingly fresh, despite being made more than a century ago, but if such radical pictures had been excluded from the art-historical canon, it begged the question: what, and who, else was left out?

Like so many Spiritualists, new technologies transfixed Houghton. In 1859, she had received a message from her archangel guides that 'the time was approaching when they would be able to impress their portraits on the photographic plate'. In 1872 she was introduced to the photographer Frederick Hudson, who took her portrait. The result astonished her. She is pictured with an ethereal woman, draped in white sheets: supposedly a ghost. Georgiana's right hand clings to the left hand of the figure, whose right hand reaches out as if to stroke Houghton's face. On the back of the photo is an inscription:

> My dear sister Zilla, on whose birthday it was taken . . . Around me, is the light binding us to each other. This is the first manifestation of the inner spiritual life. G. Houghton.

In 1882, she published a book: *Chronicles of the Photographs of Spiritual Beings and Phenomena Invisible to the Material Eye.* In the preface, she writes: 'I send them forth in full assurance that they carry a weight of evidence as to the substantiality of spirit being for transcending any other form of mediumship.'

The book was reviewed by no less a figure than Madame Blavatsky, who declared it 'a neat and curious volume' full of 'valuable testimony' from 'some of the most eminent men of science and literature of the day, who all testify to the fact that photographs have been, and are, taken from "Spirit Beings", their more or less shadowy forms appearing on the negative near or about the sitters in visible flesh and blood'. However, you can sense her scepticism: why, she wonders, the repetition of hazy rigid forms in white sheets? And why is there 'such a servile copy of the conventional ghosts in theatricals?'

In her memoir, Houghton, who never questions the veracity of the spirit hand in any aspect of her life, describes photography as full of 'fresh marvels', and explains that her fascination with it is keeping her from her easel. When she poses for Mr Hudson, she is directed by the spirits: the result is something of a human/ghost collaboration. She describes being reunited with her dead nephew Charlie, via the camera lens: 'My face is pressed against the spirit, whose veil falls partly over me, so that I am within it, and we seem locked in mutual embrace. The feeling that comes upon me when I look at it, is as if a loved relative whom I thought was dead, had suddenly appeared before me, upon whose breast I would fain weep out of my joy at so unexpected a return.'

There were so many frauds in the spirit world. Science was required to keep it respectable, and a camera was considered more objective than a pencil. Yet many of the spirit photographs look so staged it's astonishing anyone believed them. But when photography was so new, how were the uninitiated to know how simple it is to create a double exposure?

Even the inventor of the arch-sleuth, Sherlock Holmes, was deceived. A fervent defender of spirit photography, Sir Arthur Conan Doyle, who, in 1893, joined the British Society for Psychical

Research (whose members included the future Prime Minister, Arthur Balfour), mentions Georgiana in his history of Spiritualism. He writes: 'Hudson, who obtained the first spirit photograph in England of which we have objective evidence, is said to have been about sixty years of age. The sitter was Miss Georgiana Houghton, who has fully described the incident.'

Seen from this great distance, Georgiana Houghton's work - freely expressive, vividly original, strange - anticipates some of the radical art movements that were to shine so brightly in the twentieth century, such as Surrealism and Abstract Expressionism. But it's important to remember, as Simon Grant, one of the three curators of her exhibition at the Courtauld Gallery, writes: 'While to our eyes these works possess elements of abstraction (a word that did not exist in the context of art in Houghton's day), to the artist the *Spirit Flowers* and *Spirit Fruits* were representations of real objects growing in spirit regions, with each series becoming visually more complex as her own spirit became "less clogged with earthliness".'

In *Evenings at Home in Spiritual Séance* Georgiana is open about what transpired at séances. Her memoir begins with the line: 'On the 6th of October 1870, I held my first séance after the return of Mrs. Guppy from her prolonged visit to Italy.' She explains how the immense labour involved in each drawing 'would baffle any merely human artist to produce such harmonies' and describes, in a wonderfully matter-of-fact way, the most extraordinary sequence of events: visitations from angels, her dead mother, brothers, the drowned nephew, dripping with water, a General Ramsay and a Native American, a 'fair young girl' named Môtee holding a harp. In one memorable experience, floating words illuminate the dark: 'Cast thy burthen upon The Lord, and He will sustain thee: His arm will uphold thee, so that the deep waters shall not cover thee.'

In another entry, a spirit writes an 800-word 'instructive message' in eight seconds. Georgiana sees white and purple grapes shining in the ether, spirit lights glowing like stars, a crown hovering in the air, and a figure in a blue coat with metal buttons and a thin gold diamond ring; she feels 'that upon the table there was a mass of something, wet with rain' and hears 'the clatter of cups and saucers', a 'rustling of leaves', the 'fluttering of a bird's wings' and 'a perfect rainbow of sound'. She, and others, are 'tenderly touched by the loving fingers of those so dear to us'. She is kissed, given a white coat by Gabriel, and showered with flowers. A pile of 'snow-covered ice' is discovered on the table and a wreath placed upon her head. She sees a number of 'Indians' (First Nations Americans) with white cloths around them; she is sprinkled with 'delicious perfume', given a ruby, a shell, wet with sea water, and a cup of tea. At times, the table rocks so hard she fears it will be broken. She describes dying as withdrawing 'from the earth-plane to enter upon the realities of the world beyond'. She understands table tipping as 'a sign that our invisible friends had united with us'. She is dismissive of sceptics, writing: 'It also often amuses me when people say that it is "contrary to the laws of gravitation" when a table is raised in the air without visible contact, but they do not imagine that they break a law when they lift up a light table with their own hands, and yet that is an exercise of a precisely similar power.'

She explains her hair ornament: it's a 'Neapolitan tortoise-shell dagger (a gift from Mrs Guppy)'. During one séance it 'was gently withdrawn, and taken to Mrs. Chevalier, who was allowed to hold it for a time, but it was then brought back and replaced in my hair'. During another visitation, the dagger is taken from her hair and dropped into her lap.

There's a tantalisingly brief description of the artist meeting Kate Fox, one of the two American sisters who had ignited the flame of Spiritualism in the United States years earlier. Houghton writes:

I had the pleasure, later on, of meeting her one evening at Mrs. T.'s, when she willingly let us have evidence of her power with reference to the raps, which came with wonderful strength and sound upon everything on which she laid her hand: - and she puzzled the sceptics by allowing them to stand on the other side of the closed door, to make themselves quite sure that she had no mortal confederate to bestow the blows.

I imagine the two women, the artist and the 'mysterious knocker', meeting in London almost 150 years ago. Georgiana, full of enthusiasm, her faith in her spirit friends radiating from her; Kate, who a decade or so later would rail against the chains that bound her so tightly. It is impossible to know precisely what motivated them. Loss, love, the truth? In the case of Houghton, a grief for her lost family so deep that she conjured them from the air? (This does not make it any less real.) With Kate - a childish prank with her sister gone wrong? Maybe. But if so, I don't understand how a girl could make her bones crack so loudly they could startle an audience. I do understand, though, that the way art is created is mysterious. It can be as much the product of a dark room as a bright studio.

The women surely understood something fundamental: that the way we each make sense of our existence is never straightforward. Yet Kate - despite her like-minded sister Maggie and her fame - strikes me as lonely; isolated in her renunciation of the very thing that had shaped her life. By contrast, in every anecdote she tells, Houghton is part of a group, mainly of women: they came together in the dark to explore a realm that blazes with light and colour. The spirit world gave her a radiant community; she was never alone.

Oceanic States

'I had often felt, when out painting, both exalted and yet guilty, as if I were evading something that the people round me, all busy with their daily lives, were facing, that their material was real life and mine was dreams. But was it?'

Marion Milner, *On Not Being Able to Paint* (1950)

Twenty-five years after I finished writing my novel about Richard Dadd, I returned to Amorgos to write this book. In Greek mythology, a group of sea nymphs so angered Poseidon that he transformed them into the Cycladic islands, known for their raw, wild beauty. It was an act of cruelty that I, for one, can't thank him enough for.

As I wake up and look across the bay, which is graced by a statue of Erato, the muse of lyric poetry, and up at the mountain, the site of the ancient city of Minoa, and out to the turquoise sea, where the horizon shifts constantly – I'm reminded again that in Greece the possibility of a spirit world isn't so startling.

A headless statue of Nausicaa seems to float on a rock in front of the graveyard. Sitting on the beach gazing out at her, I google who she was: the beautiful young daughter of King Alcinous and Queen Arete of the Phaeacians, who Homer recounts helped the shipwrecked Odysseus by introducing him to her father. I swim out to her; it's about 200 metres or so. The waves are choppy and the sea so hypnotically, so transparently blue, I get vertigo. I finally reach the statue: her face is missing, exposing the rusted metal of the

Statue of Nausicaa, Amorgos, 2022

structure; she's perched on a slab of rough concrete embellished
with a faint inscription of her name in Greek: Ναυσικᾶ. Although
the statue was probably made in the 1980s, her posture echoes that
of prehistoric Cycladic figurines: a slender, naked female form,
her arms folded in front of her, her face, if she had one, a pale

moon with a strip for a nose. She usually can't stand on her own accord, so she was possibly made to be held. Although the Cycladic period stretches for around 2,000 years from 3300 BCE, nothing is known of its religion or what the 1,500 or so versions of the figure represent: was her self-embrace a form of protection, a symbol of nurturing or self-containment? Although we tend to think of ancient sculpture as gleaming white, the marble would have, in fact, been painted with mineral-based pigments: azurite for blue and iron ores, or cinnabar for red. She would have blazed with colour.

Floating before Nausicaa, I realise that for an old and damaged statue she looks oddly contemporary: a goddess ravaged by time, perched on a concrete plinth but still, somehow, vital. Her name translates as the 'burner of ships' or 'passion for ships'; her relationship with Odysseus is said to be one of the first accounts of unrequited love. I can't find anything online about who made the sculpture or when it was erected; I remember its presence on my first visit, when her face was intact.

As I swim, I think about an essay that my friend Shelley, a writer who is studying to be a psychoanalyst, is working on. It concerns 'oceanic states' – the theory that creativity begins during a pre-logical, pre-verbal phase of infancy – which was first mentioned as 'oceanic feeling' by the French novelist, art critic and mystic, Romain Rolland in 1927 in a letter to Sigmund Freud. Inspired by the Indian Hindu mystic Ramakrishna, Rolland was attempting to describe a 'sensation of eternity', of being one with the world.

Shelley explains how Freud ran with the idea, as did the writer, psychoanalyst and artist Marion Milner. Freud described it as 'a sense of eternity, a feeling of something limitless, unbounded – as it were "oceanic"' which . . . was most likely linked to religious or mystical experiences'. He linked oceanic states to the times 'when people first fall in love and consequently feel as if they are merged with another or are in some way transfigured by the experience'. Marion Milner struggled with becoming a painter all her life

- something she wrote about in her 1950 memoir *On Not Being Able to Paint*, which emerged from the creative experiments she undertook from 1939, when she visited an exhibition at the Guggenheim Jeune Gallery in London by the Surrealist artists Reuben Mednikoff and Grace Pailthorpe - who was a psychologist. Milner, who had studied Zen Buddhism and mystical traditions from the East and West, believed that - unlike Freud who felt that 'oceanic states' are confined to infancy - an oceanic state could be experienced in moments of artistic creativity: when the unconscious mind 'let's go of the distinction between me and not-me, between seer and seen, and does things that the common-sense, conscious mind, cannot do'.

Oceanic states is a wonderfully evocative term: infinite, expansive; something that accommodates, like tides pulled by the moon, uncommon energies - the intertwining of creativity and transcendence. I imagine a group of nineteenth-century artists in their dark rooms, linking hands, closing their eyes, diving into the unknown; their hands picking up pencils or paints and transcribing their . . . unconscious thoughts? The will of a dead person? Each other's energies? Milner wrote that 'emptiness, formlessness (the oceanic), must be the basis of new forms, almost perhaps that one has to be willing to feel oneself becoming nothing in order to become something'.

On Amorgos, I glide, immersed in blue, above and below. I'm an astronaut on Earth in my very own oceanic state.

One night we watch Mark Cousins's new film, *The Story of Looking*. It's a meditation prompted by his imminent cataract operation that explores the importance of sight and the sky, the vulnerability of bodies, of losing yourself and finding solace in what is familiar. Cousins mentions that despite frequent references to the sea and the sky in *The Iliad* and *The Odyssey*, Homer never cites the colour blue; he repeatedly describes the sea as 'wine-dark'. This is startling.

I do some reading: Homer constantly used the words 'black' and 'white'; he describes the sky as bronze; the dawn as 'rosy-fingered'; stars are copper, sheep are purple, horses and lions, red; honey, green. The Ancient Greeks, it turns out, did not have a word for blue, even though the colour dominates: you can exhaust yourself searching for the precise tone: sapphire, cerulean, arctic, azure, aquamarine, cobalt . . .

The Greeks were not alone. The only ancient language that has a word for blue is Egyptian. Of course, this does not mean that the colour did not exist; rather, that it was understood in terms of tone, intensity and even metaphor rather than pigment. Like everything we experience, how we see - and describe - colour is cultural. Words and images reflect a moment in time back on itself; Homer not mentioning blue prompts an image of a group of women in a séance on a rainy night in London 150 years ago, seeing objects I have not dreamt of, using words that do not correspond with my world view, experiencing time and space as something idio-syncratic, conjuring pictures from the ether. I remind myself that because I have not experienced what they did, it does not render what they did impossible.

The Ancient Greeks believed that our planet is composed of five elements: fire, air, water and earth - and something less solid, but no less present: a spirit world. One afternoon, my head thick with reading about the gods, I go for a swim and fall into a reverie; strange, disconnected images flit in and out of my mind: bleeding feet, an argument with a bureaucrat, a stumbling attempt to craft a sentence with a feather. I think of a young woman I worked with, an art historian and tarot reader with a sharp eye for proofing, who keeps crystals in her bra and told me she's not the only one in the office to do so. I dive deep, opening my eyes wide: the turquoise is shot through with silver shafts of light. I follow fish, hum to myself, break the surface of the waves only to descend again. As I float beneath vertiginous cliffs, the landscape as raw as a bone, my day-to-day anxieties melt away; they seem so pointless in such an ancient environment. Sitting on the beach, I line up seashells that look like galaxies.

These dry, stony hills are solidly reassuring; everything is stripped back, constant, indifferent to the petty machinations of humans. Marion Milner is right. Perhaps this is how inspiration arrives. By a letting go of expectations, of ambition, of the ego. By seeing yourself in relation to the immensity of history. By allowing unexpected elements in. By not always knowing the answer - or shifting the tenor of the question.

Down a rocky track at the end of the village we're staying in is an old white house. On my first visit to the island, twenty-five years ago, we met its inhabitants: an enigmatic American painter who, when asked his name would reply, 'they call me Tassos'. He was a gentle soul; not much given to conversation. I can't recall why we visited his home, but I do recall stacks of paintings and doors open wide to the sea; the sound of wind chimes mingling with the hiss of the waves. Tassos died a few years ago and the house is now run by a wonderful woman called Theodosia, who teaches yoga. We do a class: I feel stiff and old but she's encouraging. As we lie in the corpse position, she plays a Tibetan singing bowl and tells us quietly that the world needs to soften. All sense of irony and cynicism dissolves. It's hard to disagree.

A woman called Christina does massage in the same house. Friends have told me that she has near-magical therapeutic powers. Luke, for example, who is sometimes sceptical of esoteric talk, is vague about what happens when you visit her, but he did say, with a mix of embarrassment and laughter, that as she worked on his body he fell into a reverie and imagined her floating like the Virgin Mary above him. Just go, he tells me, and so I do.

The room she practises in is plain and white; the windows look over the sea. I tell Christina about visiting the house decades before and she explains that we are in the room in which Tassos died.

She tells me that she cleansed the room of its negative energy and it's now a place of healing. From what I remember of the room's former inhabitant, I think he might approve.

We sit on thick rugs; Christina's gaze is direct and kind. She asks me why I've come. I tell her about my anxiety and insomnia, my stiff lower back, my tight shoulders. I lie on the rugs, and she covers my eyes and asks me if I would mind if she called in my 'helpers, ancestors, angels - whatever you like to call them'. I say I don't mind at all. She lays her hands on me and is silent for a few minutes. She tells me that my family is large, that I am very loved, and she can sense the presence of two dogs. This doesn't surprise me.

Over the next hour and a half, as she gently manipulates my body, I enter something I can only describe as a trance. Images from the past flash before me; it's like a screening of a new work by an experimental video artist. Fragments of conversations, words, glimpses of people I haven't thought about for a long time - all glide in and out of my consciousness. I am both deeply relaxed and highly alert. I feel protected; my muscles and my brain unwind in equal measure. Afterwards, I am ravenous and thirsty. I don't know what just happened. That night, I fall asleep quickly. In the morning, I wake feeling oddly optimistic. I think of London, and it seems like such a harsh place: so rough, rushed, crowded, expensive, cold. I remind myself that it's easy to love and romanticise a place when you're a tourist. But still.

The Benefits of Not Knowing

'The earliest *experience* of art must have been that it was incanta-
tory, magical; art was an instrument of ritual ... The earliest
theory of art, that of the Greek philosophers, proposed that art was
mimesis, imitation of reality. It is at this point that the peculiar
question of the *value* of art arose.'

Susan Sontag, *Against Interpretation* (1966)

When I was at art school in the 1980s and 1990s, thanks to the in-
filtration of French theory there was a tacit understanding that we
should be suspect of instinct, imagination, mood: everything was
a 'construct'. While on the one hand I'm grateful to have learned
something about the power structures of the languages we were
using, on the other it was the most killjoy way to launch a creative
life. It was also elitist: without a grounding in philosophy – which
none of us had – we were somehow meant to act upon a host of
enormously complex ideas of which we had only the scantest understanding. Now, thankfully, such ideological constraints have
been flung to the winds – and it doesn't mean the work being produced is any less critical, aware or complex.

Towards the end of my time at *frieze* magazine, I became increasingly attracted to artworks that resisted my often hasty attempts to
understand, justify or ascribe value; works that slowed me down
and challenged my assumptions about art and meaning. I was held
rapt by a story that began in August 1939, in the dark, inner cham-
ber of a cave in Hohlenstein-Stadel in Germany's Lone valley. A

geologist, Otto Völzing, unearthed some fragments of a prehistoric figure carved from the tusk of a mammoth - the largest animal on Earth. It was a staggering find, but the Second World War intervened and it was decades before more pieces were discovered; in 2013, the carving was almost completely restored.

Löwenmensch *(Lion-human)* c.38,000BCE

At around 40,000 years old, it is now considered the oldest figurative sculpture on the planet - and it appears to represent a creature
that, as far as we know, has never existed in nature: a hybrid of a
human and a lion. At only 31 centimetres tall, it's estimated that it
would have taken more than 400 hours to carve with stone tools:
an indication that it was an object of significant importance.

As if ready for action, the creature stands upright on its hind
legs. Its front legs hang like human arms loosely beside its body
- parts of which are smooth, as if the sculpture were passed from
hand to hand. Above a thick neck, it gazes directly out at us across
the millennia with the kind of rough-hewn, genial expression that
wouldn't be out of place in a Disney movie: its ears pricked as if
it's listening to us, its expression thuggish, miraculous, strange.
Despite being known in German as the ungendered *Löwenmensch*
(Lion-human), in English the sculpture is commonly referred to
as Lion-man. The German archaeologist and Upper Palaeolithic
expert Joachim Hahn believes that a plate on the sculpture's
abdomen represents a 'penis in a hanging position', while the pal-
aeontologist Elisabeth Schmid - who has a theory that Lion-man
was the product of a matriarchal society - believes it to be a pubic
triangle. Eva Wehrberger - the curator of archaeology at the Ulm
Museum, which owns the statue - feels that it's been made into
an 'icon of the women's movement'. It's impossible to know who
is right. The Ulm's website states: 'We cannot know precisely the
intentions of its creators. Even though this unique relic is a fantastical creature, which draws us intuitively towards the spiritual
world of early humans living in the grip of the last ice age, we will
never be able to decipher their clearly highly complex world view.'

In many ways, the not knowing animates this small object: in
an era where we expect quick answers, we cannot reduce it to a
fixed meaning and so the imagination is given permission to roam.
Connections spark, unhindered by the anxiety that your response
might be the wrong one. While scholarship is an essential part of

decoding the evolution of art, it's important to stress that a work of art cannot be *wrong*: it is what it is. Both making and looking are unstable activities, and images are unstable objects.

Every day our real world collides with our imaginary one. It could be something you've seen or overheard, some trivial thing that, by its very displacement or emphasis, reiterates the potential vigour that lies dormant in our environment. A work of art only comes alive when someone interacts with it. While experts might be able to place a painting or a sculpture in a certain period and as-cribe certain intentions to the artist, every interpretation is a form of speculation. Being open to not knowing can inspire a different knowledge, one grounded in humility and common humanity; one that engenders readings that might contradict accepted wisdom or cultural expectation. At a time in which we are endlessly bombarded with news, statistics, information and the dreadful cer-tainties of religious and political extremism, the secrets that reside at the heart of much great art can supply a rich space for contem-plation. As the artist Paul Chan recently wrote: 'Irreconcilabilities are where insights are truly gained. When thinking becomes an active experience, it tends to create options for consideration that were neither evident nor given by initial concepts. Real thoughts occur when all the solutions on offer are wrong or are refused.'

The cave where Lion-man was discovered is one of four, all of which have now been excavated. Around twenty-five other objects have been found, including effigies of large animals, birds and fish, a polished phallus, and the earliest known musical instrument, a 42,000-year-old bone flute. In 2008, the only obviously human form was unearthed: a female figure, the Venus of Hohle Fels. Cre-ated around 35,000 years ago and only 6 centimetres tall, it is the oldest extant depiction of a person. Although it's unknown what its creator intended, it is hard not to see the figure as a representa-tion of feminine power: she has a pronounced vulva, her breasts are as sturdy as battering rams, her thighs like pylons. Her head is a tiny loop, which indicates she may have been worn as a pendant. It's possible that the figure was once graced with a head made of plant or animal fibres or that the original one is simply lost. While we can only speculate as to her meaning, symbolic or otherwise, what is known is that patriarchal religion is a relatively new invention; artefacts relating to Goddess worship pre-date male deities by millennia. But despite her immense age, this figure is not that dissimilar to women today. I look at this tiny figure, glowing in the light of my laptop, and I feel a kinship with her. She feels familiar.

Venus of Hohle Fels, c.35,000 BCE

Many famous works of art are inscrutable. Thousands flock each year to the ancient geoglyphs in the highland plateaus of Peru's Nasca Desert that depict animals, plants, zoomorphic figures and mysterious geometric shapes carved around 2,000 years ago. As with the meaning of the prehistoric ring at Stonehenge in England, or An Cheathrú Mhór, a large group of megalithic monuments on the Cúil Iorra Peninsula to the west of Sligo, Ireland - to name but a few of the many possible examples - no one knows why they were created or what they represent, and yet people visit them in their droves and many of them are inexplicably moved.

But mystery isn't the preserve of a deep past we have little knowledge of; in many ways, a desire to understand the unknown shaped the Renaissance. Catherine de Medici, Queen Consort of France from 1547 until 1559, not only exerted huge power over the politics of her time but was a student of astrology and astronomy, and rumours circulated around her interest in the 'dark arts'. Christina, Queen of Sweden from 1632 until 1654, was one of the most learned women in Europe and passionate about alchemy and astronomy, and her court welcomed scientists and philosophers. In 1625, her librarian Gabriel Naudé published *Apologie pour les grands hommes soupçonnez de magie* (Apology for Wise Men Unjustly Reputed Magicians), in 'an attempt to peel away the many legends of spells and magic that had blackened the reputations of the early philosophers'. Numerous books exploring the occult were published: Domenico Auda's *Breve compendio di maravigliosi secreti* (A Brief Compendium of Marvellous Spirits; 1655), for example, went into five editions. In 1651, what is now considered to be the world's first museum was opened by the charismatic Jesuit priest, scientist and 'great magician', Athanasius Kircher, in the Roman College in Rome. Called The Kircherian Museum, visitors from across Europe flocked to see this vast 'workshop of Art and Nature' that included musical instruments; machines of Kircher's own invention, such as magic lanterns - an early type of image projector; 'a large crystalline globe full of water representing the resurrection of the saviour in the midst of waters'; stuffed rare animals, obelisks, Etruscan art and technological artefacts. Finding connections between science, magic and alchemy, Kircher's entertaining demonstrations of the collection attempted to illuminate no less than the structure of the universe.

Yet despite the numerous attempts to understand everything, it was - and is - inevitable, especially in art, that an element of unknowing persists. The website of Florence's Uffizi Gallery admits that interpreting one of its most famous paintings, Sandro Botticelli's allegorical *Primavera* (The Birth of Spring, c.1482), 'is difficult and still uncertain'. In 1556, Sofonisba Anguissola painted a small self-portrait holding a medallion emblazoned with a mysterious monogram of intertwined letters that covers most of her body: a code that both expresses and hides a message, which has now been lost to posterity. A century later, Nicolas Poussin painted what was to become one of the most inconclusively analysed paintings of the French Baroque, *Et in Arcadia Ego* (1637-8), a portrayal of Ancient Greek shepherds conversing around a tomb. Many seventeenth-century artists, such as the philosopher/painter Salvator Rosa, mined the era's fascination with magic and monsters in paintings so popular that crowds flocked to see each new composition. Leap forward to the nineteenth century, and the literary, musical and artistic movement Symbolism, fuelled by religious mysticism, privileged mood, mystery and atmosphere over detail.

In more recent times, some artists professed themselves baffled by what they created. Paul Klee, for example, described how his hand was 'wholly the instrument of some remote power. It is not my intellect which runs the show, but something different, something higher and more distant. Somewhere else. I must have great friends there, bright ones but sombre ones, too.' Hilma af Klint spent her life attempting to decode the messages she received.

Many of my artist friends struggle to articulate what prompts them to create a work of art and groan when galleries ask them to write an artist statement, clearly outlining their intentions. I'm a great admirer of the American artist Trisha Donnelly, who generally refuses to give interviews about her enigmatic work. When she curated an exhibition at the Museum of Modern Art in New York in 2013, she gave a tour of the show and said she chose 'striking voices I couldn't let go of . . . paths of encounters and building poetic structures . . . images that go beyond the images themselves'. For her solo debut at her New York gallery, Donnelly rode into the opening on a white horse, dressed like Napoleon, and delivered the oration the Emperor intended to give if he had won the Battle of Waterloo. Her final words were: 'I am electric, I am electric.' If anyone asked what any of it meant, the gallery played them a recording of electronic beats. The contemporary art critic Martin Herbert wrote in praise of Donnelly's reticence: 'So much art today . . . comes with an accompanying explanation that actively disarms the viewing experience, rationalises it, and rationalising appears to be the last thing Donnelly wants.' Donnelly is consistent: for her solo show at London's Serpentine Gallery in 2014, there was no press release. I go to the gallery's website to see how they archived it: the information is sparse, simply that she created new video works. A single unattributed quote hovers beneath a blurry black-and-white photograph of a ray of light hitting a domed ceiling: 'I like late in the day. I like the day to night transfer, I like desaturation. It's a high-speed eternity.'

There can be comfort in not knowing: while certain things are beyond our comprehension, they are not beyond the limits of our empathy or curiosity. We cannot google the precise meaning of art because there's no precision involved. We can't predict the ways in which it might entangle with our own imaginations, or move us, or reveal something to us about ourselves, someone else, the planet. Human nature is not easily reducible. That so many women in the nineteenth century made pictures via spirit mediums and didn't always fully understand what it was they created is, in the scheme of things, nothing new.

If we can't trust the leaps and bounds of our imaginations, then how can we ever expect something new to come into being? Why do we need to rationalise an act that, in the main, depends on the suspension of reason to evolve? We don't always understand what we're compelled to do, either as artists or humans. Creation is often its own explanation. It is not always logical or well-behaved: it flowers in multitudes. Why not remain alert to the possibility that the spiritual realm, for want of a better term, might be, in the words of the novelist Angela Carter, an 'unexplored country, a brave new world'?

In her book *A Life of One's Own* (1934) Marion Milner frequently asserts that not knowing is often the best way to learn something new. My friend Shelley explained that although Milner's suggestion sounds very contemporary, she was actually following in the footsteps of a long line of thinkers, such as the third-century Saint Gregory the Illuminator who wrote: 'We make Idols of our concepts, but Wisdom is born of wonder.'

Yet to experience wonder takes time and most of us lead lives that leave little room for the solitude needed to explore the parts of ourselves that are intangible or inarticulate. We live in a world that insists we explain from the time we are teenagers: What do we want? How might we achieve it? For an artist to teach at graduate level, in many countries they're now required to have a PhD, a depressing state of affairs: to bureaucratise the arts is to shackle the wild roaming that imaginations are capable of. Why isn't professional practice as an artist considered a qualification in itself? Over the past century, works of great innovation have emerged in response to swift change. None of it was created because it was a formal requirement. To demand a very particular kind of artistic engagement in order to allow something or someone into the hallowed halls of art history is to deny creativity its often eccentric lifeblood. As the painter Bridget Riley once said: 'the worst thing that can happen to art is when radicalism is transformed into a fashionable mode of conformism'. She understands all too well that both the creation and reception of art is complicated. As she once (beautifully) put it: 'Vision can be arrested, tripped up or pulled back in order to float free again. It encounters reflections, echoes and fugitive flickers which when traced evaporate.' Artists employ art because that's the language they understand – even as it often baffles them. Riley sees the act of painting as one of translating 'a text unknown even to yourself'. This demands the ability to 'learn to listen, because it is through a special kind of listening, a sort of "listening in", that one learns how to speak'. These are words that wouldn't have been out of place in a nineteenth-century séance.

Marion Milner quotes the artist Jan Gordon, who in his 1934 book *Step Ladder to Painting* declared that:

> Everyone has two bodies, the real body, and the imaginative, whimsical, adventurous, astral self. The real body may go on with its humdrum existence while the astral body is prancing alongside, driving cars at a thousand miles an hour, strangling lions in the Strand. The astral body strolls casually into lunch at the Savoy, while the real body creeps humbly into Lyons. The ordinary man's astral body is of little use, but the artist pulls his astral body in, and sets him to work.

Milner felt that to create paintings that evoked a life force as opposed to mere imitation she needed to repudiate common sense to explore the possibilities of what she termed 'uncommon sense'. She looked at drawings in the way that Freud examined dreams and understood that we need elements of illusion to cope with reality. She defined 'psychic creativity' as the ability to form

Hildegard von Bingen, illumination from *Liber Scivias*, c.1151

Richard Dadd, *The Fairy Feller's Master Stroke*, 1855-64

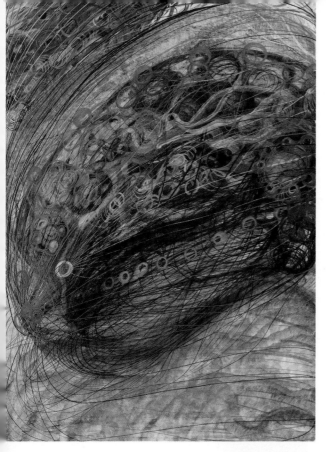

Georgiana Houghton,
*The Spiritual Crown of
Mrs Oliphant*, 1867

Georgiana Houghton,
*The Spiritual Crown of
Annie Mary Howitt Watts*,
24 April 1867

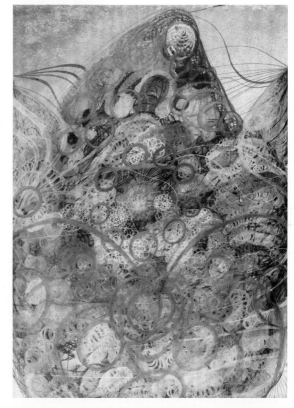

Margaret Watts Hughes, *Voice Figure*, late nineteenth century

'Astral Plane', plate from Annie Besant and C.W. Leadbeater, *Thought Forms*, 1905: a vision of Charles Gounod's music played on a church organ

Hilma af Klint,
'Adulthood', from
The Ten Largest, 1907

Wassily Kandinsky, *Composition V*, 1911

Estella Canziani, *The Piper of Dreams*, 1915

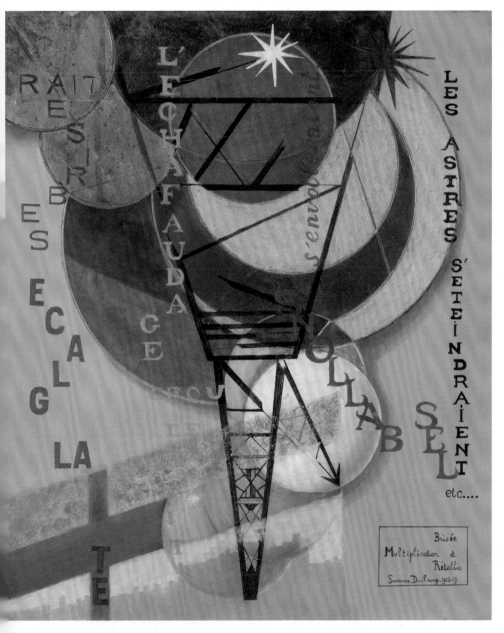

Suzanne Duchamp, *Broken and Restored Multiplication*, 1918

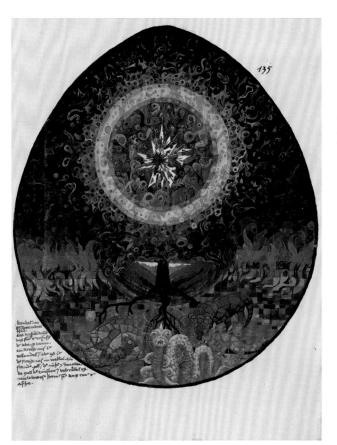

Carl Jung, 'Tree of Life', image from *The Red Book*, 1922

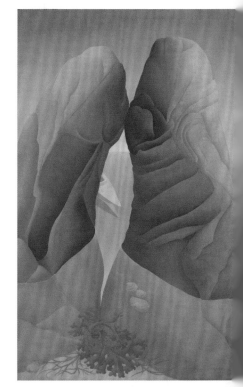

Ithell Colquhoun, *Scylla*, 1938

a symbol for the emotions in art and for knowledge in science. She subsequently developed what she called her 'free drawings' - allowing her hand to move wherever it wished, without being overruled by her conscious mind. Milner realised that the edges of objects human beings assume to be fixed don't exist in nature; nothing is clear or compact: neither the physical world nor the unconscious one.

The drawings Milner created via free association surprised her: a lamb, a mouse, a baby; a monstrous beast, ready to attack - a beast she realises is herself. The titles of her drawings are revealing and entertaining: *The Angry Parrot, Thunder Over the Sea, Blasting Witch, Horrified Tadpole, Ape in the Garden of Eden, The Pregnant Butcher.* In her book, she is at once a scientist - analysing her motivations, the nature of creativity, its precedents and potentialities - and artist: someone open to impulses that she doesn't fully understand. Her attempts to break free from the barriers of inhibition to create 'what has never been' are part of the therapeutic, mystical traditions that stretch back to the nineteenth century, not only, and most obviously, to Sigmund Freud's development of psychoanalysis but to the complicated legacy of a Russian aristocrat.

Between Mortals and Beings

'The Mind is the great Slayer of the Real. Let the Disciple slay the Slayer.'

Madame Blavatsky, *The Voice of the Silence* (1889)

A few years ago, I went to dinner at a collector's home in London. Taking off my coat, I turned and stepped back in surprise: in front of me, a veiled, middle-aged woman dressed in dark purple (the colour of mourning and magic) was levitating on her back between two wooden chairs. Her eyes were closed, her hands neatly resting on her belly. It took me a moment to realise that the woman was, in fact, a carved wooden sculpture. Titled *Madame Blavatsky*, it was created in 2007 by Goshka Macuga, an artist who has long explored different modes of knowing that, in her words, 'extend beyond the visible into the productive space of intuition'. Blavatsky believed that somnambulism - the trance-like state between waking and sleeping, when the mind roves to places it might avoid in a conscious state - was a conduit to creativity. Goshka's portrait is her homage to the sway of Blavatsky's thinking on the development of modern art and literature; like the Russian mystic, she sees the possibilities that occur when we loosen our conscious attachment to the physical realm.

Mme Blavatsky, 1877

It's impossible to read about the development of modern art and culture without coming across the name of Madame Helena Petrovna Blavatsky - or, as she preferred to be called, H.P.B. Even now, 130 years after she departed her physical body - as her followers like to describe her death - wildly differing opinions and theories swirl around her. I read so much about her, from so many angles, that I become fearful of stepping into the mire - she was extraordinary, divisive, evasive and, at times, unintentionally comic. But whatever your take, she was a lynchpin between Spiritualism and modernity. She laid the groundwork for the so-called New Age

movement and was one of the first - or at least, the most charismatic - people to direct Western seekers towards the riches of
Eastern religions. She railed against materialism and nationalism,
believing that the rejection of a spiritual life led to a gulf between
people and countries. As fascinated by the past as much as an
advocate for the future, she advised that the best way forward involved looking back. She was mired in philosophical, mystical and
religious texts - from Buddhism and Hinduism to Neo-Platonism,
Christianity and the Kabbalah and more - and it's likely that much
of her writing was, if not plagiarised, then heavily reliant on a vast
array of source material. Her life was a dizzying, often uncorrob-
orated sequence of journeys: she rarely stopped moving, literally
or figuratively, and often resorted to tricks to illustrate the veracity
of her claims; in 1885 she was accused of fraud by the Society for
Psychical Research. It's ironic that the motto of Theosophy - the
movement she was instrumental in founding - declares 'there is no
religion higher than truth'.

Her life reads like a fantastical novel. Driving around Amorgos,
I regale my friends with some of the anecdotes from H.P.B.'s life
and we can't stop laughing at her originality and audacity. She was
a trickster, a genius, an intellectual and a performer. Her appetites -
for life, love, food - were enormous. She was an aristocrat who had
great compassion for working people. She was a seeker of truth,
who was uncomfortable with facts.

In brief: She was born Helena Petrovna von Hahn into an aristocratic family in 1831, in Ekaterinoslav in the Russian Empire
(present-day Dnipro in Ukraine). In a period when even aristocratic
young women were barely educated, her grandmother, Princess
Helena Pavlovna Dolgorukov, could speak fluent Greek and was so
well-versed in classical literature, art, botany and archaeology that
they named a fossil after her. Helena's mother, Helena Andreyevna,
was a respected proto-feminist novelist who published under the
pseudonym Zenaida R-va. (That name!)

Helena's childhood was marred by tragedy. When she was ten, H.P.B.'s mother died from tuberculosis. As H.P.B.'s father, a military man, was constantly on the move, along with her sister, she was taken in by her grandparents, who lived in Saratov, a town on the Volga. Their home was old, enormous, filled with tunnels, abandoned passages, nooks and corners - and a library filled with her great-grandfather Prince Paul Dolgorukov's rich collection of books. H.P.B. devoured his tomes on the occult sciences, magic and alchemy - including *Solomon's Wisdom*, a Jewish book written in Greek in the first century BCE, which inspired her early experiments with putting pigeons to sleep. An aged serf who worked for the family, Baranig Bouyak, was a healer and magician; he taught H.P.B. about the occult properties of plants and the language of bees - and predicted great things for her future. She later recalled in a letter to a friend: 'All the devilries of the Middle Ages had found refuge in my head and soon neither Paracelsus, Kunrath, nor C. Agrippa would have had anything to teach me.' She hated the trappings of aristocratic life and the expectation that matrimony was the pinnacle of female achievement. Ballrooms, finery and dressing up were anathema to her. So extreme was her aversion to being forced into a role in which she had no interest, she once plunged her leg into a vat of boiling water so she wouldn't have to dance. Her fierce sense of self was astonishing. She wrote: 'There is nothing of the woman in me. When I was young, if a young man had dared to speak to me of love, I would have shot him like a dog who bit me.'

She inhabited an animistic world that no one else could see. She would sleepwalk, talk to friends not visible to the naked eye, had paranormal visions, encountered a mysterious Indian man who she called her 'protector', experienced astral travelling, channelled the dead, and 'heard the voices of pebbles, trees, and pieces of decaying timber'. As a teenager she had no idea what she was looking for, aside from 'the powers of nature that are inaccessible to our reason'. Her worried relatives called in priests to exorcise her. With her fierce eyes and ferocious will, she was admonished and admired in equal measure.

At the age of seventeen, she had a short-lived and, according to her, unconsummated marriage to a man called Nikifor Blavatsky, who she nicknamed 'the plumeless raven'. He was thirty-nine, a vice-governor who shared her belief in the occult, possibly in order to seduce her. She agreed to marry him to spite her family. After three months she fled, at first to Constantinople and then later to London; all she kept of her husband was his name. She possibly earned money as a jockey or an acrobat.

In 1851 she travelled again to London, as a companion to her godmother, Princess Bagration-Murransky. She was either on a crowded London street, visiting the Great Exhibition, contemplating suicide on Waterloo Bridge or walking beneath a full moon at the English seaside town of Ramsgate, when she met the 'mysterious Indian' from her earlier visions: a Hindu Master of Ancient Wisdom known as Morya, or Mahatma, who was both a 'Great Soul' and a mortal. His instructions were clear: she was to travel to Tibet and spend three years there. She always claimed to have followed the Great Soul's order, but one of her more sceptical biographers, Marion Meade, believes that it's likely she roved Europe with the Italian-Hungarian opera singer Agardi Metrovitch, who fell in love with her when he saw her perform in the circus. This is, however, refuted by many of H.P.B.'s present-day followers.

However much they admire her, some of her biographers believe that certain accounts of Blavatsky's life should be taken with a pinch of salt – which is something she might have agreed with. (Her favourite expression, which she regularly employed to dismiss something as nonsense, was 'flapdoodle'.) She even told her first biographer, the Theosophist and journalist A.P. Sinnet, that: 'From seventeen to forty, I took care during my travels to sweep away all traces of myself wherever I went . . . I never allowed people to know where I was or what I was doing.'

One account is that after travelling via Canada, the United States and South America, she spent two years in India trying to get to Tibet, but was blocked by the British Colonial administrators. After returning to England and working as a professional musician, she went back to India via San Francisco and Japan and then journeyed to Russia to see her family, where she displayed her supernatural abilities: she moved furniture, received messages, communicated with spirits via raps. She became known in Tiflis as a seer, a magician and a psychic. She lived briefly with her husband, was possibly reunited with Metrovitch, and most likely gave birth to an illegitimate child, who died at the age of five. (She described him as her ward.) In 1864 she was thrown from a horse and was in a coma for six weeks. When she came to, her paranormal abilities were even more fully formed.

She resumed her travelling through Europe and the Middle East, claiming that she fought for Garibaldi in Italy, and finally made it to Tibet in 1856, accompanied by a shaman, but 'after a number of supernatural experiences, some of a frightening nature', she was rescued 'by a party of twenty-five Lamaist horsemen and swooped back to the frontier'. In 1867, she finally achieved her goal, to reach the school in eastern Tibet where she met Master Morya and another important Master, Koot Hoomi (the spelling is changeable). She was then initiated into a system of ancient knowledge through the study of a Tibetan text called *The Book of Dzyan*, written in the sacred, and now lost, language of Senzar - something about which quite a few scholars are sceptical.

Unsurprisingly, some of H.P.B.'s biographers believe her whereas others are unconvinced. Tibet's borders were closed, its terrain wild and inhospitable, and there are no eyewitness accounts to confirm her story. For a single woman of limited means to travel so far would have been difficult, although H.P.B. was an accomplished horsewoman and as bold as they come. But she was adamant that she had spent seven years in the mountainous kingdom.

When H.P.B. left Tibet – or wherever she was – in 1871, she was one of seventeen survivors of an explosion on a ship, the SS *Eumonia*, en route to Cairo. Metrovich either died in the blaze or in Ramleh (an Arab city now in Israel), after being poisoned by Maltese ruffians in Alexandria. H.P.B. then worked as a Spiritualist in Cairo and then Europe. Although she was often called a medium, she derided the term, possibly because of its whiff of the side-show. She preferred to describe herself as 'a mediator between mortals and beings'. I'm not sure I understand the distinction.

After more travelling through the Middle East and Europe, apparently under the instruction of Master Morya, H.P.B. moved to New York. It was 1873; she was forty-two, a chain smoker, possibly an imbiber of opium and hashish and, at first, poor: she lived in a women's housing cooperative and earned a living through sewing and designing advertising cards. When her father died in 1874, her dire financial situation improved; in 1878 she became the first Russian woman to become a citizen of the United States. Investigating a news story about two brothers who claimed to manifest spiritual phenomena, she met a lawyer and journalist, Henry Steel Olcott, who lit her cigarette and promptly fell under her spell. He wrote an article about the powers of this mysterious Russian woman with the piercing azure eyes who could commune with the dead; from now on, their lives would be forever intertwined. He wrote in his memoirs that 'our acquaintance began in smoke [and] stirred up a great and permanent fire'.

By all accounts, Olcott was a man of integrity. Years later, Sir Arthur Conan Doyle observed that no one could read his autobiographical *Old Diary Leaves* without realising that this was a man 'loyal to a fault, unselfish and with that rare moral courage which will follow truth and accept results even when they oppose one's expectations and desires'. H.P.B. and Olcott called each other 'Jack' and 'Maloney' and together they founded 'The Miracle Club' to discuss esoteric matters and explore psychic happenings. H.P.B. became increasingly sceptical of American Spiritualism, believing it was her duty 'to purify the new religion from all its filthy weeds'.

At a meeting on 7 September 1875, the Theosophical Society came into being, its name a fusion of the Greek 'theos' (god) and 'sophia' (wisdom): Olcott was voted president; Dr Seth Pancoast, a student of the Cabbala, and George H. Felt, an engineer and architect, as vice-presidents; William Judge, an occultist, as counsel and H.P.B. as secretary. It was both an ambitious and a vague undertaking: an attempt to establish a universal brotherhood, conduct research into religion, philosophy and science and to investigate the laws of nature. They were guided by seven Mahatmas or Masters – who H.P.B. insisted were real men. It was not a religion and had no dogma or creed apart from a study of the laws that govern the universe, and members were accepted irrespective of race, sex, colour, nationality or religious belief. Judge's evasive claim that 'the strength of theosophy lies in the fact that it is not to be defined' sounds, in many ways, like a definition of art. It's the most accurate description of what was to transpire.

It certainly challenged expectations. Everywhere Blavatsky went, strange things happened: letters of advice from 'Ancient Masters' fell from the ceilings of rooms and train carriages, a teacup materialised in the earth, a brooch beneath a pillow. Each occurrence was a message of some sort, intended to reinforce Theosophy's wisdom and the power of H.P.B.'s connection to the spiritual realm. Yet, in her introduction to her 1,200-page book *Isis Unveiled: A Master-Key to the Mysteries of Ancient and Modern Science and Theology*, published in 1877, Blavatsky briskly stresses the reasonableness and rigour of her world views:

We believe in no Magic which transcends the scope and capacity of the human mind, nor in 'miracle', whether divine or diabolical, if such imply a transgression of the laws of nature instituted from all eternity. Nevertheless, we accept . . . that the human heart has not yet fully uttered itself, and that we have never attained or even understood the extent of its powers.

Isis Unveiled was no less an attempt than to retell ancient and esoteric knowledge for the contemporary reader. As with most of Blavatsky's texts, it is a dense and difficult read. Yet, despite mixed reviews – the *New York Herald* called it 'one of the most remarkable productions of the century', the *New York Sun* 'discarded rubbish' and the *Springfield Republican* 'a large dish of hash' – it sold 1,000 copies in ten days. *The New York Times* refused to review it as the editor had 'a holy horror of Mme. Blavatsky'.

The authorship of *Isis Unveiled* has long been debated: for some, it's a breathtaking exercise in intellectual theft; for others, a work of originality and scholarship. Like so many of the artists she was to inspire, H.P.B. claimed no responsibility for her creation, writing to her sister Vera that she was not the author of her texts but simply the conduit for her Masters:

Somebody comes and envelopes me as a misty cloud and all at once pushes me out of myself, and then I am not 'I' anymore – Helena Petrovna Blavatsky – but someone else. Someone strong and powerful, born in a totally different region of the world; and as to myself it is almost as if I were asleep, or lying . . . not quite conscious – not in my own body but close by, held only by a thread which ties me to it . . . I am perfectly conscious of what my body is saying and doing – or at least its new possessor. I even understand and remember it all so well that afterwards I can repeat it and even write down his words.

In 1878, H.P.B. and Olcott moved to India; in Benares, the Maharajah allowed the Theosophical Society to borrow his family motto: 'There is no religion higher than truth.' In 1879, they founded the periodical *The Theosophist* (a less alarming title than *Lucifer*, the publication H.P.B. launched in London in 1887). In 1882, the headquarters of the Society were established in Adyar, near Madras (now Chennai). It's still a thriving centre for study; the Theosophical Society currently has 40,000 members in sixty countries.

On a visit to Ceylon, H.P.B. and Olcott converted to Buddhism – something that could be accommodated within Theosophy, which is non-denominational. In 1885, her health fragile, H.P.B. moved to London, where she established the Blavatsky Lodge, gained an ardent follower in Annie Besant – who was to become her successor – and wrote *The Secret Doctrine*, a two-volume, 1,500-page epic search for the beginnings of civilisation that is still in print. She was to write two more books, *The Key to Theosophy* and *The Voice of Silence*. During her final years, visitors to the Theosophical Society included Thomas Edison and Mohandas Gandhi – who was interested in Theosophy's tenet of universal brotherhood but suspicious of its mysticism, and who Annie Besant called 'Mahatma' or noble soul – Oscar Wilde and W.B. Yeats, who was so inspired by what he learned that he conducted experiments to contact the other side, including an attempt to raise the ghost of flowers. In 1878, in the United States, the Civil War general, Abner Doubleday – who, after his death, was credited (falsely) as the inventor of baseball – became president of the American branch of the Theosophical Society, and in 1892, the author of *The Wizard of Oz*, L. Frank Baum, joined up. Apparently, even Albert Einstein was a keen reader of Theosophical texts. H.P.B. died on 8 May 1891 at the age of fifty-nine from a mix of influenza and Bright's disease – her 200-cigarette-a-day habit and obesity surely contributing to her early demise. Each year, H.P.B.'s death is commemorated by her followers on 8 May – White Lotus Day.

Trying to separate fact from fiction in H.P.B.'s life story is, to put it mildly, a tricky endeavour. Especially in her later years, she attempted to rewrite her past: at the age of fifty-four, for example, despite it being more than likely that she had two husbands, various lovers and a child, she insisted she was a virgin. There are contrary aspects to her beliefs, too. In many ways, she was a modernist and yet, despite her disdain for what was traditionally expected of women, she never publicly supported the burgeoning women's movement and was opposed to birth control - perhaps she considered her concerns to exist on a higher plane than the policing of gender and reproduction. It must have been a challenge for her to uphold Theosophy's claim to 'tolerate the intolerant': whatever she did and wherever she went she was pursued by fervent believers and howling critics. She was accused of self-interest, fraud, corruption, charlatanism; of lying, being psychotic; of having fanged teeth and eating meat with her fingers when she espoused vegetarianism, of being filthy and foul-mouthed. In hindsight, the attacks on her were inevitable: her association with spirit photography, levitation, raps, poltergeists, ectoplasmic materialisations, out-of-body experiences, telepathy, clairvoyance and mediumistic communications must surely have alarmed as many people as it beguiled.

While there's little question that H.P.B. resorted to theatrics to support her theories, many of her ideas, such as the need for humans to develop a closer relationship with nature, chime with a slew of contemporary concerns. Her indifference to time, place or authorship - and her openness to new ways of navigating existence - were invigorating at a time when everything, even the nature of reality, was being questioned. To agree with Theosophy's premise that surface appearances are just that - surface - and thus incapable of fully representing the rich complexity of existence meant that new ways of picturing the world were not only possible but necessary.

There is nothing rigid about Theosophy: it's too broad a system. That it's non-conformist, undogmatic and accommodating of all faiths, and – generally speaking – doesn't discriminate on grounds of gender, race or wealth, made it especially attractive to artists and writers at a time of great censoriousness. They cherry-picked ideas from across the spiritual spectrum to serve their own purposes; many of them were drawn to its belief in unseen energies, its sense of wonder, and the importance of a mystical dimension in an increasingly mechanised era. In literature, E.M. Forster has his characters discuss auras in his 1910 novel *Howard's End*, T.S. Eliot namechecks Blavatsky in his 1920 poem 'A Cooking Egg' and alludes to her in 'The Waste Land' (1922) as 'Madame Sosostris, famous clairvoyante'; Theosophical teachings partly shaped Ezra Pound's 'Cantos' (which he wrote between 1915 and 1964) and James Joyce references key theosophical figures in *Finnegans Wake* (1939). Late nineteenth-century 'New Woman' writers – feminists seeking radical change – such as Sarah Grand (who coined the term in 1894) and George Egerton (AKA Mary Chavelita Dunne Bright) were also affected by the new vistas promised by Spiritualism, in particular its gender equality and respect for intuition and the power of dreams. Despite her frequent impatience with mysticism, even Virginia Woolf softened to it after meeting W.B. Yeats in 1930. She wrote about her impressions of the poet to her sister, the painter Vanessa Bell: 'As he believes in the unconscious soul, in fairies, in magic, and has a complete system of philosophy and psychology, it was not altogether easy to understand: at the same time, I agreed with many of his views and he is also surprisingly sensible.' Numerous passages in her novels and diary describe out-of-body travel, synaesthesia and auras. In her 1931 novel *The Waves*, Woolf both mocks and examines mysticism's energies. She has, for example, a young woman, Rhoda, think that 'our eyes, as they range round this room with all its tables, seem to push through curtains of colour, red, orange, umber and queer ambiguous tints, which yield like veils and close behind them, and one thing melts into another'.

In 'Concerning the Spiritual in Art', Kandinsky admires Theosophy's privileging of Spiritualism over materialism. František Kupka was immersed in Theosophy in the late nineteenth century. Piet Mondrian joined the Dutch branch of the Theosophical Society in 1909 and Kazimir Malevich's Supremacist abstractions reflect theosophical ideas around cosmology. Countless women artists, some of whom I explore in these pages, became either followers of Theosophy or were empowered by its permission to explore dimensions hitherto denied them.

From a twenty-first-century perspective, the idea that feelings have an energy that can be transformed into images is unremarkable. In 1905, it was a different matter.

Thought-Forms

'... very few of us have any clear idea as to what kind of thing a thought is, and the object of this little book is to help us to conceive this.'

Annie Besant and C.W. Leadbeater, *Thought-Forms* (1905)

In 1905, the second generation of Theosophical leaders, Annie Besant and C.W. Leadbeater, published *Thought-Forms*. Their idea was deceptively simple: 'Every thought gives rise to a set of correlated vibrations in the matter of this body, accompanied with a marvellous play of colour, like that in the spray of a waterfall as the sunlight strikes it, raised to the nth degree of colour and vivid delicacy.' In some ways, their theory can be seen as yet another reflection of the nineteenth-century mania for inventing new methods of communication, but they were also influenced by H.P.B.'s 'auratic egg' – the idea that a life force or *prana* flows through the body via seven chakras, each of which corresponds to a different vibration or colour, that can be seen by clairvoyants. In heightened beings, such as Buddha or Christ, the aura is visible as a halo.

According to the Theosophists, thought-forms can be transmitted to others as a type of healing, but this tends to be successful only if both parties are in harmony. Besant and Leadbeater's visualisations emerged from the 'second-sight' trance states in which they experienced 'auras, vortices, etheric matter, astral projections, energy forms and other expressions from the unseen world', which they then described to three artists - John Varley, Mr Prince and Miss Macfarlane - who in turn translated them into the images which illustrate the book. (Besant also thanked Mr F. Bligh Bond for his essay on 'Vibration Figures' and 'some exquisite drawings', and a friend 'who insists on remaining anonymous', who supplied some additional notes and drawings.) Besant is clearly grateful to the artists: 'To paint in earth's dull colours the forms clothed in the living light of other worlds is a hard and thankless task; so much the more gratitude is due to those who have attempted it. They needed coloured fire and had only ground earths.'

Thought-Forms opens with a declaration that puts a stop to the idea that magic and reason cannot co-exist:

As knowledge increases, the attitude of science towards the things of the invisible world is undergoing considerable modification ... Röntgen's [X-]rays have rearranged some of the older ideas of matter, while radium has revolutionised them, and is leading science beyond the borderland of ether into the astral world. The boundaries between animate and inanimate matter are broken down.

It proceeds, via a series of chapters titled 'The Difficulty of Representation', 'The Form and its Effect', 'The Meaning of the Colours' and so on, to describe the various colours and forms that are created by different states of mind and music. It includes a colour key: lavender, for example, is 'high spirituality', purple 'devotion mixed with affection', orange 'pride', grey 'deceit' and 'love to all beings' is a radiant pink. The titles of the illustrations are at once strange and specific: 'vague intellectual pleasure' (yellow, worm-like shapes gyrating in black space) and 'grasping animal affection' (a rush of ochre-ish paint, like a bird's wing); 'radiating affection' (a sun-like explosion of pale pink, again in a black space); and 'the appreciation of a beautiful picture by a religious subject' (a harmonious sliver of moon, in various shades of pink, lemon and green). The mental anguish at witnessing 'a street accident' might result in a green disc rimmed with pale pink and coral rings; having 'the intention to' know' will emanate a yellow corkscrew and a 'greed for drink' a blob of mottled red with four protruding hooks. In the section on visualising music, Charles Gounod's compositions are rendered as psychedelic clouds erupting from church steeples while Richard Wagner's operas explode like a trippy mountain hovering over a diminished purple cathedral in a bucolic setting.

This is radical stuff, even now, but the story of how *Thought-Forms* came into being is, if possible, even more surprising. How did its co-author, Annie Besant - one of the most famous women of her day, who, for many years, was known for her political activism and atheism - come to embrace this most esoteric of theories? Who was she?

Annie Besant, c.1890

Annie Wood was born in Clapham, London, in 1847 and although her upper-middle-class family appeared to be well off, it was illusory. When she was five, her father died suddenly and she and her mother were left almost penniless. At the age of twenty she married a clergyman, Frank Besant; they had two children, but the marriage was disastrous. Increasingly distrustful of her husband's beliefs, she wrote:

> I went out into the darkness alone, not because religion was too good for me, but because it was not good enough; it was too meagre, too commonplace, too little exacting, too bound up with earthly interests, too calculating in its accommodations to social conventionalities ... the Church established by law transformed me into an unbeliever and an antagonist.

Due to their irreconcilable intellectual and religious differences, the couple separated in 1873 - a highly unusual thing to do at the time, especially for a member of the clergy. Annie's husband never forgave her: he dragged her through the courts and - because of her perceived radicalism - was granted sole custody of their children. But Besant's spirit was indomitable. She became a social and political agitator and was scathing about the hypocrisies of organised religion. She was an atheist, Freethinker, social reformer, strike leader and union organiser - she rallied the matchgirls' strike of 1888 - a women's rights activist, an educator, a philanthropist, a magnificent orator and a socialist.

In 1877, Annie and her friend the activist and atheist Charles Bradlaugh were prosecuted for publishing a pamphlet on birth control - *The Fruits of Philosophy, or the Private Companion of Young Married People* - by the American campaigner Charles Knowlton. The injustice of their treatment by the law, which was veiled in religious piety, only served to inflame her spirit further: she demanded that evidence should precede spiritual belief and declared that 'the over-mastering sway which was beginning to exercise over me drove me to seek for the explanation of all problems of life and mind at the hands of the biologist and the chemist'. Her battle-cries would not be considered unreasonable today: she was a vocal critic of British imperialism in Afghanistan, Burma, Egypt, India, Ireland and the Transvaal. She was 'against war, against capital punishment, against flogging, demanding national education instead of big guns, public libraries instead of warships - no wonder I was denounced as an agitator, a firebrand, and that all orthodox society turned up at me its most respectable nose'. Her friend, the playwright George Bernard Shaw, remembered her displays of personal courage, how she stood up for 'the over-exploited matchgirls' and helped them organise a strike. Any attempt to 'keep pace with her on the part of a mere man', he wrote, 'generally wrecked the man'.

So how did this tireless atheist and socialist activist become the leader of an esoteric movement that many people believed to be fraudulent? Her autobiography, which was published in 1893, casts some light. Besant describes herself as a child as 'mystical and im-aginative, religious to the very fingertips, and with a certain faculty for seeing visions and dreaming dreams', something she ascribes to her Celtic origins. Her mother had the gift of sight; Annie grew up believing that elves and fairies and ghosts were all very real. Yet her renunciation of Christianity was bound up in her refusal to believe without evidence; her socialism stemmed from the very real social problems and injustices she had witnessed. However, by 1886, she was beginning to feel a spiritual vacuum in her life. It's worth quoting at length the section in her autobiography that explains not only her level of disillusionment, but the kinds of new ideas to which people had to adjust in the nineteenth century:

> . . . there had been slowly growing up a conviction that my philos-ophy was not sufficient; that life and mind were other than, more than, I had dreamed. Psychology was advancing with rapid strides;

hypnotic experiments were revealing unlooked-for complexities
in human consciousness, strange riddles of multiplex personalities
and, most startling of all, vivid intensities of mental action when
the brain, that should be the generator of thought, was reduced
to a comatose state. Fact after fact came hurtling in upon me,
demanding explanation I was incompetent to give. I studied the
obscurer sides of consciousness, dreams, hallucinations, illusions,
insanity ... I added Spiritualism to my studies, experimenting
privately, finding the phenomena indubitable, but the spiritualistic
explanation of them incredible. The phenomena of clairvoyance,
clairaudience, thought-reading, were found to be real. Under all
the rush of the outer life, already sketched, these questions were
working in my mind, their answers were being diligently sought.

In 1889, she was asked by W.T. Stead - a Theosophist and editor
of the *Pall Mall Gazette*, who, in 1912, would drown in the sinking of
the *Titanic* - to review Madame Blavatsky's two-volume *Secret Doctrine*. Initially reluctant, it was to change Annie Besant's life. She
read it with a bolt of recognition:

> How natural it was, how coherent, how subtle, and yet how intel-
> ligible. I was dazzled, blinded by the light in which disjointed facts
> were seen as parts of a mighty whole, and all my puzzles, riddles,
> problems, seemed to disappear ... the light had been seen, and in
> that flash of illumination I knew that the weary search was over
> and the very Truth was found.

She opened her review with a light-hearted observation, that 'the
study of the book will begin in bewilderment and end in despair'
and that 'the average person might just as well skip it; all who did
decide to attempt it must have an intense desire to know'. But on
a deeper level, she had come home. Besant asked her editor for a
letter of introduction, met Blavatsky and immediately became her

lifelong student and disciple. Many of her comrades and former friends, in particular Charles Bradlaugh, were dismayed by what they saw as her seduction by hocus-pocus. H.P.B., though, was thrilled: to have such a renowned firebrand and public intellectual join her ranks was a coup. The two women became inseparable. Before long, H.P.B. was writing to Besant with the fervour of a lover. 'Dearly Beloved One, I am proud of you, I love you, I honour you. You are and will be yet before all men - the star of salvation.' She called Besant her 'sweet mango' and 'darling Penelope' to her 'female Ulysses'. The younger woman was 'my dove-eyed one'; her 'dearest' whom she longed to kiss 'on both your big lotus-like eyes peeping into mine'.

There are, however, aspects of Theosophy that very clearly chime with Besant's earlier socialist and atheist beliefs. The fact that its aim was to 'found a Universal Brotherhood without distinction of race or creed', and that its founders 'deny a personal god' but teach a 'somewhat subtle form of Pantheism', was attractive to her. In her autobiography, she repeatedly makes clear Madame Blavatsky's lack of personal wealth and praises her philanthropy. In 1890, H.P.B. gave Besant £1,000 that had been donated to the Theosophical Society, for her to distribute the money, at her discretion, 'for human service', especially women. After much discussion, they decided to establish a refuge for homeless factory girls in east London. On 16 August of that year, the 'Working Women's Club', 'wholly free from theological creeds and conditions' and with 'books, papers and music at hand', was opened at 193 Bow Road: fifty impoverished girls sang and danced to herald its inauguration. The club closed after four years, unable to afford its upkeep - but in those four years they had vastly improved the lives of hundreds of young women.

Besant's philosophy was essentially an optimistic, active one, an embracing of the fact that each life is in flux. She reiterates that there is nothing illogical or superstitious about Theosophy: according to her, it is no more superstitious than 'a belief in bacteria or any other living thing invisible to the ordinary human eye'. At times, her impatience leaps off the page. She suggests that people stop:

> ... and ask themselves whether they really and seriously believe that throughout this mighty universe, in which our little planet is but as a tiny speck of sand in the Sahara, this one planet only is inhabited by living things? Is all the universe dumb save for our voices? eyeless save for our vision? dead save for our life? ... Earth, air, water, all are teeming with living things suited to their environment; our globe is overflowing with life.

Although, when H.P.B. died in 1891, Annie Besant was her chosen successor, she only became the head of the Society in 1907, when Colonel Olcott died. By then she had worked as the editor of *Lucifer*, moved to India, made her home at Adyar, and would only wear white flowing robes, but she increasingly combined her esoteric beliefs with her political ones. In 1898, she helped establish what was to become one of the country's largest educational establishments, the Central Hindu School, in Varanasi - which is still going strong. In 1903, the thirteen-year-old Jawaharlal Nehru - who, in 1947, would go on to become India's first post-Independence Prime Minister - joined the Society after hearing her lecture at Allahabad but left when he became active in politics. Besant managed somehow to balance politics with her spiritual life. In 1909, she supported Leadbeater's belief that a fourteen-year-old boy he had spotted on a bank of the Adyar river, Jiddu Krishnamurti - the son of an Indian Theosophist employed by the society - was the reincarnation of the Master Maitreya, a universal teacher and a Messiah. (Leadbeater's legacy is a murky one. In 1906, he resigned from the Society after it came to light that he had been advising boys to masturbate. Besant nevertheless was vociferous in her support of him; when she became president, he returned to the fold.)

When the First World War broke out, Besant joined forces with the Indian Nationalist Bal Gangadhar Tilak to establish the Home Rule Movement, which advocated for Indian autonomy; in 1917, she became the first female president of the Indian National Congress and was briefly imprisoned by the British on account of her anticolonial activism. In 1929, however, Theosophy was dealt a blow when Krishnamurti severed his ties with the organisation, renounced all religions and gurus, and forged his own path as a philosopher.

When she died in September 1933, obituaries described Annie Besant as one of 'the most unique women of all time', placing her in the same league as Marie Curie, the social reformer Jane Addams, the ballerina Anna Pavlova and the poet Elizabeth Barrett Browning. Yet perhaps her most enduring legacy is to modern art – *Thought-Forms* is one of the earliest attempts to posit the idea that an image could represent something ineffable. It influenced not only a host of avant-garde European artists but those working in the United States, Australia, India and beyond, who were mesmerised by its commingling of art and science, politics and mysticism.

Vivienne Roberts – the curator of the London College of Psychic Studies, whose knowledge of mediumistic art is second to none – told me an intriguing theory: that *Thought-Forms* was possibly influenced by the experiments in visualising sound that were conducted in the second half of the nineteenth century by the Welsh soprano and philanthropist, Margaret Watts Hughes. I hadn't heard of her, and what I learned was astonishing.

Watts Hughes was gripped by the experiments conducted by the inventor of the telephone, Alexander Graham Bell. To get a sense of Bell's excitement in this new world, after demonstrating a device he called the 'Photophone', he wrote to his father: 'I have heard articulate speech produced by sunlight! I have heard a ray of the sun laugh and cough and sing! . . . I have been able to hear a shadow, and I have even perceived by ear the passage of the cloud across the sun's disk!'

Intrigued and inspired, Watts Hughes created a machine that would suit her purposes as a singer: an instrument she called an 'Eidophone' to measure the power of her voice. In 1876, she demonstrated her findings to the Royal Society, the oldest scientific academy in continuous existence. The society had only rarely allowed women a voice and Watts Hughes was one of the first to take up the challenge. Her idea was straightforward: she would sing into its tube to see how much she could move grains of sand, seeds or powder that she had sprinkled on an India-rubber membrane. By varying the harmonics of her voice, she discovered she could create different shapes with whatever substance she had placed on the membrane. In 1885, however, something startling happened. Rather than the seeds, as she writes, 'scattering promiscuously in all directions and falling over the edge of the receiver onto the table, as was customary when a rather loud note was sung', they 'resolved themselves into a perfect geometrical figure'. In 1891, she penned an article for *The Century* magazine describing the phenomenon, which she termed 'Voice Figures'. She was then inspired to take her experiment further: she placed various coloured pastes onto ceramic and glass plates to register her vocal vibrations - a process she described as 'singing into shape these peculiar forms'. Once completed, she would place another glass plate onto the pattern to take an imprint of it. The resultant pictures - which one of her contemporaries described as 'voice flowers' - are startlingly contemporary: luminous blue, green and yellow paintings as vivid as molecules under a microscope; they're like otherworldly ferns, bright lunar landscapes or deep-sea creatures dreamed up in the 1960s. Interestingly, Watts Hughes displayed them in the windows of the orphanage she ran in North London; the light streaming through them must have been a wonderfully kaleidoscopic sight in such a sombre setting. In 1889, the novelist Emilie Barrington visited Watts Hughes at her orphanage and wrote a letter to *The Spectator* describing how the glass pictures:

> ... are more like, perhaps, what a dream might make out of the impressions left by Nature, perfectly drawn designs of shell-like forms, photographically precise renderings of shapes of which the exact originals were never seen by human eye on sea or land; such things as *Alice in Wonderland* might have come upon, had she tumbled down to the bottom of the sea.

Her words suggest that for Watts Hughes - who was a devout Christian - the images had a significance that went beyond the purely scientific: they were proof of a 'revelation of yet another link in the great chain of the organised universe that, we are told in Holy Writ, took *its* shape in the voice of God'. It's not surprising that the Theosophists were excited. Vivienne Roberts told me that Henry Olcott had penned an article about Watts Hughes's work in September 1890, which mentions that he had learned about it from his friend W.T. Stead - the editor of the *Pall Mall Gazette*, who commissioned Annie Besant to review Blavatsky's *Secret Doctrine*. Yet, despite the obvious debt that Besant and Leadbeater owed Watts Hughes, she's mentioned only in passing in *Thought-Forms*: 'The voice-forms so admirably studied and pictured by Mrs Watts-Hughes ... should be consulted, and her work on the subject should be in the hands of every student.'

It is one of the vagaries of history that Watts Hughes's discovery, which spans music, art and science, went largely unrecognised. For many years, the series she called 'Impression Figures' was considered lost, but in 2016 it was found in the archives of the Cyfarthfa Castle Museum and Art Gallery in Wales. It's now a star attraction.

The impact of *Thought-Forms* has lingered. In 2015, the 14th Istanbul Biennale - a major exhibition on the international art calendar

- was curated by the influential Italian museum director and art historian Carolyn Christov-Bakargiev. She titled her exhibition 'Saltwater: A Theory of Thought Forms' and her introductory statement reveals her indebtedness to Besant:

> A number of drawings, paintings, installations, films, objects, books, collaborations, and research-based events will be viewable as thought forms - waves or oscillating patterns of repeating and differing lines that structure and enfold all forms of transference of energy - from brain waves to shockwaves after an explosion, from sound waves and waves of water to electromagnetic waves of different lengths and frequencies, including radio waves and light.

Once again, science mingled with art even though what constituted art and science had shifted. Once again, old ideas were reborn and bloomed anew.

Magnetic Fields

'Where war has torn up plants and killed animals there are empty spaces which could be filled with new figures if there were sufficient faith in human imagination and the human capacity to develop higher forms.'

Hilma af Klint Notebooks (1919)

Hilma af Klint, 1902

A few years before *Thought-Forms* was published, a woman in her early forties had her photograph taken. It's 1902, Stockholm. She's in a crisp white high-necked blouse; a plain, long dark skirt. She's sitting on a wooden chair: she gazes out at us with a quizzical expression, her head resting on her right hand. Her hair is pulled back. Her face is clear and strangely modern: thoughtful, open, smooth. She's surrounded by paintings: a conventional portrait of a man and what could be a watercolour of a landscape - it's hard to tell. There's a stack of paintings facing the wall. Secret paintings, perhaps. She's looking out at us. We're in the future - which is something she knew more about than most.

In an earlier photograph, taken in 1885 in her studio at the Royal Academy of Fine Arts in Stockholm, she's more animated. She's smiling lightly at someone out of the picture; she's holding a large palette in her left hand and leaning against the kind of shelf that is everywhere in art schools: grubby, lined up with flowers and old bottles and candles: subjects ripe for still life. She's dressed in black, but her head is in light and framed by dried flowers - a nod to her love of nature - and a paper parasol. Above her, the light pours through a window: it illuminates her. She glows.

Thinking back over my time at *frieze*, I can see a clear dividing line 'before' and 'after' 2013, when I crunched across the snow to the Moderna Museet in Stockholm to visit an exhibition of the Swedish artist Hilma af Klint. I had first heard about her some years previously when two friends, Donna Huddleston and Frank Hannon, paid homage to her in their exhibition 'Dear Hilma' in a series of dilapidated rooms in London's Fitzrovia. Their drawings and watercolours depicted delicate figures performing strange rites - a hand boxing or lifted in response to something out of view; a woman framed by rabbit-like shadows; a group with black hair and gloves, staring into space, as if in a trance; a lone girl holding a mysterious rope, in front of a depleted tree: atmosphere was all.

They hung their pictures on the green walls of a lamp-lit room that evoked something of a nineteenth-century Scandinavian living room. In the gloom of a cold winter's night, it was possible to imagine that Hilma had only momentarily stepped out of the room.

Donna said that when she first saw af Klint's work in an exhibition at the Douglas Hyde Gallery in Ireland in 2005, 'the energy field between the paintings was palpable and extraordinary. We wanted to name the show as if it were the opening of a letter to her. We wanted to drop her a line to say hello and thank you for the experience.' Frank told me that he felt lucky to have 'the various receptors' in his body to be able to absorb her work into his heart.

Nothing could prepare me for the shock of seeing af Klint's work in the flesh. Her exhibition in Stockholm comprised more than 200 paintings and works on paper - including the 'Ten Largest' from 1907, a monumental study of the stages of life from birth to death from a metaphysical perspective. Wandering from picture to picture was like travelling through the exalted corridors of someone's mind; they towered over me, in scale and in content. Images veered from ecstatic abstraction to hard-edged minimalism and erotic figuration: black and white swans - symbols of duality - and men, women and doves, entwined, separated, rose and plummeted in a hallucinogenic celebration of Eros and the spirit. A black room with af Klint's three enormous 'Altar Pieces' from 1915 recall the transcendent pictures of artists such as Mark Rothko and Agnes Martin fifty years later.

Who was the artist who could create such pictures?

Hilma af Klint was the fourth of five children born to an aristocratic family of naval officers in the town of Solna, near Stockholm, in 1862; her grandfather was the country's cartographer. In 1879, aged seventeen, she started taking part in séances. A year later, her ten-year-old sister Hermina died suddenly, a tragedy that most likely fuelled the devastated young artist's desire to contact the other side. She studied painting at Stockholm's Royal Academy of Fine Arts, where she became close to the artist Anna Cassel. Although women could enrol at the Royal Academy from 1864 (state-funded German academies, by contrast, barred female students until 1919), female students were expected to put down their brushes and hang up their smocks for marriage and motherhood. Even modernist movements barred women from their ranks. For example: in 1909, a group of young artists, inspired by the work of Henri Matisse, established a supposedly radical new art group in Stockholm. Calling themselves *De Unga* - the young ones - they wrote the exclusion of women into their charter.

But af Klint was unconventional, and she forged her way, despite the obstacles. Between 1886 and 1907, her work was included in more than twenty-four exhibitions; she never married and had romantic relationships with women. Like so many artists, she was fascinated by developments in science. Among the burgeoning numbers of people embracing - or at least, curious about - Spiritualism, were some of the great scientists of the day: the physicists Marie and Pierre Curie, the evolutionary biologist Alfred Russel Wallace, and the psychologist William James. Pioneers of electricity, including Nikola Tesla, the inventor of the radio and wireless technology, who claimed that his ideas came to him in flashes of light, and Thomas Edison, who invented everything from the light bulb to motion pictures, experimented with a spirit telephone that would let the living communicate with the dead. In 1932, the radical quantum physicist Wolfgang Pauli asked his friend Carl Jung for help during a personal crisis. The psychoanalyst's esoteric knowledge and analysis of his dreams opened the physicist's mind to new discoveries, not only about the nature of the universe but about the depths of his own mind. In turn, Pauli taught Jung that a basic principle of alchemy - reconciliation of opposites into a unity - is central to quantum physics. How apt, then, that in 1909 af Klint was commissioned by Sweden's Uppsala University to paint a posthumous portrait of the late physicist Knut Ångström, who had explored solar radiation, was a supporter of women's rights and, as a member of the Stockholm Academy of Sciences, had argued that the Nobel Prize be awarded to Marie Curie alongside her husband Pierre, and Henri Becquerel. The painting was hung in the building of the student society.

In 1910, af Klint became a member, then secretary and deputy board member of the newly founded Association of Swedish Women Artists; her older sister, Ida, was a member of the Fredrika Bremer Association, founded in 1884 to protect and champion women's rights. From 1918 until 1940, af Klint lived in various homes with her partner, Thomasine Andersson, who had been her mother's nurse.

Alongside her interest in Spiritualism and science, it was Theosophy and Christianity that had the most impact on af Klint's thinking. She owned a well-thumbed copy of Madame Blavatsky's *The Secret Doctrine* and her encrypted use of colour echoes Leadbeater and Besant's *Thought-Forms*. As Julia Voss - author of the first major biography of af Klint, published in English in late 2022 - observes, the Swedish translation of 'thought-forms' is *tankeformer*, a term that repeatedly appears in the artist's notes; even as late as 1934 it turns up on a page illustrated with the spirits who had inspired and propelled her work nearly two decades earlier.

For af Klint, the very air throbbed with unseen energies. The question was, how to interpret them? How to give them shape? Could they be understood more clearly via the language of art? The answer was a resounding 'yes'. Although when she graduated af Klint made a living selling portraits, landscape paintings and botanical studies - and she and Cassel produced illustrations for a veterinary textbook - from 1907, she embarked on four decades of cycles and series of works in which the mortal realm mingled with the worlds of both spirits and science. The question lingers: How did af Klint arrive at an artistic language that was so astonishingly radical for the time?

In 1891, she had begun receiving messages from the other side, but it was a few years before they took form as pictures. In 1894, it's likely af Klint saw Edvard Munch's expressionistic paintings in his exhibition - including *The Scream* (1893) - that was staged in Theodor Blanch's Art Salon close to her studio. The Norwegian artist's occult leanings, along with his close friend, the playwright - and misogynist - August Strindberg, were well known. In 1896, she and Cassel attended meetings at the Edelweiss Society, a Swedish ecumenical association, where they met three women who were to become important in af Klint's development as an artist: Sigrid Hedman, Mathilda Nilsson and her sister Cornelia Cederberg. They all shared an interest in Christianity and Theosophy and decided to form their own Spiritualist group: De Fem (The Five). Their meetings began with a sermon and bible study and concluded with a séance that occasionally resulted in clairvoyant drawings.

There's an intriguing sepia photograph of the room in which they met. It's empty, expectant, neat, with an ornate rocking chair, two other mismatched chairs and a corner sofa covered in faded velvet. The wallpaper is patterned with flowers; a large fern stretches its dry tendrils almost to the ceiling. The round table is decorated with two vases - one small, the other large - filled with fresh flowers. There's a clock, some paper and pencils, a photograph of a woman. A scattering of religious pictures - Jesus gazing skywards, two Virgin Marys - which look as if they've been torn from a book, are stuck to the wall. A cut-out of a white bird, its wings raised high, is forever stilled, mid-flight. It's an ordinary middle-class parlour, waiting for something extraordinary: communication from the other side.

The women believed that 'Masters' - spirits called Amaliel, Ananda, Clemens, Esther, Georg and Gregor - had contacted them to communicate eternal truths via drawings and writing - and together they filled sketchbooks of images made under their direction. At times, they used a 'psychograph', a device developed in the 1880s to record messages from the beyond. At first, Nilsson and Hedman were the main mediums, but in 1903 af Klint became active. To deepen her concentration, she practised a popular Spiritualist exercise that involved focusing on a glass of water for hours on end, trying to evoke the shapes and colours that existed on a higher plane.

During a séance in 1904 – the year she formally joined the Theosophical Society – af Klint was contacted by the spirit guide Ananda, who predicted she would create 'astral paintings', warning her not to 'expect the signals and symbols that you have developed with much effort will be understood by the brothers that you meet but to work hard for the future'. She spent months preparing for what lay ahead with cleansing, rituals, meditation and vegetarianism. (In 1902, her guides had told her 'you cannot imagine what great harm you are doing to yourself by eating meat'.) As the curator Aaron Lister noted, her valorisation of 'slow looking, communal exchange, mind and body connectivity and the restorative powers of nature' chimes with much contemporary thinking around wellness.

In 1906, the spirit guide Amaliel offered af Klint a commission to create a suite of paintings. She immediately said yes. It was, in her words, 'the one great task that I carried out in my life'. Under Amaliel's direction, af Klint unrolled a three-metre long and two-metre-wide piece of paper on her studio floor and began. It was the beginning of a sustained period of work that resulted in the stupendous series 'The Paintings of the Temple'. A total of 193 works were comprised of thematic groups: Primordial Chaos, Eros, the Ten Largest, Evolution, The Swan, The Tree of Knowledge, the Dove and Altarpieces. 'The pictures were painted directly through me,' said af Klint, 'without preliminary drawings and with great force. I had no idea what the paintings were supposed to depict; nevertheless, I worked swiftly and surely, without changing a single brushstroke.' The artist had become a transmitter, like a human radio or telegram. That said, she was far from passive. The process was one of exchange between the artist and her spirit guide. In 1906, Hilma af Klint wrote in her journal: 'The experiments I have undertaken will astound humanity.' But her task wasn't a solitary one. The paintings emerged from the support she received from her spiritual community, in particular Anna Cassel. Most likely lovers, they called their togetherness 'Vestalasket', a fusion of their alter egos in which gender was as malleable as space and time. Af Klint was 'Asket' (a masculine ascetic), and Cassel was 'Vestal', after the female virgins who guarded the Temple of Vesta in Ancient Rome.

'The Ten Largest' was intended to 'give the world a glimpse of the system of four parts in the life of man'. These enormous egg-tempera works took af Klint two months to create; at times, she was assisted by Cornelia Cederberg. Some of the pictures bear faint traces of footprints, which indicate that she painted them on the floor. The first in the series, *Childhood, Group IV*, is as happy as a summer's day: rapturous flower-like shapes mingle with looping, curling letters and enigmatic words that tumble across the lower part of the image like drunken bass notes; dusty pink blossoms pulsate against a parched blue sky. In *No. 2, Childhood, Group IV*, an orange and an indigo ball fuse in a meeting of dark and light, while euphoric spirals dissolve in a dream of pale fresco blue. In *No. 6, Adulthood*, cryptic words and letters float across a stony pink background, while circles and helixes hover like trippy eyes. By *No. 10, Old Age*, harmony reigns, in the air, the earth and the sea, in the body's journey from material to matter: time without end is suggested in an expanse of delicate, scumbled pigment and a grid of calm ochres and blue. Intimations of Theosophy's belief in the universe as a single unit is expressed in swirling atoms that morph into planets: the suggestion of 'oneness' as the way of healing a world wracked by division - between good and evil, men and women, substance and spirit - is clear. The near-musical invocation of

elation is palpable - and contagious. Many of the pictures appear to
have been painted swiftly: parts of the surfaces are left bare, paint
stains, runs, leaks. Hilma often wrote cryptic notes and dates on
her pictures; messages to herself, or to others. Her work expressed
the belief that each human has a soul mate - on the mortal or astral
plane - and that universal harmony would result when equality
had been achieved between men and women. When her work
on the series was finished, af Klint recorded that the spirits were
happy, telling her: 'You've now completed such glorious work that
you would fall to your knees if you understood it.'

In 1908, af Klint stopped making paintings for four years to look
after her mother. It was the same year she attended a lecture on
Rosicrucianism - which combines occultism, Jewish mysticism and
Christian Gnosticism. The artist's allegiance to the movement was
apparent in the silver cross necklace she wore, which was engraved
with a rose within a circle: the Rosicrucian symbol. The lecture was
given by the man who was to become one of the most influential
people in af Klint's life: Rudolf Steiner, an Austrian clairvoyant, philosopher, educator and architect. She showed Steiner her works around
1909 or 1910, but it's not clear what transpired. What is clear is that for
the rest of her life af Klint admired him and sought his counsel.

In 1912, she returned to the studio to complete another eighty-
two works; by 1915, her task was complete. From then on, until
her death in 1944 (curiously, the same year that Kandinsky and
Mondrian died), Hilma af Klint painted mainly without the help
of her spirit guides, although she remained in contact with them.
Considering she lived through a calamitous time - two world wars
- her longing for 'universal harmony' was not just spiritual. The
violence that erupted across Europe was echoed in af Klint's cycle
'The Swan', which she began in 1914. Black and white swans - birds
that migrate between cultures - clash with terrible violence. Blood
and flames emanate from their bodies; gradually, though, their
physical forms dissolve into symmetrical, geometric abstractions:

circles, squares and triangles; abstract approximations of harmony. Julia Voss points out that the symbolism of the swan was probably influenced by Madame Blavatsky's *The Secret Doctrine*, in which the swan 'was not just the animal form of Brahma for the Hindus' but 'connects the elements, living both in the water and in the air, and it was important to the ancient Greeks, as in the myth of Leda and the Swan'. In 1917, thanks to a loan from Anna Cassel, af Klint had a studio and home built on the island of Munsö, where she lived with Thomasine and her mother. In 1920, her mother died and af Klint travelled with Thomasine to Dornach in Switzerland, where Steiner had designed an extraordinary domed building, the Goetheanum. It was named after Goethe, who Steiner revered; he was especially guided by the German writer's belief that works of art, like works of nature, are produced 'according to the divine necessity of true and natural laws' and that 'the Beautiful is a manifestation of secret laws which otherwise would have remained hidden forever'. The building named after him - which was rebuilt after a fire - became the global centre for Anthroposophy, which Steiner founded as 'an association of people whose will it is to foster the life of the soul both in the individual and in society, based on a true knowledge of the spiritual world'. In 1912, Steiner had argued with Annie Besant and left the Theosophical Society; his focus had shifted from the Eastern traditions in which Madame Blavatsky and Besant were so absorbed, to the philosophical and esoteric traditions of European culture. Essentially, he believed that Christianity, above all others, was the religion worth investing in. At the Goetheanum, equality of the sexes ruled. Both men and women shared equal responsibilities. Hilma and Thomasine both joined up.

Af Klint wanted to show Steiner the watercolours and black-and-white photographs she had taken of the 193 'Paintings for the Temple' that filled ten 'Blue books' - a kind of suitcase museum of her work in miniature. It's likely she wanted to exhibit her work in the Goetheanum but she didn't manage to meet Steiner and returned home. In 1921 Hilma and Thomasine once again visited Dornach and af Klint finally managed to show Steiner the ten volumes of her work. The women recorded his words, which are terse: one picture 'belongs to the astral world', particular images are 'the best symbolically', and so on. It's lukewarm encouragement, at best.

In 1924, af Klint wrote to Steiner with a blunt question: 'Should the paintings executed by me between 1906 and 1920, of which you, Doctor, once saw several, be destroyed, or can they be used somewhere?' Although his reply is lost, later that year af Klint gave a lecture in which she explained that he had told her it would be a shame to destroy them and they could be useful.

Steiner died in March 1925, although af Klint continued to communicate with him posthumously. According to a letter she sent to the Swedish symbolist artist Tyra Kleen in 1943, he was more supportive than has long been assumed, if still rather ambiguous in his response to what she had achieved. 'Steiner has not warned me about the path I have taken. On the contrary, he has encouraged me, and he will probably help me to complete the work.' Af Klint owned more than 120 books by Steiner, and her notebooks make clear that she considered herself a devoted disciple.

Af Klint's work of the 1930s embodies something of Europe's increasing turmoil and included her flaming 'maps': forewarnings of the destruction that would soon engulf the world. In 1932, her watercolours included *The Blitz Over London*, *The Outbreak of War in Spain* and *Naval Battles in the Mediterranean*. These she made alongside kaleidoscopic land-and-sea-and-cloudscapes, heads enveloped in rays of light or spewing fire; bodies entwined amidst a pulsating expanse; abstract colour experiments, nature studies, spectral beings, and the occasional reference to her spirit guides. On 30 July 1936, for instance, a watercolour titled *Ananda's Guidance* includes a very faint outline of an ambiguous naked figure reclining beneath a radiant yellow light.

In spite of af Klint's evident comfort with the solitude necessary to the creative life, it's clear that she would have liked to show her work to those she felt were sympathetic to Spiritualism; she even designed an unrealised spiral-shaped temple that she intended to build on the Swedish island of Ven in the Øresund strait in order to display her paintings. Although seventeen of her more representational works were exhibited at the Seventh Congress of the European Federation of the Theosophical Society in Stockholm in 1913, and an unknown number of 'Paintings for the Temple' at the World Conference on Spiritual Science in London in 1928 – something that came about thanks to the zeal of a Dutch Anthroposophical devotee and dancer, Peggy Kloppers-Moltzer – af Klint found it difficult to muster the support and enthusiasm needed to exhibit her work more widely. Apart from Rudolf Steiner and her close friends, few people were privy to what she had achieved. Later in her life, Tyra Kleen proposed that af Klint's work could be housed in a new building she was funding for the Sigtuna Foundation, a centre for learning run by the Lutheran Church. Hilma, however, was adamant that her drawings and paintings could only be displayed in a context sympathetic to Anthroposophy – and declined. Although she experienced some frustration at her work's lack of visibility, af Klint was insistent that it had to be in the right context. Also, she was so absorbed in her exploration of a new language and so bolstered by her spiritual community, it's possible she was indifferent to the petty machinations of the art world – and incapable of the hustling that the life of a professional artist often entails.

We don't know af Klint's thoughts on the matter, although it's possible we might in the future: she left behind 27,000 pages of notebooks, which are currently being studied. In many of her notes, she attempted to decode the messages she had received; she often came up with multiple meanings for a single symbol. In 1917-18 she filled 1,200 pages on 'Studies on Spiritual Life' ('Studier over Själslivet'), which she edited and probably rewrote in 1942. In it, she clarifies that spirals signify evolution; 'U', the spiritual world; 'W', matter; and overlapping discs, unity. Yellow and roses represent masculinity, and blue and lilacs femininity, but the rule is malleable: as in her 1916 series 'Parsifal' - 144 works on paper - the Swedish words for 'forward, backward, downward, inward, outward, and upward' recur amidst images that morph between severely geometric and figurative: the hero is male and then female. Rigid definitions had no part in af Klint's philosophy; in her pictures, she moves as fluidly between genders as she does between cosmic and physical realms; between botanical studies and geometry; from the body of a human to a bird to the roots of a tree. In her notes, she coins new words: 'womanman' and 'manwoman' and observes: 'Many who fight in this drama are dressed in the wrong clothing. Many female costumes conceal a man. Many male costumes conceal the woman.'

In 1932, at the age of seventy, af Klint wrote that any works she marked '+x' should not be viewed until twenty years after her death. Her directive included the blue books that contained reproductions of the 'Paintings for the Temple'. She obviously felt the world wasn't ready for the complexity of her message - a feeling that was surely compounded by her inability to find a home for her paintings and drawings. 'The experiments I have conducted,' she wrote, 'that were to awaken humanity when they were cast upon the world were pioneering endeavours. Though they travel through much dirt they will yet retain their purity.' In 1937, she gave a lecture in which she declared she didn't know who the beings were who had, for so long, guided her.

In 1938, af Klint's sister died, leaving her a generous legacy; finally, she could relax about her finances. In 1940, Thomasine died. Four years later, af Klint was injured in a fall; she never recovered. On 9 October 1944, she penned her last sentence: 'You have service to the mysteries before you and will soon understand what is required of you.' She left her paintings and notebooks to her nephew, Erik af Klint, with whom she was close. She requested to be buried alongside Thomasine. Her request was not carried out. Her ashes were interred in the family plot.

Unlike most of their female colleagues, the male artists who were guided by Spiritualism or Theosophy were commercially ambitious. Confident in their radicalism, they formed or were part of radical artist societies, were backed by art dealers, museum directors and collectors. They regularly showed their work and insisted on its status via articles and manifestos. In 1911, Paul Klee was a founder of the Munich artists' union Sema, and he joined the editorial team of Der Blaue Reiter almanac; by 1917, his work was selling well. In the same year, Mondrian co-founded De Stijl (The Style) art movement, which proposed pure abstraction, and he coined the term 'neoplasticism' to describe non-representational forms. František Kupka was a co-founder of Orphism, an offshoot of Cubism, and was financially supported for twenty years by the art collector and industrialist Jindřich Waldes. By the 1930s, works by male members of the group were lauded and collected. In 1931, Alfred J. Barr curated 'German Painting and Sculpture' for the Museum of Modern Art in New York. Its press release declared it 'the most important exhibition of German art ever held in America'. Of the twenty-eight artists - including Paul Klee and Franz Marc - only two were women: Paula Modersohn Becker and Renée Sintenis. Gabriele Münter was nowhere to be seen.

Due to her expressed wish that her paintings couldn't be sold, there are no af Klints in major public collections. (She did allow for individual works to be released to support the upkeep of the archive, but only to an institution. This has not yet happened.) In 1970, Pontus Hultén, the then-director of the Moderna Museet - the most important modern art museum in Sweden - was offered the af Klint estate but he turned it down: for Hultén, the fact that she was a Spiritualist was a sign that she wasn't to be taken seriously. (He was possibly also daunted by the sheer volume of paintings, drawings and notebooks.) Similarly, af Klint wasn't even a footnote in the 2013 show 'Inventing Abstraction, 1910-1925' at the Museum of Modern Art in New York: the show's curator, Leah Dickerman, justified the artist's exclusion because she wasn't convinced that af Klint saw her paintings as art. This, despite the fact that 'secret' paintings were informed by mysticism, mathematics, science and religion - all of which inspired Kandinsky, Mondrian, Kupka and Malevich, who were all stars of the MoMA show - and their paintings, it's important to note, are part of the museum's collection.

A quote from Kandinsky's essay 'Concerning the Spiritual in Art' from 1911: 'The true work of art is born from the Artist: a mysterious, enigmatic, and mystical creation.' Dig deep and it becomes clear: when a male artist explored spirituality it didn't necessarily harm his career, but when a woman followed the same path, she was dismissed as, at best, eccentric, at worst, a maverick. (A friend who has a PhD in magic lanterns observed to me that women are usually seen as clairvoyants, the men, magicians. I'm still thinking about what this means.) But it's not so long ago that a woman's expressed interest in other realms might have ruined her reputation or even killed her - we all know the tales of women being branded as witches, cast out from society or burnt at the stake. For millennia, magic was seen as a very real, and possibly malevolent, power, one that might undermine or even overrule patriarchal power. Women with a close connection to nature and animals, who had great intuition and sensitivity, who possibly understood things that weren't immediately obvious, were often literally demonised. 'The land is full of witches,' Chief Justice Anderson, a witch-hunter, told an English court in 1602, 'they abound in all places.' It's startling to discover that the last person convicted under the Witchcraft Act in Great Britain was the Spiritualist Jane Rebecca Yorke in 1944. But it's a persecution that continues in thirty-six countries in Asia,

Africa and South America. It's such a serious problem that in 2020 the Pope declared 10 August as World Day against Witch Hunts. Activists and Feminist artists across the globe have pushed back. As the American writer Anya Ventura observed on the eve of Hilma af Klint's Guggenheim show:

> The witch, like af Klint, represents bodily and psychic independ-ence - a figure in possession of secret knowledge gleaned outside the traditional structures of power. Like af Klint, the witch's wisdom, expressed through incantations and herbs, is rooted in the natural world and in collaborations with other women. Why does af Klint speak to us in the present? Perhaps because she rep-resents values - female, spiritual, ecological, collectivist - eroded by the rise of industrial modernity, values we desperately need to reclaim.

In 2018, 'Hilma af Klint: Paintings for the Future' opened at the Guggenheim Museum in New York - a building that could have been dreamed up especially for her. Its design was influenced by the German artist and Baroness, Hilla Rebay, who, as well as being guided by astrology, Buddhism and Zoroastrianism, was a Theos-ophist who had been involved in Der Blaue Reiter; in 1946, she translated *On the Spiritual in Art* into English. A year after emigrat-ing to the United States in 1927 with the intention of opening a gallery of abstract art, Rebay had accepted a commission to paint Solomon Guggenheim's portrait; they formed a close friendship, and the artist eventually became his art adviser; it was through her introductions that he was to buy more than 150 paintings by Kan-dinsky for his collection.

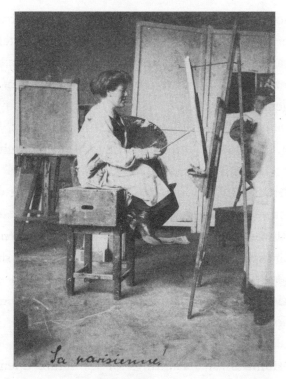

Hilla Rebay, 1911

Rebay believed that the translation of spiritual feelings into abstract, or 'non-objective' art would serve the betterment of mankind. In 1937, she declared: 'Non-Objectivity will be the religion of the future. Very soon the nations on earth will turn to it in thought and feeling and develop such intuitive powers which lead them to harmony.' In 1939, Rebay was appointed director and curator of the newly founded Solomon R. Guggenheim Museum in New York; its first location was called the Museum of Non-Objective Painting and opened in a temporary space on East 54th Street. For its inaugural exhibition, alongside abstract artworks, the baroness burned incense and played music by Bach and Beethoven; the art critic for *The New York Times* described it as 'an esoteric, occult place in which a mystic language was spoken'. Rebay dreamed of a 'museum-temple' filled with abstract art and in 1943, she found the architect who could turn her vision into a reality: Frank Lloyd Wright. She told him she was seeking 'a lover of space, a fighter, and originator' and he rose to the challenge -- although it took sixteen years for the museum to be built. In 1959 the Solomon R. Guggenheim Museum opened, and no one had seen anything like it before: an organic, biomorphic, light-filled gallery, 'one great space on a continuous floor', in the words of the architect, that forces visitors to spiral skywards.

Notwithstanding their shared interests, Rebay and af Klint never met. But it's fair to assume that the Swedish artist would have approved of Lloyd Wright's modernist temple for her first major exhibition in the United States.

In late 2022, Julia Voss's majestic biography of af Klint was published in English and the artist's complete *catalogue raisonée* was released: seven enormous volumes of drawings, paintings and notes. Her output is staggering. To keep going without public recognition must surely have entailed enormous self-belief, yet it's clear that for af Klint, her pictures weren't something that she depended upon to make a living, but an extension of who she was. Her pictures were part of her.

In recent years, more and more curators have supported af Klint's work; as I write this, a major exhibition of af Klint and Mondrian has been announced for Tate Modern. Quite apart from the sheer beauty of her paintings, it's hard not to see the near-feverish interest in her as a reflection of the widespread hunger for new ways of inhabiting the planet. Given the crises we've collectively experienced in recent times, it's apparent that long-held assumptions around art, politics and gender, the natural world, religion - and even what constitutes time itself - are being challenged. In her creation of a new language, af Klint suggested that some of the truths we assume to be fixed are, in fact, straitjackets of our own making.

She Danced a Goldfish

'. . . in the early 20th century, new spirits would wander abroad, conjured up by Armageddon, out of its blasted foxholes and damaged minds, from the Angel of Mons to the Cottingley Fairies. As the weed and wildflowers overran those scarred sites of annihilation, new suburban visionaries saw both Apocalypse and Utopia in England's past, present and future.'

Philip Hoare, 'This Dis-Remembered Land' (2009)

When I was at art school in Canberra in the mid-1980s, I worked in a poster shop called Frame-Up. Situated on a dead-end street in a suburban wasteland, some days no one came in and I fell asleep on the counter. On the rare occasions when customers did appear, they usually wanted to buy a picture to match their furniture. Sometimes, though, they confessed that what they wanted was a glimpse of somewhere else; another life, place or state of mind. I would steer them towards our bestsellers: 'abstracts' (usually blue); photographs of New York or Paris in the 1940s and 1950s of people running hand-in-hand down foggy streets full of promise or kissing with abandon in the kind of dim-but-golden bars you never found in Australian suburbs; or nature, especially photographs of waves or lightning, or animals, who were either 'spiritual' (dolphins) or absurd (monkeys). Nineteenth-century flower paintings were popular, as were reproductions of Matisse, Chagall, Rothko and, in particular, Edward Hopper's melancholy *Boulevard of Broken Dreams*. The racier customers went for erotica, especially Herb

Ritts's semi-naked supermodels dished up like a mixed grill. On the bus home, I always felt morose and a little grubby. Despite the fact that I was selling pictures, none of it seemed to have anything to do with either art or with my life. And yet, years after I quit and found work piercing teenage earlobes in a chemist shop, I couldn't pass a poster shop without stopping and checking out the wares.

Decades later, soon after I joined *frieze*, for some reason I remembered that job and wondered what the popularity of certain images signified about particular moments in time. I pitched an article asking that very question. While researching it, I came across a heartbreaking story.

In 1915, as battles raged across Europe and young men were being slaughtered in their millions on the Western Front, a small painting was exhibited at London's Royal Academy. It depicts an elf-like child, probably a boy. His legs are crossed and he's leaning against a tree. He's playing a pipe, his face obscured by a dark-blue hat adorned with a peacock feather. He's in a forest glade; perhaps it's early spring, as a scattering of yellow primroses and purple crocuses surround him. A robin perches on the toe of his left boot; a squirrel has paused, possibly to listen to the music. Tiny silver fairies swirl above the child's head. The picture's title is *The Piper of Dreams*, and it was painted by the British-Italian artist and writer Estella Canziani – one of the two women artists whose work I had seen in the fairy painting exhibition at the Royal Academy.

Curiously, in her 1939 autobiography *Round About Three Palace Green* – which was published on the eve of another calamitous war – Canziani mentions that she exhibited the painting before it was finished. She gives no reason for displaying it in such a state, but then art history is full of gaps and elisions. Soon after *The Piper of Dreams* was first displayed, The Medici Society snapped up the rights to its reproduction. In 1916 – the year conscription for British men was introduced – 250,000 copies of the picture were sold; it also inspired a composition for piano by Daisy Wilson-Gunn.

As all hell rained down upon the Western Front, it would seem that every muddy trench had a copy of the painting pinned to its walls - a talisman of a better place, where animals and humans co-existed in harmony, and everything stopped for music. It was popular back home, too; its gentle unreality a distraction from the state-sanctioned carnage across the Channel. During the dark years of the war, fairy fever was endemic in London. Productions of *A Midsummer Night's Dream* and a revival of the Edwardian play *Bluebell in Fairyland* sold out, while *Peter Pan* - J.M. Barrie's work first created as a play over a decade earlier - never waned in popularity. 'To die will be an awfully big adventure': that famous cry of the 'boy who wouldn't grow up' must have been unbearably poignant. Unsurprisingly, however, some writers and artists fulminated against what they saw as the escapism of fairy mania. In 1917, Robert Graves's poetry collection *Fairies and Fusiliers* was published: its title a mockery, its tone elegiac; the guns had blasted innocence to smithereens. In his poem 'Babylon' he observed that:

Wisdom made him old and wary
Banishing the Lords of Faery . . .
None of all the magic hosts,
None remain but a few ghosts

But Graves was in a minority. In the same year his lament was published, the poet and folklorist Rose Fyleman's poem 'There are Fairies at the bottom of the garden' ran in *Punch* magazine and was later set to music by the popular soprano composer Liza Lehmann. Fyleman's saccharine collection of poems *Fairies and Chimneys* (dedicated to the 'Realest Fairy of My Childhood: My Mother') came out in the final year of the war - and was reprinted more than twenty times:

Yesterday in Oxford Street, oh, what d'you think, my dears?
I had the most exciting time I've had for years and years;
The buildings looked so straight and tall, the sky was blue between,
And, riding on a motor-bus, I saw the fairy queen!

New worlds demand new languages, but in England it would seem it was the old worlds for which the populace longed.

In the early-1990s, I was enrolled in a postgraduate course at an art school in Melbourne. We painted in shabby studios in a decrepit building on St Kilda Road; rumour had that it had once been a medical ward as we could turn on the taps with our elbows and each room had an internal gutter. Back home in Canberra for a holiday, I came across an old wooden box in the depths of a cupboard. I opened it up; it was full of newspaper clippings and faded photographs. A leaflet fell out. Something about it looked familiar. It was advertising a new hospital for soldiers returning to Australia from the battlefields of the First World War. I was staring at a photograph of my studio.

I asked my dad about it. He told me that the box was my grandfather's and he had been hospitalised in Melbourne. On 19 and 20 July 1916, Poppa had taken part in the Battle of Fromelles on the Western Front. The Australian War Memorial describes it as 'possibly the worst 24 hours in the country's history'. Soldiers of the 5th Australian Division, along with the British 61st Division, were ordered to attack German frontline positions near the Aubers Ridge in French Flanders. In a single day, more than 5,500 Australians became casualties; almost 2,000 of them were killed in action or died of wounds and 400 or so were captured - the greatest loss by a single division during the entire war. According to official records, the battle was a 'disastrous failure' and 'had no impact whatsoever upon the progress of the Somme offensive'. Poppa returned to Australia with shell shock, amputated toes, tuberculosis and mental-health issues. He was just twenty-one. He never talked about what happened but in 1970 he penned a memoir for the family. It was decades before I read it. He wrote: 'It was, indeed, a hell of a time . . . I lost many of my mates. Good mates, whom I often remember with sadness.' He was an infinitely kind man. I cannot imagine how he managed not to go mad with the horror of it all.

Sheet music for 'Smile All the While', 1922

Yet somehow, he coped. A few years after the war ended, he composed the words and music to a 'vocal two step' that became something of a hit in Melbourne. It was called 'Smile All the While' and includes the refrain:

Smile, Smile, Smile all the while
It's easy when skies are blue
Tho' the clouds you find
Are not all silver lined
This motto in life's always true . . .

Be content and you'll never repent
The clouds aren't always grey
You'll forget all your sorrow in the joys of tomorrow
So, smile all your troubles away . . .

I wonder if Poppa knew *The Piper of Dreams*? I suspect he would have liked it. In her autobiography, Canziani wrote that her original title for her painting was *Where the Little Things of the Woodland Live Unseen*: a more literal description of her interests in other realms. She was uninterested in modernism: unlike many of the avant-garde artists inspired by the spirit world, such as af Klint and Kandinsky, she was content to represent other dimensions in an easily recognisable fashion.

A quaker whose lifelong interest in different spheres never waned, as well as being an artist and illustrator, Canziani was a regular contributor to *Folklore* magazine and donated 700 objects - such as a carved wooden pipe, ornately decorated thimbles and scent bottles - to the Pitt Rivers Museum in Oxford. She tells of her astonishment at hearing that reproductions of her picture were selling not only across the United Kingdom, but in Egypt, India and France; they were 'in the trenches, everywhere'. She had painted *The Piper of Dreams* in the woods behind her home; the son of a friend modelled the piper. Canziani's family was no stranger to the spirit world. Her mother, Louisa Starr, was a well-known portrait painter who had been one of the first women admitted to the Royal Academy and the first female student to win a gold medal.

Although there is scant information about her, one source claimed
that in the late nineteenth century, facsimiles of Starr's painting *A
Fairy Tale* sold like hot cakes. She didn't live long enough to witness her daughter's success with *The Piper of Dreams*.

So, why was it so popular?

Canziani was born in 1887, at the tail-end of the so-called 'golden
age' of nineteenth-century fairy painting. Sobriety, piety and rationalism had, supposedly, triumphed – until the devastation of the
First World War, when a grieving populace turned to Spiritualism
in a desperate attempt to contact the people they loved who had,
so cruelly, been taken from them. Millions were denied the closure
of seeing a body or laying their sons, fathers, brothers, lovers or
friends to rest. Human beings crave rites of passage; but during
and after the First World War it was not only the dead who could
not rest: grief was a collective activity, and many of the leading
intellectuals of the day believed in the possibility of an afterlife. In
1916, the renowned physicist Sir Oliver J. Lodge published his bestselling memoir *Raymond, Or Life and Death*, which documented his
communication with his son Raymond, who was killed in Flanders
in 1915. Sir Oliver was convinced of the veracity of mediumship
when, during a séance, he was told of a photograph of his son's
regiment that the family were unaware of, and which they subsequently received in the post. In his preface, Lodge justified writing
his book:

> I should not have done so were it not that the amount of prema-
> ture and unnatural bereavement at the present time is so appalling
> that the pain caused by exposing one's own sorrow and its allevi-
> ation, to possible scoffers, becomes almost negligible in view of
> the service which it is legitimate to hope may thus be rendered to
> mourners . . . Some few more perhaps may be thus led to pay crit-
> ical attention to any assurance of continued and happy and useful
> existence which may reach them from the other side.

At the beginning of his chapter titled 'Supernormal Portion', Lodge quotes the beautiful lines from Shelley's *Adonais: An Elegy on the Life of John Keats*: 'Peace, peace!/He is not dead, he doth not sleep/ He hath awakened from the dream of life.' Lodge is clear that despite his grief at the loss of his son, he is driven by science, while 'the family scepticism, which up to this time has been sufficiently strong, is now, I may fairly say, overborne by the facts'.

By 1917, Spiritualism's popularity was such that it challenged the dominance of the Anglican Church. In 1914, some 145 societies were affiliated to the Spiritualists National Union. In 1917, Sir Arthur Conan Doyle – whose wife was a medium who channelled a spirit guide called Phineas, who advised the couple on everything from global disaster to train timetables – had given his first public lecture in support of Spiritualism. When his son Kingsley was badly wounded at the Somme and then died of pneumonia in London in 1918, Conan Doyle's fervour for spirit communication increased. So vehement was he in his beliefs that he became embroiled in discussions debating photography's relationship to truth.

The year before Kingsley died, a sixteen-year-old girl, Elsie Wright, had taken a snapshot of her nine-year-old cousin, Frances Griffiths, gazing at a small group of fairies cavorting and playing musical instruments in an idyllic glade in front of a waterfall in Cottingley, Yorkshire. It was the first photograph Elsie had ever shot and it was to become one of the most hotly contested images of the early twentieth century. Three weeks later, Elsie took another photograph; this time, her cousin appears to be communing with a dancing winged gnome. The girls found a champion in Elsie's mother, who was interested in Theosophy. Convinced that the photographs were real, she took them along to a meeting in Bradford and showed them to Edward L. Gardener of London's Theosophical Society, who excitedly declared that the fairy photographs were proof that humanity was at last opening itself up to supernatural energies. He supplied the girls with two new cameras and more evidence appeared. By now, Conan Doyle had seen the photographs. In 1920, he wrote enthusiastically about them in the pages of *The Strand* magazine and then again in 1922, in his book *The Coming of the Fairies*. He believed that if the images were real, it would 'mark an epoch in human thought'. He continued: 'The recognition of their existence will jolt the material twentieth-century mind out of its heavy ruts in the mud and will make it admit that there is a glamour and a mystery to life.'

It wasn't until 1983 that Elsie Wright confessed that the Cottingley fairies were a hoax: she explained that the girls had copied the figures from *Princess Mary's Gift Book*, which had been published in the first year of the war, added wings to them and propped them up in the garden with hat pins. However, Frances Griffiths insisted that the last photograph they had taken - *Fairies and their Sunbath* in 1920 - was real and that they had staged the other photographs to make people believe in the little people, which she insisted they had seen. Interestingly, *Fairies and their Sunbath* is unlike the girl's other prints in that neither of them is in it. It's moody, textured, semi-abstract. The fairies' translucent wings shine like dewy cobwebs.

Looking at them from this distance in time, the photographs seem like unequivocal fakes. But something about them, despite their strange sweetness, is deeply modern - especially their stubborn insistence that there are many ways of making sense of the world - a feeling that was widespread in the immediate aftermath of the Great War.

In 1918, Conan Doyle's essay 'New Revelation' was published as a book by Hodder & Stoughton: its cover asked 'Can we, or can we not, speak with our beloved dead? Sir Arthur Conan Doyle answers YES.' That year, Spiritualism's popularity soared: men and women flocked to séances, which were held in venues as large as London's Royal Albert Hall, desperate to contact their loved ones, and yet another bestseller spurred even greater enthusiasm for

contacting the other side. Frederick Bligh Bond - former chief archaeologist at Glastonbury Abbey - explained in his memoir *The
Gate of Remembrance* that his successful excavations of the foundations of the Chapel of the Loretto at Glastonbury had been guided
not by his scholarship, but by the interception of sixteenth-century
monks which he received via automatic writing. In 1918, the book
was republished twice, and then again in 1920 and 1921. In 1919,
the cover of Conan Doyle's *The Vital Message* declared: 'Sir Arthur
Conan Doyle speaks with authority . . . the ascent of the material
plane to the spiritual, is shown as the gate to that wonderful land
which stretches so clearly before those eyes which are open to see
it.' In 1925, he became President of the London Spiritualist Alli-
ance, which had been founded in 1884; it's now called the College
of Psychic Studies. In 2021, I became a member.

It is hard from this distance to imagine the challenges that the First
World War presented to artists. What kind of image could ade-
quately respond to something so unprecedented, so catastrophic?
The Piper of Dreams, while charming in its own way, is a vastly diluted version of the wild imaginings that fairy painting, at its best,
was capable of. Richard Dadd and his contemporaries - in particular, John Anster 'Fairy' Fitzgerald - pictured fairies as complex, and
as potentially malevolent as humans; for them, the nightmare was
as rich with potential as the dream. Canziani's piper, by contrast,
is predicated on reassurance; a child inhabiting a refuge forever
stilled on a sunny spring day. Death is absent, time unmoored.

The sweetness of Canziani's image doesn't render it irrelevant.
There's room for a multitude of artistic responses to whatever life
throws at us. Openly criticising the government for the violence
enacted upon an entire generation was a risky position to take - you
could be jailed for being anti-war or anti-conscription. Instead, *The
Piper of Dreams* gently posits a psychic space that was desperately
needed in 1915. It's a safe image - but its popularity surely betrays a

widespread desire to be elsewhere. The piper is the face of socially acceptable escapism – hope visualised as a woodland populated by mystical beings, nature a place of refuge and consolation. While it's usually the artists who have discovered new, radical ways of representing the world who have been deemed the worthiest of acclaim, modest art forms have a power, too. At times of great distress, they allow the imagination to roam unchallenged to kinder places. Help can be manifested in untold shapes and forms.

Sophie Taeuber dancing, 1917

Modesty had no place at the Cabaret Voltaire in Zurich, Switzerland, where, on 20 March 1917 an unknown photographer took a portrait of a twenty-seven-year-old woman. Her face is hidden by a large, rectangular mask comprised of huge Cubist eyes, a nose like an alp, and a ferocious mouth topped with a crown as jagged as a saw. Her arms, raised as if to fend off blows, are encased in robot-like tubes; her gyrating body, which appears to jerk like a giant mario-nette, is draped in a patterned fabric that looks at once ancient and futuristic. Although more than a century old, the image crackles with energy. Inside the costume is its creator, the Swiss artist, designer, dancer, puppeteer and architect, and co-founder of the Zurich Psy-chology Club, Sophie Taeuber; she's performing a series of 'abstract dances' to the Dadaist Hugo Ball's cycle of phonetic poems at the opening of the Galerie Dada at Bahnhofstrasse 19 in Zurich. She pre-sents herself as something of a totemic celebration of the individual over the mass carnage of the Great War. Her husband-to-be, the artist Jean (also Hans) Arp described her performance: 'She danced a goldfish losing all its gold and swimming poor and miserable away. She danced darkness, evil growing bored with itself and wanting to turn into its opposite but unable to decide whether it should become a child or an angel. She danced questions, too.'

One of the twentieth century's most radical art movements, Dada soon erupted across Europe, before migrating even further afield. This first iteration comprised a group of young artists who, via absurdity, performance and a bleak, raging humour, railed against convention - a mindset that had given the world permis-sion to go to hell. Restless, despairing, provocative and yet often madly funny, their improvised art, poems and performances re-flected human experience in all its messy, irrational glory. They censored nothing: they honoured the unconscious mind at every turn. After all, it was conscious minds and governments that had agreed to the mass slaughter: Why should they be trusted?

In Britain, the short-lived modernist art movement Vorticism - named by Ezra Pound and fired by Cubism, Futurism and, to some extent, mysticism - echoed some of Dada's aims. The founder, the artist and writer Wyndham Lewis, edited and wrote much of the only two issues of the movement's publication *BLAST*, which was published just before and then during the war; it died along with one of its significant contributors, the French sculptor Henri Gaudier-Brzeska, who was killed in the trenches at the age of twenty-three. The Vorticists ostensibly supported the women's movement, and two women artists, Helen Saunders and Jessica Dismorr, were official members. (Dorothy Shakespear, who was married to Ezra Pound, was an unofficial member.) Saunders was one of the first British artists to work in a non-figurative style; how ironic, then, that during the First World War she found work in the Government Censor's office. *BLAST*, issue 2, includes Dismorr's fragmented, impressionistic short story 'June Night', in which the unnamed narrator escapes a man and wanders alone, describing herself as 'a strayed Bohemian, a villa resident, a native of conditions, half-sordid, half-fantastic. I am the style of a feuilleton cherishing a hopeless passion for Latin prose.'

It's easy to imagine how irritated the women might have been by Lewis's message in *BLAST*, issue 1:

TO SUFFRAGETTES: A Word of Advice. In Destruction, as in other things, stick to what you understand. We make you a present of our votes. Only, leave works of art alone. You might someday destroy a good picture by accident . . . You and artists are the only things (You don't mind being called things?) with a little life in them.

With its bright pink covers and wild typography, the magazine included poems, short stories, artworks, a positive review of Kandinsky's 'Concerning the Spiritual in Art' and a list of things to 'blast or bless' – 'Curse the flabby sky that can manufacture no snow but can only drop the sea on us in a drizzle like Robert Bridges!' Its manifesto boasted: 'We fight first on one side and then the other, but always for the same cause, which is neither side, or both sides and ours . . . we only want humour if it fought like tragedy'. Its rage was palpable. It sold far fewer copies than *The Piper of Dreams*.

New Worlds

'The word Transcendental has been chosen as a name for the group because it best expresses its aim, which is to carry painting beyond the appearance of the physical world, through new concepts of space, colour, light and design, to imaginative realms that are idealistic and spiritual.'

Transcendental Painting Group manifesto (1938)

One of my favourite times in Greece is twilight; the moment when the hard edges of daylight begin to dissolve, the air cools, birds fall silent, and the indigo sea ripples with pinpricks of star light. I'm not sure if the artist Agnes Pelton, who was born in 1881, ever travelled to the Cyclades, but standing on the terrace looking out over the darkening landscape, it occurred to me that her paintings of the Californian desert evoke something of a Grecian blue hour. While her paintings are cosmic, in many ways they're also purely modern – at least, they are if you understand modernism to be a way of anticipating the future, while responding to the present and understanding the past.

So, what happened? Why was spirituality excised from the founding story of modern art? In many ways, a single exhibition can be held responsible. In 1936, Alfred H. Barr Jr., the first director of the Museum of Modern Art in New York, curated 'Cubism and Abstract Art': 400 works of art, architecture and design by around 120 artists – of which only a tiny percentage were women. It also included two unattributed African masks and three 'ancestral figures'.

Regardless of the inclusion of countless artists whose abstract work was fired by various esoteric beliefs, in the essay Barr wrote for the catalogue that accompanied the show, he declared that 'the more adventurous and original artists had grown bored with painting facts'. Yet many of these self-same artists would have argued that they were, in fact, 'painting facts' – about new ways of articulating inner worlds. In 'Concerning the Spiritual in Art', Kandinsky made this clear, writing: 'The artist must have something to say, for mastery over form is not his goal but rather the adapting of form to its inner meaning.'

In 1888, in *The Secret Doctrine*, Madame Blavatsky had announced, with great prescience, that: 'It is in America that the transformation will take place and has already silently commenced.' When Hitler came to power in January 1933, New York saw an influx of European artists and intellectuals, many of them – such as Leonora Carrington, Marcel Duchamp, Max Ernst and Piet Mondrian – bringing with them ideas that were to influence the course of modern art, especially abstraction.

In the 1930s, three groups devoted to abstraction dominated the American art scene. The American Abstract Artists group – which included Josef Albers, Lee Krasner, Jackson Pollock and Charmion von Wiegand – was formed in 1936 in the New York studio of the sculptor Ibram Lassaw in order to foster a greater public understanding of abstraction. Non-Objective painting, by contrast – whose followers included Hilla Rebay, Rudolf Bauer, Fernand Léger, Alice Trumbull Mason and others – arose from the desire to release art from representation and manifest spiritual truths.

A year later, in Albuquerque, New Mexico, nine artists united to form the short-lived Transcendental Painting Group (TPG). They believed in the power of archetypes, symbols, the collective unconscious, Theosophy, Zen Buddhism and yoga, and they devoured the writings of – among others – Carl Jung, Friedrich Nietzsche and Kandinsky. They declared that they were 'concerned with the development and presentation of various types of non-representational painting; painting that finds its source in the creative imagination and does not depend upon the objective approach . . . The work does not concern itself with political, economic, or other social problems. Methods may vary.'

Agnes Pelton by Alice Boughton, 1909

One of the members of the TPG was the artist Agnes Pelton, a visionary Symbolist and lifelong Christian who was interested in numerology, astrology, faith healing and Theosophy. Born in Stuttgart, Germany, in 1881 to American parents, her early childhood was itinerant and marred by tragedy: her father died of a morphine overdose when she was nine. Her mother supported the family by opening a music school in Brooklyn, which she ran for thirty years. Agnes enrolled at Brooklyn's Pratt Institute, where she was taught by Arthur Wesley Dow, who was influenced by Eastern philosophies and believed in art as a radical force for everyday life. (Interestingly, he also taught Georgia O'Keeffe.) Later, she studied at the British Academy in Rome. Her work was included in the influential 1913 Armory Show in New York – the first major exhibition of modern art in the United States – and in 1914, she was elected to the Association of Women Painters and Sculptors in New York; she took part in their shows throughout the 1920s. The year 1917 saw the beginning of Pelton's lifelong interest in Theosophy and the writings of Madame Blavatsky, but she was also drawn to New Thought, an alternative feminist theology that had been developed by the spiritual teacher Emma Curtis Hopkins. In 1919, Pelton travelled to Taos, New Mexico, at the invitation of the legendary philanthropist, Mabel Dodge, who also invited, at various times, D.H. Lawrence and O'Keeffe to stay. Pelton loved travelling. In Hawaii she saw lava pour from the volcano of Kīlauea, 'a clear sign that the physical world was animated with hidden, life-affirming energy'; from there, she travelled to Syria and Lebanon. She moved to the Hamptons on New York's Long Island, where she lived in seclusion in 'a mystical house reaching into heaven' and made her first abstract paintings: swirling, dreamy canvases, inspired, in part, by Kandinsky.

In 1932, at the age of fifty, Pelton settled in Cathedral City, a desert town a few miles from Palm Springs on the West Coast of the States; although she only intended to stay a year, she lived there until her death in March 1961. 'The two mountains – San Jacinto and San Gorgonio are so gorgeous, and I have a feeling that there is some special reason for being here,' she wrote to a friend. She was attracted not only by the clean lines of the desert, the dry heat and the clear air but by California's tolerance towards the burgeoning New Age movement. She studied Buddhism and Hinduism, copied symbols from *Thought-Forms*, read the works of Rudolf Steiner and Carl Jung, and became a practitioner of Agni Yoga – the Sanskrit word for 'fire', a purifying symbol. It was developed by the Russian émigré artist Nicholas Roerich and his wife Helena, who had channelled seventeen volumes of instruction from Madame Blavatsky's Tibetan master, Master Morya. Apparently, with practice, the yoga sequences would contribute to the evolution of planetary unity.

Pelton built a meditation room, burnt incense, prayed and practised rituals in order to deepen her abstractions. She allowed images to come to her in moments of reverie which she quickly sketched and worked into paintings. She was uninterested in the trappings of fame or wealth; although, with their cool palette, sleek forms and immaculate finish her paintings look decidedly modern, they're also somehow very old. She combined pure abstractions – biomorphic forms, light-filled, shimmering mists and fountains of vibrational energy – with elements of the visual world, desert landscapes, white swans (a symbol of femininity), doves, flames, vessels, flowers and stars. She kept copious notebooks throughout her life. In one, she copied two quotes onto a single page: John Keats's sonnet 'Bright Star, would I were steadfast as thou art'; and Friedrich Nietzsche's 'I tell you, you must have chaos in you, if you would give birth to a dancing star' from *Thus Spoke Zarathustra*.

Agnes Pelton's hypnotic, deeply mysterious works evolved from myriad sources: debates around abstraction, occultism and mysticism; dreams, reveries, her meditation practice and her therapeutic needs, a belief in female empowerment, the power of the desert and her love of solitude. As in Greece, the horizons she depicts are unstable; the promise of something just beyond reach. The veil between the heavens and the Earth is flimsy; an intense, waiting calm dominates. She described her paintings as her 'especial light message to the world'; they were 'little windows, opening to the view of a region not yet much visited consciously or by intention – an inner realm, rather than an outer landscape'.

Pelton's later life was not without its challenges. She struggled financially and painted desert scenes for tourists. After her death, her work was largely forgotten; although she exhibited regularly, and many of her paintings were acquired by museums in her lifetime, she had no gallery representation. The fate of an abstract painting she bequeathed to the Santa Barbara Gallery is telling: it was sold in a white elephant sale for $15. It's only in recent years that her work has achieved its proper recognition. In her 2020 review of Pelton's recent Whitney Museum retrospective for *The New York Times*, critic Roberta Smith praised the paintings for their 'magical, inherently musical animation, subtly comedic wit and even jubilation'. She reminds the reader that 'the history of modernist abstraction and women's contribution to it is still being written' and that 'the Whitney show underscores too tellingly the lesson of the Guggenheim's Hilma af Klint exhibition, that the largely all-male narrative of modernist abstraction needs reworking, with much more credit to female artists and their implicitly feminist embrace of spirituality'. She concludes: 'Let's put it this way: Hilma af Klint and Agnes Pelton did not act alone.'

Even though so many superb artists were making abstract paintings inspired by Spiritualism, Alfred H. Barr Jr. chose to ignore them – and misrepresent a historical moment. The damage was done. His influence stretched far and wide. According to Charlene Spretnak, post-war art historians were taught that 'modern art began in earnest' when the Impressionists' first exhibition, in

1874, 'signalled a grand leap into modernity, leaving behind tradition, religion, community and bourgeois values'. As the theorist Rosalind Krauss wrote in 1979, for modernist art historians it was 'indescribably embarrassing to mention art and spirit in the same sentence'. Her sentiment is supported by the art historian Maurice Tuchman, who curated the ground-breaking 'Spiritual in Art: Abstract Painting 1890–1985' at the Los Angeles County Museum of Art in 1986, which included more than 250 works by 100 or so artists, including Agnes Pelton and Hilma af Klint. He wrote: 'to use the word "spiritual" in the 1930s and 1940s . . . was near heresy and dangerous to an artist's career'. Barr had his champions, in particular, the critic Clement Greenberg, who dominated much of the discourse around modern art from the 1940s to the 1960s. As a result, for too long, discussions around abstraction tended to focus on a painting's formal qualities: its texture, colour, light, line, shade and so on. Appearance was privileged over content, male expression over female, and if esoteric or religious beliefs were acknowledged, they were framed as youthful aberrations.

In the 1960s and 1970s there were dissenting voices - the art historians Barbara Rose, Annette Michelson, Meyer Schapiro and Sixten Ringbom, in particular, pushed against Greenbergian formalism - but they were a minority. Modernity was assumed to be cool, sleek, rational: an art movement that eschewed the superstitions of the past - even though some of the artists who the critic championed, such as Jackson Pollock, had come under the influence of esoteric teachings. As a young man, Pollock had attended meetings of Jiddu Krishnamurti. This in turn had led him to Carl Jung's theories of the unconscious.

But these men weren't the only influences on Pollock.

In the Museum of Modern Art's collection in New York is a painting titled *The Milky Way*. As much an evocation of the depths of the sea as it is the infinity of the night sky, it could also be read as an image of an atmosphere or spirit. At just over a metre long and 50 centimetres wide, it's a vivid study in pale blues, watery greens, soft pinks and ochres that recall cobwebs and coral; the enamel paint is applied to the canvas in drips, swooping lines and thin washes. At once abstract and figurative, gestural and detailed, when it was made, it was, in its delicate way, revolutionary. It was painted in 1945 - two years before Pollock's famous 'drip paintings' - by an untrained artist in her fifties: Janet Sobel. Her life and work are yet another example of a gifted woman being excluded from the narrow lens of the art-historical canon.

Janet Sobel in her studio, c.1940s

Born Jennie Olechovsky to a large Jewish family in Ekaterinoslav, Ukraine, in 1893, after her father was killed in a pogrom, at the age of fourteen, Janet - as she renamed herself - along with her mother and sister, emigrated to New York. She had ambitions to be an actress but marriage at seventeen, five children and supporting her widowed mother put an end to her dreams.

The story goes that when Sobel was in her forties, her art-student son Sol brought home his brushes and paints. His mother picked them up and, without further ado, became a phenomenal artist: intuitive, inventive, original. According to Sol, his mother 'would prepare a ground, which would invariably suggest or trigger some "idea" for her, whose sudden conception was matched by an equally rapid execution. She would pour the paint, tip the canvas, and blow the wet lacquer.' Her automatic technique echoes that of the Surrealists but she arrived at it via her own route. She described her motivation: 'I only paint what I feel.' Her grand-daughter Ashley Shapiro vividly remembers seeing Sobel at work:

> In 1942, I'm a tot sitting on the floor next to Gram. She's working on a long canvas. She poured paint on the canvas and took out a vacuum cleaner . . . she used the black hose to blow the paint around the canvas. No one had ever done this before. Her face is shining and her blue eyes intent. She's smiling and I remember it perfectly. I can still breathe the air coming in from the open window.

Sounds often dictated Sobel's images; she never painted in silence. In one interview she explained that: 'I don't think that ever would I paint a picture without music to listen to. All humans must have something like that, that warms them inside.' Her major work *Music* (1944) - a complex abstract work made with dripped enamel paint - was, in her words, her 'impression of the music of Shostakovich, created in a world torn by war and bloodshed. Shostakovich has captured the power of the Russian people and given them strength.'

Everything she made is shot through with a great tenderness. Glimpses of faces and flowers emerge from a tangle of under-growth rendered in marbled enamel; patterns on dresses evoke the Jewish folk traditions of Sobel's Ukrainian childhood and the mood and technical innovations of contemporary painters such as Marc

Chagall and Jean Dubuffet. Occasionally, in dense, elegiac works such as *The Illusion of Solidity* (c.1945) and *Hiroshima* (1948), Sobel alludes to the horrors of war, while in other paintings, exuberant layers of colour suggest the promises of the New World. In *Untitled* (1944) a face - represented in thick black lines - materialises from a jumble of red, blue and yellow marks floating on a translucent blue ground: it's like a hallucination on a summer day. In *Artists at the Preview* (1943), three figures, as weighty as totems, sit in a lush red/ gold environment, their eyes enlarged in order, perhaps, to see the visions they can conjure. A crimson blush creeps over their bodies and sprouts like an animate crown from the central woman's head; it's an image that is at once, somehow, very ancient and very new.

Sobel was tireless in her exploration of materials. As well as using enamel - which lends the surface of her works the soft sheen of a stained-glass window - she became adept in crayons and pencils and in some instances incorporated organic elements such as sand to lend texture to her surfaces; she also used glass pipettes from her husband's business to distribute paint. Again and again, she drew faces like masks - floating, disjointed, rhythmic. In *Untitled* (c.1942) four characters, their features simplified and bold, glow like moons in a verdant undergrowth of deep orange and blue leaves that seem to bend and quiver as if in a high wind. Often the rich variety of materials evokes the aged, lovely patina of old walls, flaking in the sun. For example, in two untitled mixed-media-on-cardboard works from 1948 and 1946/48 blunt herringbone lines define androgynous, slightly smiling figures as dark as spiders' legs against a background of swirling red and pinks. The direction of the paint makes clear that it was applied from all angles: dripped from above and pushed about with a brush. Photographs of Sobel show her working, like Pollock, on the floor.

Sol was his mother's great champion, writing to anyone he felt could help her - from Chagall, with whom she could converse in Russian, to the Surrealists André Breton and Max Ernst, the Jungian psychologist John Dewey and the gallerist Sidney Janis. It paid off. Janis included a painting by Sobel in his show of American Primitive paintings at the Arts Club of Chicago in 1943 and wrote in *The Brooklyn Daily Eagle* that: 'Janet Sobel will probably eventually be known as one of the important surrealist artists in this country.' In the same year, she had a solo show with the artist and dealer Fernando Puma. Word got about. In 1944, Peggy Guggenheim called Sobel 'the best woman painter by far in America'; in 1945 her work was included in the legendary exhibition of thirty-three female artists, 'The Women', at Guggenheim's Art of This Century gallery in New York, alongside that of Louise Bourgeois, Lee Krasner, Kay Sage and others. A solo show followed at the same gallery in 1946. A decade or so later, Sobel was the only woman out of thirty or so artists mentioned by Clement Greenberg in his seminal 1955 essay, 'American-Type Painting':

> Back in 1944, however, he [Jackson Pollock] had noticed one or two curious paintings shown at Peggy Guggenheim's by a 'primitive painter' Janet Sobel (who was, and still is, a housewife living in Brooklyn). Pollock (and I myself) admired these pictures rather furtively: they showed schematic little drawings of faces almost lost in a dense tracery of thin black lines lying over and under a mottled field of predominantly warm and translucent color. The effect – and it was the first really 'all-over' one that I had ever seen [. . .] was strangely pleasing. Later Pollock admitted that these pictures had made an impression on him.

A 'primitive painter' and 'housewife', Sobel was a working-class, untrained, intuitive female artist in her fifties. Everything was stacked against her.

Her family's relocation to New Jersey in 1946 and Peggy Guggenheim's concurrent move to Venice was disastrous for Sobel: in a heartbeat, she disappeared from the art world. After the death of her husband Max in 1953, she ran the family's costume jewellery business. Ashley Shapiro is blunt about the hurdles placed in her way, declaring that her grandmother 'had to create art - until she was squashed by the way men thought about women and the way she thought of her duties as a woman . . . People thought she had allergies to paint . . . She had allergies to suburbia.'

In spite of the far-sighted MoMA curator William Rubin's belief in the artist - he bought two paintings from her in 1968 - it would be half a century before her ground-breaking originality was fully recognised. In a 2012 talk given at the San Diego Museum of Art, the educator Brian Patterson described Sobel's untitled painting from 1946 - which at first glance looks like an early Pollock - as 'perhaps the most important in the collection' because it challenges the biases of the white, male art-historical canon. Since then, Sobel's work has been rightfully included in landmark exhibitions such as 'Women in Abstraction' at the Pompidou Centre in Paris in 2021. When Sobel died in November 1968, she left behind a thousand or so pictures. As she told the *Brooklyn Daily Eagle* in 1946: 'It is not easy to paint. It is very strenuous. But it's something you've got to do if you have the urge.' Ashley Shapiro, who describes Sobel as 'a magical human being with an immense spiritual dimension', remembers her grandmother as 'bursting with a flow of creativity that couldn't be stopped'.

The Vibrations of Different Souls

'Cinema consists of the eye for magic - that which perceives and reveals the marvellous in whatsoever it looks upon.'

Maya Deren, 'Magic is New' (1946)

How strange it is that, for so long, modernism was understood as a cool rebuttal of the irrational past. Yet, the life and art of arguably the most influential artist of the twentieth century, Marcel Duchamp, refutes such a reading. Over the last hundred years or so, his 'invention' of the readymade - repurposing an everyday object as an artwork - has shaped so-called 'conceptual art', which operates from a position that privileges an action or a thought over objects. 'I was interested in ideas,' he said, 'not merely in visual products.' But despite Duchamp's reputation as a dry conceptualist, he wasn't an artist who always championed intellect over intuition: his origins were in Dada. He was as playful and ironic as he was analytical - his alter ego was Rose Sélavy, a woman whose name loosely translates as 'eros is life' - and he welcomed the unknown with open arms.

In 1957, he declared: 'To all appearances, the artist acts like a mediumistic being who, from the labyrinth beyond time and space, seeks his way out to a clearing.' Throughout his life, Duchamp read widely on alchemy, tarot, Spiritualism and astrology; his interest in the occult, and its focus on the shift of one state or material to another, most likely had an influence on the development of his conceptual artworks. His famous dictum that 'the spectator completes the work of art' chimes, in many ways, with the notion of the artist as medium: Duchamp posits the creative act as one of active reciprocity. In 1912, as he was conceiving his best-known work, the enigmatic glass sculpture, *The Large Glass* (1915-23), he bought Kandinsky's 'Concerning the Spiritual in Art' and translated it into French.

In 1944, Duchamp starred in an unfinished film, *Witch's Cradle*, by the experimental filmmaker Maya Deren. She believed her films could 'make the world dance' and that cinema 'consists of the eye for magic - that which perceives and reveals the marvellous in whatsoever it looks upon'. Transformation was part of her life. Anti-Semitism had forced her family to cross oceans.

Born Eleanora Derenkowska in 1917 in what is now Kyiv, her family fled the pogroms in 1922 and arrived in the United States the same year. Her father, who abbreviated their surname to Deren, was appointed psychiatrist at the State Institute for the Feeble-Minded in Syracuse, New York; from an early age, his daughter was made acutely aware of the power of the unconscious mind to shape daily life. A socialist who studied journalism, in 1939, Deren was employed as a researcher for William Seabrook, who was writing *Witchcraft - Its Power in the World Today*. He, in turn, had worked with the notorious occultist and magician Aleister Crowley - known as the 'wickedest man in the world' who called himself 'The Beast' - and had contributed articles to Georges Bataille's Surrealist magazine, *Documents*. Deren then got a job as an assistant to the African American dancer, choreographer and anthropologist Katherine Dunham, whose interest in Haitian culture and Vodou had a marked impact on the young filmmaker's thinking.

In 1942, Deren married the Czech-born cameraman and photographer Alexandr Hackenschmied (later known as Alexander Hammid), who was to become her artistic collaborator. In 1943, her father died and with her inheritance she bought a 16mm Bolex camera. Increasingly drawn to all things esoteric, she changed her name from Eleanora to Maya in homage to both the mother of Buddha and Maya, one of the seven Ancient Greek nymphs of the constellation Pleiades and the goddess of nursing mothers, whose child Hermes was the herald of the gods. In Roman myth, Maia was the embodiment of growth and in Sanskrit, 'Maya' translates as 'magic' or 'illusion'. The trilogy of short films she wrote, starred in and directed over the next three years - *Meshes of the Afternoon* (1943), *At Land* (1944) and *Ritual in Transfigured Time* (1946) - explore, via the use of double exposures and slow motion, the fractured journeys of a woman through her inner worlds of magic and dreams.

Maya Deren in Meshes of the Afternoon, *1943*

In 1946, Deren wrote a long essay titled 'An Anagram of Ideas on Art, Form and Film', which outlined her ideas on what she saw as the disastrous split between science, magic, religion and philosophy that happened in the seventeenth century. A year later, she travelled to Haiti and filmed, photographed and recorded hours of Vodou ceremonies, which she occasionally participated in: she was spellbound by their melding of art, music, dance and ritual. On her return to New York, she practised Vodou herself, wrote a book *Divine Horsemen: The Living Gods of Haiti*, which includes the declaration 'myth is the facts of the mind made manifest in a fiction of matter' and concludes with her own possession by the Vodou goddess of water and femininity, Erzulie. After her death in 1961, Deren's third husband, the Japanese composer and performer Teiji Ito, edited the footage she had shot in Haiti and, in 1977, released a film with the same title as her book.

Deren's work was to have a huge impact not only on feminist artist-filmmakers, such as Joan Jonas, who represented the United States in the 2015 Venice Biennale, but also on auteurs including Orson Welles and Stanley Kubrick. Her influence, however, wasn't limited to her creative vision: she championed independent cinema production, seeing it as a viable alternative to Hollywood, and tirelessly distributed – and lectured on – her films.

Deren shot *The Witch's Cradle* in 1943 in Peggy Guggenheim's Art of This Century Gallery at 30 West 57th Street in New York City. With a running time of just over ten minutes, it's considered unfinished. (But as one critic pointed out, when you're dealing with material this imaginative, what does that even mean? After all, Franz Kafka's three novels, *The Trial*, *The Castle* and *Amerika*, are considered incomplete.) It's unclear how Deren knew Duchamp, but he was living in New York, and they shared friends in André Breton and Anaïs Nin. It wasn't his first foray into cinema: Duchamp had played chess in René Clair's 1924 Surrealist film *Entr'acte* and in 1926 he made his own film, *Anémic Cinéma*: six minutes of swirling, hypnotic shapes, which he called Rotoreliefs, interspersed with puns in French.

Peggy Guggenheim believed that the design of the gallery should be as compelling as the work it displayed. She commissioned the artist and designer Frederick Kiesler - a friend of Duchamp's - to dream up a space with only one stipulation: that paintings must be displayed unframed. Kiesler didn't disappoint: he transformed a simple room into a dynamic stage with walls that curved like a cave and lights that turned on and off without warning and were replaced with the sound of a train. Paintings were hung from white ropes suspended between the floor and the ceiling: an echo of Duchamp's web-like installation *His Twine* of the year before that comprised a mile of string weaving in and around the 'First Papers of Surrealism' exhibition.

Witch's Cradle stars a young woman, the actress Pajorita Matta, and a middle-aged man, played by Marcel Duchamp, both of whom, with no explanation, inhabit a gallery. Matta, a barefoot, spectral presence in a flimsy nightgown - or possibly a Grecian robe - wanders through the darkness, her body softly illuminated as if by moonlight. Occasionally, glimpses of Surrealist artworks emerge from the gloom; Matta peers through one biomorphic sculpture, shines a torchlight on another; switches on a mysterious machine - Kiesler's *Vision Machine*, an incomplete contraption that was supposed to screen psychic visions and demonstrate the processes of perception. A wheel spins and child-like cubes, which seem to roll of their own accord, spring up. Images appear and dissolve in hallucinatory fragments: a piece of string has a life of its own, crawling over a shoe, a sculpture, the back of Duchamp's head, shining softly. In a heartbeat, they are outside and Duchamp is playing cat's cradle with scholarly intensity but the string is tangled; it clearly won't behave. At various points, we see a close-up of a raw, beating heart that recalls a serpent, and a pentacle drawn on Matta's forehead inscribed with the words 'in the end is the beginning is the end . . .'; a hand hennaed with the shape of a tree.

Deren screened footage of *Witch's Cradle* for her friends, and drafted programme notes. She clarified why she wanted to film her protagonists among surreal art objects, which she calls 'cabalistic symbols of the twentieth century'. She described the Surrealists as 'feudal magicians and witches', who were 'concerned with the defiance of normal time (mainly projection into the past and divination of the future) and with normal space (disappearance one place and appearance another, or the familiar broomstick)'. She concluded that 'it seemed to me that the camera was peculiarly suited to delineate this form of magic'. Why the footage ends abruptly on a close-up of string is unclear.

Marcel was not the only Duchamp dabbling in other realms. Three of his five siblings became avant-garde artists, too: his brothers, Raymond Duchamp-Villon and Jacques Villon, and his younger sister Suzanne Duchamp. Throughout her life - she was born in 1889 and died in 1963 - Suzanne explored the limits of painting, from abstraction to figuration to drawing, collage and poetry. Working as a nurse in the First World War, she witnessed terrible scenes and when Raymond, a successful sculptor, died of typhoid after active service, her grief prompted her to look at things from different angles.

In her paintings, such as *Vibrations of Two Distant Souls* (1916–18) and *Broken and Restored Multiplication* (1918–19), nothing is stable, least of all the physical plane, which mingles with a more abstracted one formed of symbols denoting different levels of meaning: stars, springs, triangles, circles and cryptic phrases such as 'the mirror would shatter, the scaffolding would totter'. In one of her many self-portraits, *Give Me the Right to Life* (1919), Suzanne pictures herself disembodied, flanked by an enormous pair of scissors that is cutting the mesh that encases her head. Surrounded by a bird, a

moth, a lantern, twigs, she peers out from a single eye. In paintings such as *Factory of My Thoughts* (1920), she was one of the first
female artists to incorporate what was known as 'mechanomor-
phic' references in her work: the notion that machines themselves
can become transcendent, both symbolically and literally: she
loved driving fast along the roads of the Côte d'Azur. She and her
husband, the artist Jean Crotti - a friend of Marcel's who she married in 1919 - became part of Paris Dada. In 1920, Suzanne took part
in the first major Dada exhibitions in Paris and, in 1921, she and
her husband organised a retrospective of their work at the Galerie
Montaigne. The translated invitation, which was decorated with
an image of a heavy-lidded eye, instructs visitors:

> To understand the misunderstood: evening and morning, walk 30
> minutes on your head. Go dressed only in a few tiny roses: 2 in
> front and 1 behind.

In 1921, Suzanne and Jean rejected the nihilism of Paris Dada and
founded their own philosophical movement: Tabu Dada. They
wanted to communicate 'the unknowable and invisible' aspects of
existence. They believed that art was a mystical endeavour and was
the best way to free the mind and gain access to different levels of
meaning. In this, they were far from alone.

Demeter in Paris

'I should be among the wild Nagas of the snake-like name, who might once have been at home in Avebury, the serpent town, with their ivory and spears, feathers and bangles; whose women have all the mates they choose. But how to get there?'

Ithell Colquhoun, *The Living Stones* (1957)

In 1932, a twenty-six-year-old woman walked across Paris with a sheaf of wheat. She was on her way to have her portrait taken by the famous Surrealist photographer, Man Ray. Her name was Ithell Colquhoun; an artist, writer and occultist, she was born in India in 1906 to a British colonial family, had seen fairies since she was a child, believed in the spirit world, and was enthralled by belief systems she wasn't taught in school: the zodiac, the magical properties of perfumes, symbols pertaining to plants, birds and planets – all fascinated her.

Man Ray portrait of Ithell Colquhoun, 1932

There are a few iterations of Man Ray's black-and-white portrait, but in all of them Ithell Colquhoun's expression is faraway. She is elegant. Her eyebrows are plucked as thin as a swallow's wings, her eyelids and lips are painted, and her hair is pulled back with an elaborate woven band; she's adorned with heavy earrings and an ornate bracelet. Her white, puff-sleeved dress is decorated with delicate bows. She holds the sheaf of wheat as tenderly as she might cradle a baby.

Man Ray's portrait employs a classic Surrealist technique: single image, double meaning. His photograph depicts a scene that is at once straightforward - an elegant young woman holding a sheaf of wheat - and deeply strange. *Why* is she holding a sheaf of wheat in the middle of Paris? According to the Colquhoun expert, Richard Shillitoe, the wheat was her idea. She wanted Man Ray to depict her as a modern Demeter, the Olympian goddess of the harvest, who presided over the fertility of the Earth. But she has updated the goddess's appearance: she's no visitor from Olympus, but a smart young woman who, wheat aside, wouldn't be out of place at a cocktail party. I suspect her intention was to declare that the spirits of the Ancients still walk among us; time and space were, to her, far more malleable than they were to most people. She could also be nodding to her belief that women have special magical powers because of what she saw as their affinity with nature. As if to emphasise the ambiguous nature of the image, Man Ray printed a negative along with the more conventional prints: he's making very clear that there are two sides to everyone, and especially young occultists. In it, Colquhoun appears like a ghost, her eyes white in her shadowed face.

One highlight of the plague year of 2020 was my daily bath. Like most people I know, I was wracked with anxiety about everything from finances to my future; how to live a creative life and still pay the bills. In the midst of a London winter, at 7 p.m. every day, I

filled the bath, added oil and scents, put on music, and placed a
stack of reading by the tub. Things immediately looked up. Often,
I didn't emerge for two hours.

My love of baths is why I was stopped in my tracks by a
Colquhoun oil-on-plywood painting from 1938: *Scylla*, in the collection of Tate Britain. It depicts two large, rocky outcrops in the
sea that touch at their extremities; beneath a pale blue sky, a small
white boat zooms towards the gap between them; tangled red and
green seaweed can be seen in the translucent water. However, look
at it again, and the image shifts: now it's the view of a female body
from the perspective of someone lying back in a bath. Her thighs
are rocks, her pubic hair, seaweed, the white boat a phallic promise
of a sexual encounter. The painting's title refers to the six-headed
female monster of Greek mythology who terrified passing sailors
and ate quite a few of them. Colquhoun herself was quite clear that
the image was a *double entendre* - and that, perhaps on some level,
she is identifying with the monster. It is the earliest in a group of
seven works she created over a year all subtitled *Méditerranée* after
the sea the gods loved so well.

Scylla is a nymph-turned-monster who lives on one side of a
strait of water, opposite another sea monster, Charybdis. The story
- as with so many myths, a mix of utter cruelty, strange wisdom
and wild transformation - appears not only in numerous Renaissance paintings, but in literature, too: in Homer's *Odyssey* most
famously, Ovid's *Metamorphoses*, Keats's poem *Endymion* and James
George Fraser's *The Golden Bough: A Study in Magic and Religion*.
Colquhoun owned a copy of the latter; first published in 1890, it's
a key text of esoteric literature that was to impact on modernist
literature: the poet T.S. Eliot cited it as a central reference for *The
Waste Land* (1922). In 1952, he gave a lecture in Nice titled 'Scylla
and Charybdis'. In it, he declares:

The myth [of Scylla and Charybdis] belongs to that Mediterranean world from which our culture springs; it refers to a well-known episode in Mediterranean pre-history; like other myths in the story of Ulysses it is what I believe Professor Jung would call a universal archetype of human experience. It responds to some of the deepest desires, and terrors of all human beings: it is the experience of life itself. It is applicable to almost any subject one can discuss.

When the Tate bought the painting, Colquhoun was asked if the image was 'the result of a dream'. In reply, the artist cited the Homeric myth, stating: 'It was suggested by what I could see of myself in a bath – this, with a change of scale due to "alienation of sensation" became rocks and seaweed. It is thus a pictorial pun, or double-image in the Dalíesque sense – not the result of a dream but of a dreamlike state.' In 1957 she penned her memoir *The Living Stones: Cornwall*, about her relocation from London to the West Country. (It's something of a sister publication to her travelogue about Ireland, *The Crying of the Wind*.) In it, she writes: 'For an animist is what I am; not even a pantheist, though so I pretend when I feel the need for some veneer of urbanity.'

This time in Amorgos, I don't read Homer. I'm immersed in a novel about the nymph Circe, written by a classicist, Madeline Miller, and Charlotte Higgins's new compendium of the Greek myths seen through the lens of female characters. I learn more about the origins of the subject of Ithell Colquhoun's *Scylla*, the painting that had fascinated me in the bath on the long winter's nights only months earlier.

Higgins and Miller are part of a new wave of writers countering the all too familiar male-centred stories in which women, be they mortal or holy, are the downfall of men (Eve), the root of all evil (Pandora), turn sailors into pigs (Circe), murder children (Medea) or stir cauldrons to conjure wicked spells (witches). 'In the compendia of mythical stories produced in the nineteenth and twentieth centuries,' explains Higgins, 'particularly those for children, the camera was usually pointed firmly at the figure of the hero. These characters – Heracles, Perseus, Jason, Theseus – were often subtly, or unsubtly, co-opted to offer models of male virtue for their young readers. The females were frequently relegated to the background as defenceless virgins, vicious monsters, or grotesque old women.'

Miller's novel opens with Circe, the daughter of the sun god Helios, declaring: 'When I was born, the name for what I was did not exist.' She falls in love with Glaucus – a mortal who is transformed into a sea god by eating a magical herb – but he only has eyes for the beautiful goddess Scylla. In a fit of pique, Circe transforms her love rival into a six-headed monster with twelve feet, who devours sailors and dolphins. When Circe's powers of witchcraft are discovered, she is banished to the island of Aiaia in the Tyrrhenian Sea where she befriends birds and beasts, studies nature, hones her alchemical powers and weaves – cloths, spells, stories.

I ask my friend Sylvia what she remembers of Circe from her schooldays in Athens in the 1980s. She thinks hard. 'She was the witch who turned sailors into pigs.' I ask her if she recalled being taught anything positive about her. She answers quickly. 'No. Nothing.' In Miller's telling, Circe transforms sailors into pigs because she was raped when she offered them refuge; her isolation and lack of male support is used to justify her violation. She conjures her revenge from spells made of plants and words. Never again will she let her guard down. For millennia, in stories and paintings, her power has been pictured as malevolent: a seductress, a deceiver, a woman driven by revenge. A popular subject in the Renaissance, Circe was shorthand for 'whore'.

Julia Margaret Cameron, Circe, *1865*

In later centuries, sympathetic exceptions appeared. In 1865, the English photographer Julia Margaret Cameron - Virginia Woolf's great-aunt - shot a head-and-shoulders portrait of a young girl in a wreath made of grapes. She looks directly out at us, her face soft, young, melancholy. The photograph is titled *Circe* - her crown of grapes hints at the wine Helios's daughter used to disguise her spell to drug the sailors and turn them into pigs. The print owned by the Victoria & Albert Museum in London is inscribed with a quote from the poet John Milton: 'Who knows not Circe/daughter of the sun.' Cameron doesn't include the following lines: '. . . whose charmed cup, whoever tasted, lost his upright shape, and downward fell into a groveling swine . . .'. In an era when photography's function was to document reality, Cameron – who always portrayed female subjects in a nuanced light – trained her lens on an historic reality: the ambivalent role of women across time. She pictures Circe not as a witch but a vulnerable girl – someone both mythic and all too human. Her model was Kate 'Kittie' Keown, who Cameron used in numerous photographs. I can't find out much about Kate, apart from her dates – 1857-1922 – and the fact that she married a granite merchant named Bernard Augustine Freeman. She would have been eight years old when Cameron cast her as Circe.

Marion Milner describes the opposite of the freedoms found in the oceanic state as 'catastrophic chaos' – a letting go and a transcending of boundaries that, if allowed to go too far, could be potentially a 'dangerous plunge into a sea of pain'. I wonder how it's possible to know when you've crossed such a border. Whether gods or mortals, we all lead such precarious lives. Everyone is, at various times, touched with tragedy, serendipity and grace. This is the crux of Colquhoun's explorations: how to make sense of the short time on Earth each of us is granted.

At one point in *The Living Stones* she discusses where to live, asking: 'Where am I, between east and west? A lost soul indeed.' She could have been talking about the dizzying range of belief systems she was to explore throughout her life. (As the writer Alun Rowlands observes: 'There is bookishness within magic and the occult. Part of the hermetic advocacy is encyclopaedic, building libraries that conflate language and codes, textual entities and connections.') Colquhoun was at once an artist and a magician, a mystical Christian, a scholar and practitioner of the occult with a deep knowledge of both Eastern and Western religions. She immersed herself in Druidry, goddess worship, freemasonry, tarot, Theosophy and the Kabbalah, and argued that all matter must bear a trace of the creator and so must be considered living. She took the idea of 'mother earth' literally: the land was as vivid to her as a human; a rock was as alive as a bird or a flower and Cornwall was abundant with all of them. She evokes her chosen home with something akin to ecstasy:

> Valley of streams and moon leaves, wet scents and all that cries with the owl's voice, all that flies with a bat's wing, peace! Influences, essences, presences, whatever is here - in my name of a stream in a valley I salute you; I share this place with you. Stirrings of life, expanding spores, limbo of germination, for all you give me, I offer thanks. Oh, rooted here without time I bathe in you; genius of the fern-loved gully, do not molest me, and may you remain for ever unmolested.

Scylla - a strange, faceless painting so full of personality - is, in fact, something of a self-portrait: alienated, learned, sensual, this thirty-two-year-old artist was all too aware that the female body has long been a symbol for too many things to name: from fertility and virtue, to fallen grace and vanity. Despite the number of talented women who are now recognised as Surrealists - the movement with which Colquhoun is most associated - at first, they occupied an inferior role. All too often, they were dismissed or patronised by the men who saw them either as muses, savage girl-children, or the embodiment of nature - the antithesis of the intellectual male. That Colquhoun depicts herself as a landscape is possibly a sly critique of the Surrealist equation of women as nature.

Take, for example, René Magritte's 1929 collage: *I Do Not See the (Woman) Hidden in the Forest*. It depicts a naked woman looking to one side and covering one of her breasts with a hand. Sixteen head-and-shoulder photographs of men with closed eyes surround her, dressed formally in suits and ties. They are the core Surrealists - a curious mix of brilliance, innovation and conservatism.

The French writer André Breton, known as 'the Pope of Surrealism', had founded the movement in 1924 with his first manifesto.

He believed we live in – and are hampered by – a 'reign of logic', believed there 'are fairy tales to be written for adults', wanted to 'deepen the foundations of the real' and to unite our interior realities with exterior reality. Influenced by Sigmund Freud, he felt that dreams are too neglected, their power ignored. 'I have always been amazed,' Breton wrote, 'at the way an ordinary observer lends so much more credence and attaches so much more importance to waking events than to those occurring in dreams.' The sense lingers that he aimed his words at a male audience. By 1929, when Breton wrote his second manifesto, the swelling numbers of female Surrealists obviously stumped him. 'The problem of woman,' he wrote, 'is all that is marvellous and troubling in the world.'

This was what Colquhoun, and so many other women artists, were up against.

In *Scylla*, Colquhoun refutes herself as a one-dimensional being: she is complex, intellectual, her legs are fleshy and phallic; she's a landscape, a monster, a sea nymph, a woman. She will not be reduced to a type; her gender is not a one-liner. Nothing is uncomplicated here, but then nothing ever is. That said, *Scylla* is also an homage to something straightforward: the bath hour and the reveries its steamy depths can prompt.

When Man Ray took his portrait of Colquhoun, her first solo exhibition was still four years away. In 1926, she had enrolled in the Cheltenham School of Arts and Crafts, where she wrote, designed and performed a one-act play, *Bird of Hermes*, which was based on alchemical manuscripts. In photographs of her performances, she is dressed in a white, legless leotard, decorated with snaking, swirling patterns. She strikes poses, gazing upwards, her face a study in concentration, her strong, bare legs as supple as a dancer. In group shots, she poses with three performers, whose costumes she designed: striped trousers, knickerbockers edged in gold, a body suit wrapped like a parcel in tape. She moved to London and enrolled in the Slade School of Art, where she was considered gifted. In 1936, she visited the International Exhibition of Surrealism at the New Burlington Galleries in London - a show so popular it stopped the traffic on Piccadilly - which included 392 Surrealist paintings and sculptures by seventy-one artists, including Pablo Picasso, Magritte, Max Ernst, Marcel Duchamp, Meret Oppenheim and others. Although the English painter Sheila Legge caused a stir - in an ivory satin gown, her face obscured by roses, she was covered with ladybirds and brandished a pork chop - the star of the show was Salvador Dalí, who attempted to give a lecture on 'Some Authentic Paranoiac Phantoms' while dressed in a diving suit, holding a billiard cue and two wolfhounds on a leash. However, his helmet was bolted down, and he ran out of air. Luckily, he was saved by an artist with a wrench, but before the performance was over, Colquhoun had become a devotee of Surrealism: its questioning of the nature of reality chimed with her own relationship to the world. She briefly joined the British Surrealists but was expelled when she refused to give up her membership of secret occult societies. (It's amusing how censorious and authoritarian the Surrealists could be.)

While still a student, Colquhoun joined the Quest Society, a breakaway group from the Theosophical Society, which aimed to foster an 'undogmatic approach' to the study of religions, philosophy and science. Her first piece of published writing, 'The Prose of Alchemy', appeared in the society's quarterly journal in 1930. Over the next few years, she lived in Paris, Rome and Greece, and regularly exhibited her paintings: exquisitely painted biomorphic forms that merge with wild landscapes and sensual bodies. In 1946, surprisingly, she designed a cover for the June issue of *Ideal Home* magazine; in the same year, she bought Vow Cave Studio, a cottage without running water or electricity in the Cornish village of Paul. It was near the Cove of Lamorna, which she loved for its 'relaxed and other-worldly air'. She learned to respect her new home's lack of amenities, believing that the tension of modern life is due 'to the fact that people surround themselves day and night with the pulsations of electricity in one form or another, and these tend to disturb the subtle body'.

For Colquhoun, Cornwall - an area long associated with super-natural energies, soaked in Celtic myth and magic, and for much of the twentieth century, a beacon to artists - became her spiritual home. It had, she felt 'an attraction for the seeker, bearing as it does traces of those sunken countries Lyonesse and Atlantis, which are lost in the depths of every mind'. She believed the ancient arrange-ments of stones that punctuate the landscape contain 'earth energy' that travels in lines and that 'where an earth current meets a sea current a whirlpool develops that stimulates health and visionary capacity'. Her deep connection to the land anticipated our current ecological crisis. In her introduction to her 1973 poetry collection *Grimoire of the Entangled Thicket* she wrote:

> ... in 1971, I made a number of drawings based on the automatic process known as decalcomania, which evoke the spirit of various trees - Beech, Rowan, Ash, Willow, Oak, Vine and Silver Fir. Some of these ... I offer to the White Goddess as a time when wasteful technology is threatening the planet life (and with it all organic life) of earth and the waters.

When she died at the age of eighty-one, Colquhoun was relatively unknown and had sold very few artworks: a rather lonely and ec-centric old lady whose closest companions were the plants in her garden. Yet she left behind an enormous body of work, includ-ing coded paintings of uncanny scenes that explore her esoteric beliefs and the limitless space of her unconscious. As well as her travelogues, she authored thinly veiled novels about her spiritual search that have marvellous titles such as *The Goose of Hermogenes*, an alchemical tale which is dedicated 'To the Azores - unvisited islands'; *I Saw Water*, which is set in a convent on the island of the dead and is mainly sourced from her dreams; and a book of poems, *Grimoire of the Entangled Thicket*. I tried to read *Sword of Wisdom*, her biography of Samuel Liddell MacGregor Mathers, a founder of the Hermetic Order of the Golden Dawn, but struggled to understand its bewildering references to Christian mysticism, Paganism, Eastern religions, Egyptian myths, various alchemical practices and magical traditions. Her writing is dense, often personal, and assumes a depth of erudition only a handful of readers might possess. But what shines through is Colquhoun's openness to the possibilities around her, and her belief that there is much more to being an artist than describing their surfaces. She devoted much of her energy to an exploration of gender, examining its various manifestations in the human, natural and celestial realms; she railed against the strictures placed on female agency and repeatedly drew and painted the male body - often naked, occasionally castrated, never more powerful than a woman. She thumbed her nose at convention: she was bisexual, took lovers, didn't have children, and while she believed in the power of the 'divine feminine' she held that at some time in the distant past masculine and feminine energies had been united. The website devoted to her, which is run by Richard Shillitoe, who made a pilgrimage to visit the artist in the 1970s, declares that Colquhoun's ambition was no less than 'to transcend all divisions' - between mind and body, spirit and earth - and describes her as a 'magician born of nature', a line taken from Mathers' wife, Moina Mathers: 'Woman is the magician born of nature, by reason of her great natural sensibility, and of her instinctive sympathy with such subtle energies as these intelligent inhabitants of the air, the earth, fire and water.'

Many of Colquhoun's ideas - about the importance of myth, the environment, identity and sexuality - chime today. As the anthropologist and folklorist Amy Hale writes in her wonderful recent biography, *Ithell Colquhoun: Genius of the Fern Loved Gully*: 'Her idea of what it would take to get humanity back to [a golden age] would require radical shifts and her vision of enlightened and genderless beings seems oddly progressive.' It is only in recent years that people have begun to 'awaken to the real scope of her vision . . . no longer the lost surrealist, she is now being rediscovered as a mystic and an esoteric artist'. When Amy and I meet on Zoom, she tells me that she understands Colquhoun's thinking as 'transcendent' - not just 'receiving but also calling' - and that her focus was less in contacting the dead than in trying to understand the various energies that govern existence. In recent years, Colquhoun's name keeps cropping up as an influence among a new generation of artists: in 2020, her work was included in the Liverpool Biennial, alongside paintings and sculptures by artists born decades after her. A highlight was the work of Linder - renowned feminist artist and former lead singer of the Manchester-based post-punk band Ludus - for whom Colquhoun has long been an inspiring presence: Linder is often guided by what she calls 'the Hand of Ithell'.

In 2016, Linder created a ballet which imagines an encounter between Colquhoun and the sculptor Barbara Hepworth - another migrant to Cornwall - at the Penwith Arts Ball in 1956. It's titled *Children of the Mantic Stain* after Colquhoun's 1952 essay of the same name, which concludes with the question: 'Does not all inspiration come from the multitudinous abyss?' For Linder, the essay 'details the full range of techniques of automatism within the visual arts. Mantic is of Greek derivation, it means "oracular, divinatory", it also points towards a state of divine possession.'

Linder used the phrase to describe the process of making marks upon paper in a dreamlike state. She had been thinking about the glossy abstract works that Colquhoun painted with Humbrol enamel towards the end of her life. Linder and her son, the musician and composer Maxwell Sterling, worked on a score for the ballet, discussing how certain rhythms, instruments and chord progressions might create the kind of hallucinogenic effects that would mirror Colquhoun's own processes and works. (Linder explained: 'He's the only composer on the planet with the patience enough to ponder the sonic possibilities of what Ithell Colquhoun describes as "a treasure of symbolic scenes of mind-pictures . . . dredged up from the depths of the phantasy-life, that dream-world of which many are hardly aware in waking consciousness".') Along with the choreographer Kenneth Tindall and the fashion designer Christopher Shannon, they 'wanted to extend Ithell Colquhoun's rallying call to automatism into all arenas of creative practice'. The result was a ballet filled with otherworldly sounds and smells; the 'children' danced upon a carpet that could shapeshift, Linder says, 'at the same speed that the Humbrol enamels spill across found imagery. It's a different way of seeing a carpet, a tracksuit and a ballet dancer.'

Linder says 'Where Ithell Colquhoun leads, I follow', and she credits the artist for her return to using paint after a four-year abstinence. Linder creates 'Rorschach-like marks' that have a beauty quite different to that created by scissors and scalpel. 'I love this new form of experimentation,' she says. 'The lack of control drives me half-crazy, but if I let go of all notions of a desired outcome then the magic begins to happen, as if Ithell herself were spilling the paints quite wantonly.'

I first heard of Ithell Colquhoun in 2009, when the writer Michael Bracewell asked me to pen something for the catalogue of a group exhibition titled 'The Dark Monarch: Magic and Modernity in British Art' he was co-curating at Tate St Ives. Exploring the influence of folklore and mysticism on a cross-section of historical and contemporary British artists, the show included collages by Linder and *The Trees* from 1941 (two tree stumps linked by a rainbow) and *Double Figure* from 1942 (two embracing, androgynous figures, one yellow, one red) by Colquhoun, who at the time was known by very few people. *The Dark Monarch* took its title from a 1962 novel of the same name by the artist and writer Sven Berlin; recognisably

based on the St Ives artists' colony, which he renames 'Cuckoo',
he reimagines the populace as the mortals of Greek mythology
who have become the playthings of the gods. The influence of
the geological, magical and mythical properties of landscape on
the development of British art in the twentieth century become
clear - in particular how artists used it as a springboard to respond to the 'anxieties, trauma and instability of a turbulent and
uncertain world'.

Re-reading *The Living Stones* reminded me that Colquhoun had
just lived through six years of war when she moved to Cornwall.
For her, the county was deeply restorative. She wrote:

> When the war was over, and I could partially escape from my own
> entangled life, it was to this region, this 'end of the land' with its
> occasional sight of the unattained past, that I was drawn. There is
> some balsamic quality in the air that never fails to bring healing;
> after years of Blitz, I felt that here I could find some humble refuge
> from the claustrophobic fright of cities. I determined that I would
> never be so trapped again.

Healing is a theme that recurs again and again. So many of the
women whose artworks explored spirituality were coping with
trauma, war, rapidly changing societies, the death of loved ones. If
spirituality was the escape route, art was the vehicle.

If an artist makes a statement that is too easily understood, it risks
being propagandistic or dull: one prerequisite of a good work of art
is that it can't be expressed in any other language. While Colquhoun
was vocal that women must be artistically, emotionally, mythically
and sexually empowered, her work is never didactic or even em-
phatic. Rather, it reiterates that despite our protestations, human
beings are more open to different energies than we realise and it's
up to each person to discover the ones that suit them.

I'm sure that Ithell Colquhoun was uninterested in converting anyone to her ideas, least of all a fashionable art audience - her quest for knowledge was too wide-ranging and deeply felt for such superficialities - which is possibly why, along with the fact that she lived in remote Cornwall, she was ignored for too long by the art powers that be: hers is not an art practice that is easily grasped. When she died, she left a few paintings to Tate and the bulk of her archive to the National Trust. In 2019, it entered the Tate collection. It comprises 5,000 sketches, drawings, commercial artwork, charts, doodles, photographs, scraps of paper.

November 2021: I visit the Ithell Colquhoun archive, which is held at Tate Britain. I arrive at the same time as a research student who is as excited as I am about what we are about to see. The sheer amount of material is staggering, and what we glimpse is only a fraction of it: Colquhoun must have never rested. There are boxes and boxes of newspaper clippings, research papers, invitations, journals; sketches of bodies, of flames, of alchemical symbols; paintings of fountains that spurt water like octopus tendrils; diagrams of the tree of life with Earth underscored with words such as 'Olamh Ha-Olipoth'. The curator, Victoria Jenkins, pulls a picture out at random, and we're confronted with a naked, multi-coloured female body, her legs and arms outstretched, with rays of energy erupting from her vagina; another, with an ejaculating penis, breasts framed by light blue wings, a face that could be growing wheat. I open a file: it's a poem of sorts titled 'The Decade of Intelligence'. The first lines read:

Beginning of the whirling motions
Root of elemental air
Crown an ancient, bearded king . . .

There are piles of abstract paintings on paper: one, in glossy enamel paint, is a delirium of deep blue and swirling black. It's titled, or captioned, 'The Princess of the Echoing Hills, The Rose of the Palace of Earth'. Another is formed of swirling black lines that could be a screaming head. The curator tells me she thinks it's titled 'Depression'.

Abstraction here isn't about nothingness; it's about giving the psyche a shape. I don't begin to pretend to understand everything about Colquhoun's practice: to do that, I would have to study her, and the occult, for years. But what is infinitely rewarding about her work is its restlessness and curiosity; the way she used art as a conduit for a deep exploration into the recesses of her mind, into history, into how we might better navigate our planet, and its often-enigmatic energies.

The absorption of Colquhoun's archive into Tate's collection heralds a new chapter: one in which the contributions of artists whose work doesn't fit into the traditional canon of art history are finally being recognised. I ask Linder about Colquhoun's relevance to the here and now. She thinks for a moment and says: 'There's such a wealth, an abundance of investigation and deep pleasure in the world in her writing and artwork.' Then she laughs and says that 'there's also something very liberating about an artist who was answerable to no one and who, when you dive deep into her work, gives you permission to time travel'. She adds: 'Colquhoun knew that the veils between worlds are very thin. She was someone who could see the veil - and see through it.'

In the Cards

'But tarot, as you'll see if you have not already, provides a path toward reclaiming the imagination from the grips of doubt and rationalism. Toward reawakening the part in us with the audacity to know without material evidence.'

Jessica Dore, *Tarot for Change* (2021)

In 1977, Ithell Colquhoun staged an exhibition of seventy-eight enamel abstract works at the Newlyn Art Gallery in Cornwall. In high gloss, the vivid colours swirl, stain and drip: a bright orange ovoid shape with a red centre floats in a blue expanse; a cerulean smudge, edged in brown, is flanked with the suggestion of a bird wing; an explosion of yellow throbs amidst indigo. Colquhoun wrote a dense - and to the uninitiated, near-incomprehensible - page of explanation to accompany her exhibition; she spells tarot as 'taro' as she (most likely erroneously) felt it better reflected its Egyptian ancient origins. In her book *Taro as Colour*, which she published a year later, Colquhoun was more concise: 'This design for a Taro pack is both personal and traditional. It renders the essence of each card by the non-figurative means of pure colour, applied automatically in the manner of the psycho-morphological movement in Surrealism.'

'Psycho-morphological' is a branch of psychology concerned with metamorphosis; it recognises that the mind is in constant flux. The Surrealists - especially Robert Matta and Salvador Dalí - embraced it. Colquhoun's abstract tarot reflects her belief that each person will discover the meanings they need in the swirling patterns of colour and line – as Amy Hale told me, the cards, for the artist were not about prediction but were 'portals for contemplation'. It's a radical departure from traditional tarot, which is divided into seventy-eight cards decorated with archetypes that are divided into twenty-two Major and fifty-six Minor Arcana: The Fool, The Prophetess, The Hangman and others. While its meaning is open to interpretation, certain narratives hold steady: we are born fools, need to embrace change and accommodate stillness, strive for human connection, kill off bad habits, honour the unknown, choose empathy over violence, live in hope and so on. Colquhoun, however, decided to dispense with familiar narratives in favour of something more transcendent: the idea that the unconscious will reveal truths and images if the conscious mind allows it to. She wanted the deck to be used for meditation, not prophecy; she eschewed logic for instinct. She believed that the profound potential of the tarot had for too long been corrupted by its popularity as a tool for fortune-telling, a state of affairs which she described as 'decadent'. While her set of tarot cards might initially look abstract, their colours are highly coded – Air (Swords, pale yellow); Water (Cups, deep blue); Fire (Wands, scarlet); and Earth (Discs, indigo) – and she is clear that, although her use of automatism might seem unconventional, she combined her Surrealist techniques with instructions drawn from the Hermetic Order of the Golden Dawn, in particular, *The Tarot: Its Occult Signification, Use in Fortune-Telling and Method of Play*, which was written and published in 1888 by Samuel Mathers. Colquhoun's rationale concludes with an acknowledgement: 'After I had completed the pack, I saw some slides showing nebulae in outer space and the birth of stars. These recalled my designs and confirmed my conviction of their cosmographic function.'

It's extraordinary to think that tarot cards could only be freely printed and sold in England after the Witchcraft Act was repealed in 1951. In the last few decades, hundreds, even thousands of new decks have been produced. A search for 'tarot' on Amazon results in more than 50,000 products – there are now something in the region of 100 million copies in circulation in twenty countries – and it's enormously popular not just as a predictive tool but as a meditative and therapeutic aid. As Jung wrote in his 1933 text *On the Uses of the Tarot in Analysis*: 'These are psychological images, symbols with which one plays, as the unconscious seems to play with its contents. Tarot represents archetypal ideas, and therefore it is applicable for an intuitive method that has the purpose of understanding the flow of life.'

In this, Colquhoun's abstract Taro was prescient. She was just one in a centuries-long line of artists who have been fascinated by tarot's intertwining of image, self-exploration, archetypes and divination. Its origins are obscure: it possibly grew from Turkish or Middle Eastern card games or derived from the ancient Chinese divination text the *i-Ching* – also known *as The Book of Changes* – or from the visual language of the Egyptian *The Book of Thoth*, which some believed was written by the god himself and contained the secrets to all esoteric knowledge.

The tarot's meaning is communicated via images that have developed over time, reflecting the sensibility not only of the artist who designed them but aspects of the culture in which they were produced. As Jessica Hundley writes in a new book on tarot: 'Like all esoteric traditions, the Tarot is mutable and elastic, allowing each new generation to rediscover, and ultimately rework, its classic structure and iconography.' Early decks incorporated Christian and Hebrew symbols, such as the 'tree of life' from the Kabbalah, and many of their archetypes are influenced by sacred geometry and numerology. In the Renaissance, delicate gilded and detailed decks reflected the widespread interest in Ancient Greek and Roman mythology. One of the earliest and best-known decks is the Visconti-Sforza from early fifteenth-century Italy, which was most likely designed by the artist Bonifacio Bembo. Exquisitely hand-painted and gilded with gold leaf, the cards depict worlds within worlds, skeletons who ride horses, women who float above cities and angels who dwarf humans. Their beauty inspired Italo Calvino's 1973 novel *The Castle of Crossed Destinies*, which recounts the story of a group of travellers who are inexplicably rendered mute and can only communicate via tarot.

In the 1600s, the Tarot de Marseille was created in the south of France, where the quality of the printing presses was renowned. In bright, primary colours and clear, black-outlined drawings, it's one of the most influential and recognisable decks; the moon shines above baying dogs; a naked girl gathers water beneath stars; monkeys spin on a wheel of fortune; an elegant woman prises open the jaws of a wolf. In 1770, the French Occultist and first professional tarot reader, Jean-Baptiste Alliette - who coined the term 'cartomancy' and whose pen name was the reverse of his regular name - published *Etteilla, or Way to Entertain Yourself with a Deck of Cards*, and it was a hit. By the nineteenth century, tarot was central to several secret societies and in the early 1900s the Rider-Waite-Smith - arguably the best-known deck - was released by the Rider publishing company. It was a collaboration between Arthur Edward Waite, a scholar, poet, mystic and editor of the magazine *The Unknown World*, and a young artist, illustrator and suffragette, Pamela Colman Smith. Variously known as 'Pixie' and 'Gypsy', Waite described her as 'a most imaginative and abnormally psychic artist'.

Like Colquhoun, Smith was a member of the secret society the Hermetic Order of the Golden Dawn, and they both wove aspects of the group's ideas into their interpretations of the classic arcana. Unlike Colquhoun's deeply enigmatic deck, Colman Smith's de-signs are full of stories; although influenced by the Marseille Tarot, they're shot through with details that bring the whole alive. A couple, their children dancing beside them, gaze with joy into the heavens where the ten of cups floats like a rainbow; a laughing baby straddles a white horse in front of a field of sunflowers and beneath a serene sun. The High Priestess sits on her throne against a backdrop of patterned wallpaper, a crescent moon at her feet. The Fool, an androgynous figure in a flowered robe, is on a journey: with a white rose in one hand, a staff in another, and accompanied by a faithful white dog, they walk towards a precipice, gazing at the golden sky. The journey, however precarious, is festive, not frightening.

Pamela Colman Smith was born in London in 1878, lived in Jamaica and New York - where she studied art at the Pratt Institute - and, when her mother died, then her father, she returned to England for good in 1899. She illustrated twenty books, including a collection of poems by W.B. Yeats, whose work is rich in occult imagery and who, in 1901, introduced her to the Isis-Urania Temple of the Hermetic Order of the Golden Dawn. She opened a shop in London to sell prints and paintings, started a magazine called *The Green Sheaf*, and travelled the country with a theatre troupe, designing costumes and stage sets.

Pamela Colman Smith, 1912

In 1912, an unknown photographer shot a portrait of her: even from a distance of more than a century, she crackles with charm. She's thirty-four, smiling, an impish expression in her dark, lively eyes. She's wearing a silky, patterned dress and four thick ropes of beads around her neck. Her arms are crossed jauntily in front of her and she appears to have feathers in her hair. She had famous friends: the actress Ellen Terry, the impresario Henry Irving, the author of *Dracula*, Bram Stoker, and the photographer Alfred Stieglitz, who exhibited her work in his New York Gallery 291: watercolours of fairy tales and folklore populated with human/animal hybrids.

She garnered a sparkling review in the *New York Sun*: 'Pamela Colman Smith is a young woman with that quality rare in either sex - imagination ... "Death in the House" is absolutely nerve-shuddering ... Munch (he of the expressionist painting, *The Scream*), himself a master magician of the terrible, could not have succeeded better in arousing a profound disquiet.' The prominent journalist and poet Benjamin de Casseres described her paintings as 'curious and fascinating', declaring, 'She is a blender of visions, a mystic, a symbolist, one who transfigures the world she lives in by the overwhelming simplicity of her imagination.'

Like Kandinsky, Colman Smith experienced synaesthesia and she listed her works as if they were pieces of music, sonatas, overtures and concerti. In a 1908 article for *The Strand Magazine*, she wrote:

What I wish to make plain is that these are not pictures of the music theme ... but just what I see when I hear music. Thoughts loosened and set free by the spell of sound ... Subconscious energy lives in them all ... When I take a brush in hand and the music begins it is like unlocking the door to a beautiful country ... with plains, mountains and the billowing sea.

Her parties were famous; her sense of fun was infectious, she dressed in orange robes, told folk tales and sang songs. Her love for humanity was clear. In an article for *The Craftsman* magazine in 1908 titled 'Should the Art Student Think?', she declared:

> Learn from everything, see everything, and above all feel everything! And make other people when they look at your drawing feel it too! . . . Think good thoughts of beautiful things, colours, sounds, places, not mean thoughts. When you see a lot of dirty people in a crowd, do not remember only the dirt, but the great spirit that is in them all, and the power that they represent.

She railed against convention and challenged her readers to seize life:

> Lift up your ideals, you weaklings, and force a way out of that thunderous clamour of the steam press, the hurrying herd of blind humanity, noise, dust, strife, seething toil - there is power! The imprisoned Titans underneath the soil, grinding, writhing - take your strength from them, throw aside your petty drawing room point of view.

In 1909, A.E. Waite commissioned Colman Smith to design a tarot deck. Despite its enormous popularity, during her lifetime the originality of her drawings was largely unacknowledged and until recent years her name was left off most editions of the deck.

After illustrating Bram Stoker's last book *Lair of the White Worm* in 1911, Smith converted to Catholicism and - like Ithell Colquhoun - moved to Cornwall, where she died in Bude in 1951, penniless and unknown, at the age of seventy-three. As far as we know, the two women never met. Apparently, Colquhoun didn't approve of the Rider-Waite-Smith deck; she felt it distorted Mathers' research and 'introduced a gender balance into the court cards by substituting knaves for princesses'.

*

In the decades since the Rider-Waite-Smith deck, tarot gradually
grew in popularity. In 1969, Aleister Crowley's Thoth Tarot was
released; it was painted between 1938 and 1943 by the aristocrat
artist Lady Frieda Harris, who followed Crowley's updating of the
symbolism and numerical systems. The Anthroposophical writings of Rudolf Steiner inspired it, among other esoteric teachings.
Although they worked together on the deck for years, neither
Harris nor Crowley lived to see its publication.

The 1970s and 1980s saw the emergence of several feminist tarot
decks created by women who were looking for new ways of living
outside patriarchal logic. In 1976, the artist Penny Slinger - whose
work was included in the exhibition 'The Dark Monarch' at Tate
St Ives and who feels that tarot gives us the 'opportunity to explore
not what separates us but what connects us' - designed the Secret
Dakini Oracle, the first collaged deck, and in the same year, Womanspirit Circle in California published several decks, including A
New Woman's Tarot and the Amazon Tarot. In 1981, Rachel Pol-
lack's *Seventy-Eight Degrees of Wisdom* - one of the most influential
guides to tarot - came out, as did the circle-shaped, goddess-inspired
Motherpeace deck, by Vicki Noble and Karen Vogel. In 1984, Ffiona
Morgan published Daughters of the Moon, yet another feminist
tarot deck conceived by the Santa Cruz Womanspirit Circle.

However, by far the most ambitious tarot ever to be made was
dreamed up by the French American artist, Niki de Saint Phalle,
who was famous for her large-scale, psychedelic sculptures of vo-
luptuous, goddess-like women which she called 'Nanas' - French
slang for young women. In 1974, she was offered a plot of land
by friends in Tuscany, 100 kilometres north of Rome. She spent
the next couple of decades designing and building her Giardino
dei Tarocchi - the Tarot Garden - which opened to the public
in 1998. Designed as much to touch as to look at and get lost in,
de Saint Phalle created twenty-two enormous, vividly colourful

biomorphic figures which represent the major and minor arcana; many of them are covered in tiny mirrors, which the artist believed rejected 'all kinds of bad influences'. Created from reinforced concrete, steel, ceramics and mosaic, and inspired by the organic architecture of Antonio Gaudí in Barcelona, these giant human/ animal/mystical hybrids populate a labyrinth of magical caves and tumbling fountains. The characters are at once delicate and robust; monstrous, inviting, eccentric; some spin on their axis amid a pool, while others you can enter. In 1983, during the construction of the garden - which was a labour of love for many artists, including the renowned sculptor Jean Tinguely, and local residents - de Saint Phalle moved into The Empress, which was designed in the shape of a Sphinx. She lived there for seven years; her bedroom was in one of the breasts, the kitchen in the other. She asked her friend Mario Botta to 'make the entrance of the garden in contrast to what was inside' and wrote that he created 'a masculine fortress-like wall of local stones which marks clearly the separation of the world without and the world within. The wall symbolizes for me a protection like the dragon who protects the treasure in fairy tales.'

The Tarot Garden opened to the public on 15 May 1998: a lush, sun-dappled haven, filled with winding paths, trees, flowers and running water. You can visit it in person in summer or online, where a photograph of each sculpture is accompanied by de Saint Phalle's explanation, which is handwritten in her distinctive looping script. Justice is a black woman as a building, a prison door between her legs, her enormous breasts the scales. 'Real justice,' declares the caption, 'is not blind, it brings a vision of universality.' Death is a golden woman on a blue horse, decorated with stars: a beautiful grim reaper, 'who allows new blossoms to grow'. The Moon - which 'can be perilous or offer great imaginative power' - is the outline of a woman's face gazing upwards, held by strange creatures. The High Priestess has a mouth like a cave that opens onto a pool. 'Those who wish to explain events by reason or logic alone,' explains de Saint Phalle, 'remain on the surface of things, without the depth of instinctual vision and imagination.' The Empress rises from the midst of a forest like something from a dream: a benevolent, Black, psychedelic sphinx, with breasts like enormous flowers, feet like the claws of trippy dinosaurs, colourful, her vagina a doorway. De Saint Phalle writes: 'She is Queen of the sky. Mother. Whore. Emotion. Sacred magic and civilisation. The Empress which I made in the form of a Sphinx. I lived for years inside this protective mother. She also served for headquarters for my meetings with the crew. It was here we all had coffee breaks. On all, she exerted a fatal attraction.' Although Niki de Saint Phalle died in 2002, her legacy lives on in her joyful garden and her artworks. In one of the many interviews she gave, she said, laughing: 'I'm not a person who can change society - except through showing some kind of vision of these happy, joyous, domineering women. That's all that I can do.'

In Greece, the days passed by in a sunny haze. For the first time in years, I had time to reflect on my years at *frieze*: on the good (a world without art is not somewhere I want to live); the bad (art made for all the wrong reasons - propaganda, self-interest, material gain, sensationalism); and the ugly (billionaires competing for the most expensive artworks in order to show off). Navigating these three categories, making judgement calls, and assessing who to believe and what to trust, was a minefield.

Niki de St Phalle's declaration that she wanted her art to spark joy seems almost naïve today: the role and function of art is so hotly contested. Not many artists I know would admit to such a seemingly simple aim, even if it's something their work engenders; in a world wracked with terrible happenings, the ambition to make something happy could be seen as an indulgence. But to my mind, what could be more useful, more defiant than an art that declares there are other, better, ways of living? (Just think of the clips of musicians playing their instruments amid the rubble of devastated cities in Ukraine.) The work of artists who insist that this earthly realm is not all there is embodies the idea of possibility - surely, an offshoot of joy.

Witch Dance

'What is magic?
Little cracks coming in, small flaws in the glass'

Rebecca Tamás, *WITCH* (2019)

In 2013, my friend Donna Huddleston (one of the most joyful people I know) invited me to compose a piece of music for the triangle. I am not, I hasten to add, much of a composer; but as I had been in a band in my early twenties with my sister Suzie and had once studied piano, Donna felt I was qualified. She was creating a performance called *Witch Dance*, featuring a group of young women gyrating like glamorous ghosts in clouds of smoke, observed by a man sitting on a rock, wall paintings, sculptures and a revolving platform. I was one of three friends she invited to collaborate on a score.

Like many artists, Donna's approach is intuitive; she thinks in images, atmospheres and sounds. She once told me she feels things 'three-dimensionally'. The triangle, for her, is at once an object and a form rich with symbolic and sonic possibility; it's replete with alchemical associations of earth, fire and air, and as an instrument, it emits an ethereal tone. She's never doubted the existence of different realms and has always been a believer. However, as a lapsed Catholic, Donna's is a belief that is open-ended; it's about possibility, not dogma; about seeking new ways of living that are personally, and aesthetically, liberating. About finding the joy in the mundane.

To get my creative juices flowing, Donna emailed me a short collage of scenes of what she calls 'cinema magic': film clips by directors including Almodóvar, Cassavetes, De Palma, Fassbinder and Tarkovsky, auteurs whose work highlights the power of the imagination and non-verbal communication. A clairvoyant girl moves a glass of water with her mind; two hands create the shadow of a flying bird; a camera pans through a building like a disembodied eye; women break into a dance routine in prison.

Mary Wigman performing Witch Dance, *1926*

She also sent me a short, choppy clip of the German expressionist dancer and choreographer Mary Wigman performing her own *Witch Dance* (or Hexentanz) in 1926. In it, Wigman - who believed in dance as the 'visualization of the incomprehensible' - sits on the floor in a loose dress, moving like a cosmic crab. Her next move was only captured in photographs: she leapt into the air. She's wearing a mask, although it's difficult to see it in the degraded footage, and her feet are bare. Her black hair is loose; it shakes like a storm cloud as her raw-boned body jerks and gesticulates; her roving hands are splayed like starfish. There is no soundtrack and so her gestures erupt within a malevolent silence. The witch she embodies is the antithesis of idealised femininity: she's hardly human, enigmatic, powerful, angry, possibly violent. Like Sophie Taueber-Arp's Dada dance, there's nothing seductive about Wigman, but she's mesmerising. She's a creature of her own making.

Wigman first performed professionally with the pioneer of modern dance Rudolf Laban. His influential school in Monte Verità in the hills above Ascona in Switzerland was part of a nature-loving, vegetarian community of artists, musicians, writers and performers who had loosely come together under the *Lebensreform*, or Life Reform movement. It aimed to rescue the human body from bourgeois society, which its proponents perceived as unnatural, sterile and materialistic. In many ways, it was a precursor to the counter-cultural groups of the 1960s. Wigman helped to develop what became known as *Ausdruckstanz*, or expressive dance, which was a reaction to the rules-based rigours of classical ballet. She summed up her approach as: 'Dance is unity of expression and function; physicality filled with light, giving soul to form. Without ecstasy no dance! Without form no dance!' She saw her role as a communicator of fundamental truths and often performed without music to emphasise the primacy of movement. While she wasn't religious, she did believe in the idea of a god, or higher power, and she was often overcome by visions of something or someone - an energy that she attempted to channel in her performances. In 1916, she wrote in her diary: 'I am the dance/And I am the priestess of dance/. . . The pain of all things striving/is my pain./The joy of all circling movements/is my joy./Lord of the space I am./The priestess of high dance./ I am the soul of dance.' In an essay on 'Composition', Wigman outlined her approach to choreography: 'The mystic dance . . . will only emerge from a state of spiritual awareness. It will renounce anything of theatrical

nature . . . The mystic is the pure medium for a pure idea, sacerdo-
tal in nature.'

Unsurprisingly, her work divided critics. In 1919, one German
reviewer described Wigman's performances as 'ridiculous', 'idiotic',
'a mad frenzy' and 'an imbecilic dislocation of the joints'. When she
toured the United States in 1930, an enthusiastic writer described
her first season as 'one of the most memorable adventures in the
history of dancing in America', while the *New Yorker*'s correspond-
ent mocked her: 'Miss Mary Wigman suddenly dashed out, giving
one an impression that she might be trying to escape from an irate
or perhaps amorous stagehand.'

Her legacy is complicated. Mining familiar archetypes such as
witches and reimagining them for the twentieth century, Wigman
was both an arch-modernist and deeply connected to mysticism and
pre-Christian paganism. In the early 1930s, many of these ancient
stories appealed to the Nazis as they co-opted the revival of interest
in German folklore into their advancement of Aryan supremacy.
There is debate around Wigman's complicity with the regime;
much of it focuses on the perennial question of how to distil the
politics of avant-garde artists from their artworks or performances,
many of which are intensely enigmatic. As she famously said: 'If I
could say with words what my dances express, I wouldn't have a
reason to dance.' The power and innovation of her choreography
embodies the fact that the evolution of art is often as chaotic as it
is transformative; it frequently looks as much to the deep past as it
anticipates a future in which creative freedoms might flourish.

In 1979, the ecofeminist Starhawk – whose book *The Spiral Dance*
was an impetus for the Goddess movement – wrote a powerful
riposte to accusations that the revival of witchcraft was somehow
sympathetic to Nazism:

The Nazis were not Goddess worshippers; they denigrated women, relegating them to the position of breeding animals whose

role was to produce more Aryan warriors. They were the perfect
patriarchy, the ultimate warrior cult - not servants of the life force.
Witchcraft has no ideal of a 'superman' . . . all people are already
seen as manifest gods, and differences in colour, race, and customs
are welcomed, as signs of the myriad beauty of the Goddess. To
equate Witches with Nazis because neither are Judaeo-Christians,
and both share magical elements, is like saying swans are really
scorpions because neither are horses and both have tails.

Wigman stayed in Germany between 1933 and 1945 and received
funding from the state between 1933 and 1936, when she performed the prophetic 'Lament for the Dead' at the Berlin Olympic
Games. However, with Goebbels's 1937 edict that 'dance must be
cheerful and show beautiful female bodies and have nothing to do
with philosophy', her work fell out of favour, and she refused to
choreograph a performance in honour of Hitler. In a 1940 article,
her work was declared degenerate and 'non-Nordic'; the following
year, she was prevented from lecturing and performing, and her
school closed in 1942. After the war, it reopened and her innovations were key to the modern dance revival in Germany.

Donna Huddleston told me she thinks of influence as 'a necessary guide that chaperones and magnetises you' - an apt summary
of her version of Witch Dance, which was performed in a small
London East End gallery. Over thirty-eight minutes, her performance embodied how the art of the past morphs and mutates in its
journey to the present. The origins of 'glamour' pulsated throughout the work. Originally, it was a word that alluded to sorcery,
witches, occult knowledge and magical spells; now, it's been diluted
to describe a person who is good-looking and elegant; someone
who might put a spell on you. The original meaning of 'fascinating' is relevant here. The word derived from Pliny the Elder, who
described a group of people from 'faraway places' (he was possibly
referring to the Balkans) who had two pupils in each eye and who

could kill with a single glance. Pliny called their power 'fascinatio': its meaning also alluded to spellcasting or possibly enchantment.

Donna's cast of eight female dancers formed a chorus, protagonists, ghosts and a wandering woman whose sharp style wouldn't have looked out of place in a Weimar nightclub. Wigman's spirit mingles with veiled allusions to a group of radical artists, writers and filmmakers, dead and alive, who share a belief that minds and bodies should be free to do whatever they see fit. In particular, the legacy of that great critic of everyday fascism, the German filmmaker Rainer Werner Fassbinder, haunted *Witch Dance*. Fassbinder redefined glamour as a political tool; his female actors repeatedly communicate through movement and gesture. He also adored Hollywood, something Donna referenced. She directed her witches to click their fingers like the dualling gangs in *West Side Story* and to tap their canes like the troupes of dancers in so many of the movies from the golden days of cinema.

Scenes unfolded as if in a trance; a *mise en scène* in which time and place were as vague as each other. Against a projection of a full moon and a wall of painted plants, young women – fashioned in simple dresses from different eras, some with gloves, and one with a cape – moved in and out of light and through smoke. At times they struck poses that echoed Wigman's long-ago gestures: hands splayed in an evocation of terror, tension or power, fingers pointing to the sky, arms raised in supplication. The least movements seemed loaded with significance, but what, precisely, they signified was unclear: sometimes mystery is an end in itself. ('Why,' Donna asked me, 'should we explain everything?') Five fake porcelain vases, like a very old still-life painting made flesh, slowly rotate on a platform; eventually, a dancer, directed by a priestess in silk gloves, smashes four of them as furiously as if she were shattering the past itself. When she slams the final vase into another dancer's back, the shock is palpable. That the violence is enacted to my piece for the triangle – which I accompanied with a simple, repeated phrase on a basic Casio keyboard - made it a curiously intimate experience.

One of the most cryptic aspects of Donna's *Witch Dance* is the ponderous actor she employed to sit on a large rock as if to oversee the proceedings: a stand-in for the writer J.G. Ballard - a critic of the worst excesses of humanity. In his prose poem 'What I Believe', he declares that the role of the imagination is 'to release the truth within us, to hold back the night, to transcend death, to charm motorways, to ingratiate ourselves with birds, to enlist the confidences of madmen'. Who could argue with that?

Witch Dance ends with a jolt: the trance-like atmosphere blown apart by the blasting of Led Zeppelin's cover of an old blues tune about a flood, 'When the Levee Breaks'. Each of the women - in silk dresses, leotards, gloves and bustiers - echo Mary Wigman's movements before finally dancing alone. As they gradually disappear, a line from the song rings out starkly: 'When the levee breaks, mama, you got to move': an apt motto for art, as well as life.

Fast forward eight years. Donna is working on a new exhibition of drawings. She texts me photographs of her work in progress. I gaze at the images on my phone, tiny in the palm of my hand, but containing worlds: a piano beneath an eclipse; a woman draped in flowers, another flanked by crows; a necklace formed of two crystals, suspended like tears in a cleavage. I don't know precisely what any of this means but I am drawn to its strange joy. Like mediums, this is what artists do: they conjure images from the air and the earth, and then send them into the ether, gifts for anyone willing to receive them.

Trees of Knowledge

'Though lowly, the plant kingdom reaches high, soaring like giants
above us, great trees that hold court with birds - ethereal creatures
associated with the spirit realm.'

Gina Buenfeld, 'The Ur Plant' (2020)

When the first London lockdown hit in March 2020, I had just
returned from Australia. My family and I had been caught up in
the catastrophic bushfires that decimated an area larger than the
Amazon. Almost 3,000 homes and 20 per cent of the country's
forests were destroyed; thirty-three people and more than a billion animals died. The year 2019 had been the driest and hottest
year ever recorded in Australia and the long-running drought
had turned the land into a tinderbox. Most climate scientists are
convinced that global warming has increased the frequency of
extreme heat events and droughts, longer fire seasons, hotter and
more acidic oceans, and rising sea levels. Yet again and again, as
the forests burned, towns were wiped out and roads melted in the
heat, climate sceptics - including those in government - said that
Australia has always had bushfires, and that this was nothing new,
even though fires on this scale had never been witnessed before.

We had been on holiday at the coast when the fire surrounded
us. We were in no real danger - the house we were staying in was
next to the beach - but we lost electricity and were stranded for
four days, as fires blocked the roads out. The sky was thick and
dark, the horizon a bloody scar. The beach was black with ash and

strange storms kept erupting: the extreme heat was wreaking havoc with weather systems. Anxious text messages flew around until we no longer had phone coverage: later, two friends told me their homes narrowly avoided incineration because the wind changed direction when the flames were metres from their front doors. On New Year's Eve, we played Scrabble by candlelight, drank warm champagne, and ate sandwiches. As 2020 was ushered in, my niece Alice read my tarot cards.

At dawn on the fifth day, glued to the radio - the only way we could get information as the internet was down - we heard the highway was briefly open. Only hours before the fires erupted back and the roads were once again closed, we drove to Canberra through a landscape thick with smoke that recalled the unspeakable images of the Western Front after the First World War. Familiar lush, semi-tropical forests had become a ravaged moonscape of burnt exclamation marks. The silence was eerie, the sky dead; it was like being in one of Leonora Carrington's nightmares. When we finally reached Canberra, 200 kilometres away, the smoke was still so thick you could hardly see your hand in front of your face. When I visited my sister's home in the countryside, the normally abundant fields surrounding her garden looked like the Sahara. It was as if the earth itself had died.

A few weeks later, I returned to London and repurposed the mask I used to filter smoke for a new kind of wildfire: Covid-19. Although its origins are still being debated, the consensus is that, like the bushfires in Australia, this catastrophe lies in human mistreatment of the natural world.

After the trauma of the bushfires, my small, damp, green London garden became a place of consolation. For the first time, I loved England's rain and heavy grey skies; the quiet chores of pruning and weeding in the damp earth were deeply therapeutic. Everything felt different: the intensity of confinement lent daily life a peculiar, sharp-edged introspection. The world I assumed we could trust had become markedly unstable. My dreams intensified. I read the artist and filmmaker Derek Jarman's memoir, *Modern Nature* (1991). His wondrous garden in the shadow of a nuclear power plant on Dungeness Beach in Kent was as much a metaphor for memory and hope as it was earth and plants. Even as he was fading, a victim of another terrible pandemic, AIDS, he cultivated plants that could withstand the shingle and the savage, salty winds: alexanders, foxgloves, periwinkle, poppies, purple iris, sea kale and viper's bugloss bloomed brightly. 'My garden's boundaries,' he wrote, 'are the horizon.'

The ten weeks of 2021 that I spent not leaving my home in London were the longest time I'd stayed put in decades. When I arrived in the United Kingdom from Melbourne on a painting scholarship in the mid-1990s, being itinerant was the norm. I came for nine months and am still here. I had a new address every few years and never stopped travelling for work. (Oh, the irony that my great love is painting, the stillest of artforms.) As well as the pleasure my garden afforded me, it made me starkly aware of my ignorance: I discovered that I was inhabiting a space of which I had no real understanding. I'd lived in my home for three years, but it took a pandemic to recognise and greet my neighbours over the back fence. It took a pandemic to make me see the cosmic connections between where I'm from and where I live.

My flat in London is just off the unlovely Holloway Road, which weaves its way north up a hill to Highgate and Hampstead. A few streets away is Seven Sisters Road, a charmless, busy thoroughfare, filled with choking fumes and shabby shops. Yet until the pandemic, I had never connected the road to epic sagas, faraway places and ancient stories. In London, its name refers to the seven elm trees that were planted in a circle, surrounding a walnut tree, on a piece of common land in the eighteenth century. But the myth of the seven sisters recurs in various cultures as an origin story about the Pleiades, the nearest star cluster to Earth.

In Greek mythology, the stars represent the daughters of the Titan god Atlas and the Oceanid goddess Pleione: Maia, Electra, Taygete, Celaeno, Alcyone, Sterope and Merope. For First Nations Australians, the Pleiades are sisters who transformed themselves into stars to escape a lecherous magician, Wati Nyuri, who left his footprint in the nearby constellation of Orion. The story is told by, in the main, women in song, painting and performance via songlines or dreamings, a mnemonic system that, in tracing the journeys of Ancestral spirits, conveys crucial information - known as *Tjukurpa* - about survival on the vast continent. (How curious it is that both Ancient Greeks and First Nations Australians - two cultures that never met - refer to the Pleiades as seven sisters. And that the word 'mnemonic' is named after the Greek goddess of memory.) From the location of waterholes and the identification of medicinal plants and food to kinship, marriage rules and codes of behaviour, the songlines must be told in a way that holds the listener, so that each generation will remember and retell them. Aboriginal culture is oral: if the songline is lost, then so is memory and meaning.

In 2017, on a visit home to Canberra, my sister Suzie, a musician who works at the National Museum of Australia, said I had to see the exhibition that had just opened there: 'Songlines: Tracking the Seven Sisters'. The show had come about because Suzie's colleague, Margo Neale, the senior Indigenous curator at the museum, was in a meeting with a group of elders from Anangu in the Central Deserts when one of them, David Miller, made a heartfelt plea: 'You mob gotta help us . . . those songlines they been all broken up now . . . you can help us put them all back together again'. The old people were dying, and the young people weren't returning to Country - the site of belonging, information, stories and secrets - to learn their *Tjukurpa*.

Rising to the challenge, over the next seven years Margo travelled 7,000 kilometres, assembling a 'curatorium' of twenty custodial elders from across the Central and Western Deserts of Australia: the lands of the Martu, Ngaanyatjarra and Anangu Pitjantjatjara Yankunytjatjara (APY) peoples. They brought together 300 paintings, sculptures, ceramics, weavings, installations and films by over a hundred artists and collectives, most of them women. The story of the seven sisters was chosen as the show's focus because, in Margo's words:

> It's a tale of tragedy and comedy, obsession and trickery, desire and loss, solidarity and sorrow that touches on life's moral dimensions: how to live with each other on this earth in a sustainable way; how to care for each other and share resources equitably. It also instructs on gender relations, kinship, marriage rules and other codes of behaviour . . . It's a saga of mythological dimensions and meanings.

A sense of great joy and pride pervaded the show: projections of Elders welcomed you into their space, which was signposted as if you were moving across the land itself. Questions weaved in and out of the displays: What is the relevance of ancestral stories to the twenty-first century? What are songlines and why are they significant? Languages (there are around 250 spoken by Aboriginal Australians) and details changed with locations. Paintings, many of them made collectively by women, are some of the most beautiful maps in existence. The monumental *Yarrkalpa* (Hunting Ground; 2013), for example - one of the most staggering paintings I've ever seen - was created by a group of women: Kumpaya Girgirba, Yikartu Bumba, Kanu Nancy Taylor, Ngamaru Bidu, Yuwali Janice Nixon, Reena Rogers, Thelma Judson and Ngalangka Nola Taylor. It's a stylised view of a kaleidoscopic land, intricately detailed, seen from above and up close, throbbing with flashes of yellows, ochres, watery greens, cornflower blues. The Seven Sisters (the Minyipuru) fly across the left-hand side of the canvas, chased by their pursuer.

It's at once an abstract picture, an impression of a landscape and a highly codified record of Country - a culturally specific term that encompasses law, language, place and belief systems.

The Aboriginal peoples of Australia weren't included on the national census until 1967 and the ruling of terra nullius - 'land belonging to no-one', a legal fiction which the British used as a justification to colonise the continent - wasn't thrown out until 1992. Since then, the songlines - painted, sung, performed - have been used in land claims to assert a connection to place. These vast lands don't belong to any single person: to First Nations Australians, the Earth is a community, as intimate as skin; the past and future are all part of a continuous present. Women's creativity and power are intrinsic to its nurturing and knowledge.

Ironically, much of the art I've written about over the past few years has been about community, collective responsibility and re-discovering the local, but it took a pandemic to make me realise what I've missed because I've been too busy being elsewhere. I learned that London is the planet's largest urban forest, with more than eight million trees comprised of 319 species - and I could name about three of them. I was like the baddie in the famous letter that William Blake wrote to a critic: 'The tree which moves some to tears of joy is in the eyes of others only a green thing which stands in the way.' A friend asked me about the quality of my garden's soil, and I was stumped; I couldn't separate the weeds from the non-weeds because I had no idea what a weed was. The only flowers I could name were geraniums and roses - tulips at a pinch. I became a little obsessed with filling the bird feeder. A friend mentioned that I could boil the rosehips and drink them, and I was astonished; my garden was like a medicine cabinet, but I didn't have the key. I exchanged glances with bright, strange birds. If I discovered anything in those long dark months, it was that it was time to tend to my own garden.

In his 2017 book *The Hidden Life of Trees* the German forester Peter Wohlleben writes about what trees have taught him and asks us to observe the dramas being played out in the woods. He explains that a forest is a social network, and that trees are sentient, communicate with one another, help each other out, experience pain and memories. To be in the company of trees is not unlike what has been imagined in the countless fairy tales and cartoons where trees are as full of personality as humans.

I came across an article that mentioned the Ancient Greek 'Doctrine of Signatures', the idea that a plant that resembles part of a body could be used to heal it. While its science is discredited – birthwort, for example, looks like a uterus and was used to treat pregnancies, but it actually damages kidneys and causes cancer – there's something mind-expanding about the echo of the human form in the plant world. In her 1912 history of herbals, the botanist Agnes Arber wrote: 'Each plant was a terrestrial star and each star was a spiritualized plant.' Gazing at my lovely tangle of a garden, I didn't exactly understand what she meant but I liked the sound of it.

During the months of lockdown, I discovered a whole new relationship to food and, like many people, spent much of my time cooking. To cope with my anxiety, I went to sleep to a soundtrack of a 'cleansing crystal bowl' that I found on a free meditation app with over seven million subscribers. I did yoga with a teacher whose classes have been watched more than 900 million times. I cut back on my drinking. Although I've been a vegetarian since I was a teenager, my diet became predominantly vegan: I could not – cannot – bear the cruelty of humans to different species. (As Leonora Carrington wrote in her novel *The Hearing Trumpet*: 'I never eat meat as I think it is wrong to deprive animals of their life when they are so difficult to chew anyway.') I had never spent so much time in my kitchen.

Leonora Carrington at home with ING

In 1994, my friend, the writer Chloe Aridjis, took a photograph of Carrington, aged seventy-seven, steely and alert, at her home in Mexico City. She's standing next to one of her sculptures, which, Chloe explains, Leonora called ING (c.1994) 'as in cook-ing, paint-ing, see-ing: a sort of Golem figure, it represented the verb incarnate. In her world, everything might possess a soul; even grammar becomes an entity.' Chloe remembered that, as they sat having tea, the pots and pans hanging behind Leonora cast shadows that evoked 'claws, shovels, tridents, horned creatures'. They were, she felt, 'imbued with a *Fantasia* sorcerer's potential' and she 'half expected them to come alive and start marching around'. 'I've always had access to other worlds,' Carrington said. 'We all do because we dream.'

Chloe describes the door to Carrington's kitchen as 'a charged threshold'. It was, for the artist – who had a lifelong interest in mythology, spirituality and the occult – a sacred place that celebrated the feminine sphere. In her biography of Carrington, Susan L. Aberth coined the term 'the alchemical kitchen' in relation to her work. When the writer Joanna Moorhead discovered in middle age that Carrington was her cousin, she travelled to Mexico to meet her. She describes how the artist led her into 'the inner sanctum' of her kitchen, 'tabernacle-like at the centre of her fortified island', where they spent five days 'drinking sometimes tea and sometimes tequila, listening to an unfolding story that brought together magic and madness, love and disappointment, bravery and single-mindedness'.

In her 1956 painting *Ab Eo Quod*, Carrington depicts a kitchen furnished with a table covered by a white cloth. A large, glowing white egg – known in countless cultures as a symbol of fertility and birth – sits on top of it, along with bread, two glasses of red wine, a delicate decanter, grain, grapes and a pomegranate, a fruit redolent with metaphorical power. Although Persephone was condemned to the Underworld for eternity to reign as Queen of the Dead because she ate a few of its jewel-like seeds, the fruit is also, in many cultures, a signifier of fertility.

In the painting, butterflies and moths flutter about; a white rose, suspended from the ceiling like a light fitting, drips liquid onto the egg. The walls are graffitied with delicate drawings: a man and a woman intertwine, a goat rears, a circle hovers within a square. The Latin words 'Ab eo, Quod nigram caudum habet abstine terrestrium enim decorum est' are embroidered on a screen: according to Susan Aberth, 'it's a fragment from the Asensus Nigrum, an obscure alchemical text from 1351' that translates as: 'Keep away from any with a black tail, indeed, this is the beauty of the earth.' Ever defiant, a long black tail emerges from the embroidery – possibly detached from the menacing, furry beast whose face peers from beneath the table. I suspect that Leonora Carrington always looked what is forbidden or frightening straight in the eye. But that is me surmising. Carrington didn't like to explain her work. Analysis, she felt, would dilute its power.

With the pandemic raging its way across the planet, an eerie stillness gripped London and everyone flocked to the parks; nature had never been so popular. I went for long walks on Hampstead Heath with Shelley and her dog Henry. As we tramped through the mud, she told me of the interest many early Freudians shared in the occult and how Carl Jung believed that the unconscious was part of a shared, or collective, unconscious which communicated in archetypes - images and symbols from myth and alchemy, one of which was the 'tree of life', an organism that supports every aspect of the cosmos. Freud and Jung were to fall out, in part because Jung challenged Freud's theory that all neuroses had a sexual basis; Jung believed that social or personal factors could cause them too. They also disagreed about spirituality: in his autobiography, Jung recalled Freud telling him 'never to abandon the sexual theory. That is the most essential thing of all. You see, we must make a dogma of it, an unshakable bulwark.' Jung replied, 'a bulwark - against what?' Freud answered: 'Against the black tide of mud . . . of occultism.' Jung's response is unequivocal:

> I knew that I would never be able to accept such an attitude. What Freud seemed to mean by 'occultism' was virtually everything that philosophy and religion, including the rising contemporary science of parapsychology, had learned about the psyche. To me the sexual theory was just as occult, that is to say, just as unproven a hypothesis, as many other speculative views. As I saw it, a scientific truth was a hypothesis which might be adequate for the moment but was not to be preserved as an article of faith for all time.

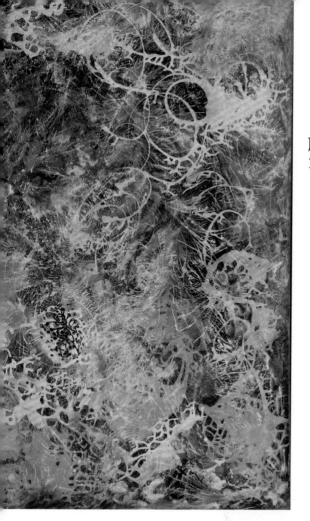

Janet Sobel,
The Milky Way, 1945

Madge Gill, *untitled*, 1954

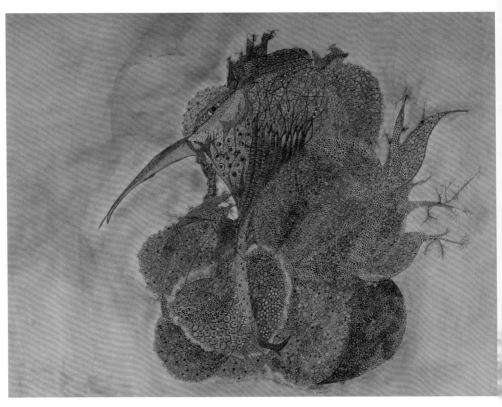

Unica Zürn, *untitled*, 1955

Lenore Tawney, 1959,
portrait by Yousuf Karsh

Minnie Evans, *untitled*, 1968

Liliane Lijn, *Conjunction of Opposites:
Lady of the Wild Things and Woman of War*, 1986

Niki de Saint Phalle, *The Empress*, The Tarot Garden, 1998

Goshka Macuga, *Madame Blavatsky*, 2007

Ngamaru Bidu, Yikartu Bumba, Kumpaya Girgirba, Thelma Judson, Yuwali Janice Nixon, Reena Rogers, Karnu Nancy Taylor, Ngalangka Nola Taylor, *Yarrkalpa (Hunting Ground)*, Parnngurr Area, 2013

Linder, *Children of the Mantic Stain*, 2016

Sheila Hicks, *Escalade Beyond Chromatic Lands*, installation at the Venice Biennale, 2016-17

Donna Huddleston, *Brighter*, 2021

Jung collated accounts of the psychological experiments he undertook between 1913 and 1916. Via self-induced trances, he attempted
to activate and illuminate the neglected corners of his mind. He
produced a series of extraordinarily vivid and detailed illustrations
of his visions - both waking and sleeping. He believed he had a
spirit guide: an old man called Philemon, and Salome, who he believed to be the personification of his 'anima' - the feminine part of
a man's soul. Each day he would paint a mandala - a universal form
that appears in countless cultures that represents individuals as
microcosms within a unified whole. Returning to the shape helped
him 'observe my psychic transformations from day to day'. In his
autobiography, Jung wrote: 'My 21 were cryptograms concerning
the state of the self which were presented to me anew each day. In
them I saw the self - that is, my whole being - actively at work.'

Although commonly known as *The Red Book* - titled because
of its red leather binding - Jung's formal title for the work is the
Latin *Liber Novus* (The New Book). A deeply personal investigation,
it wasn't published in his lifetime, possibly because he was concerned that, as he wrote, 'it is ironical that I, a psychiatrist, should
at almost every step of my experiment have run into the same psychic material which is the stuff of psychosis and is found in the
insane'. *The Red Book* wasn't made public until 2009. Jung considered it to be incomplete: the last word he wrote in it is 'moglichkeit'
- possibility. In 2013, the Italian curator Massimiliano Gioni was
appointed the artistic director of the largest art exhibition in the
world: the Venice Biennale. The exhibition he dreamed up, 'The
Encyclopedic Palace', privileged the imagination over academicism, abandoning a linear representation of time and traditional
demarcations between art, craft and anthropology - all of which
prompted wonderfully unexpected conversations and connections
between materials, eras and cultures. As you entered the show, you
were greeted by *The Red Book* in a glass vitrine: Gioni's idea pivoted
on an investigation of the psyche and its role in the creation of art.

Jung's theory of the 'active imagination' - the idea that to achieve self-knowledge, the conscious mind must plumb unknown depths via dream analysis and the creation of intuitive drawings or paintings - could be a description of the process that resulted in artworks created via channelling spirit guides. Jung was aware that what he was proposing was challenging. In his 1951 book, *Aion: Researches into the Phenomenology of the Self*, he wrote: 'No tree, it is said, can grow to heaven unless its roots reach down to hell.'

In 2021, I went to see an exhibition, 'The Botanical Mind: Art, Mysticism and the Cosmic Tree' - visionary work inspired by plants spanning five hundred years - at London's Camden Art Centre. Soon after it opened, another lockdown forced its closure and so it went online, revealing a treasure trove of ancient and modern artworks, maps, texts, audio pieces, video; each leaf and branch was more than the sum of its parts; every plant a metaphor for growth, a symbol of hope, a cryptic code. The curators of the exhibition, Gina Buenfeld and Martin Clark, summed up something that many of us were feeling: 'During this period of enforced stillness, our behaviour might be seen to resonate with plants: like them we are now fixed in one place, subject to new rhythms of time, contemplation, personal growth and transformation.'

The show travelled from the giant *Yggdrasil*, which connected the Nine Worlds of Norse mythology, to the Tree of Knowledge in the Garden of Eden, to contemporary artists composing meditations around plant life and exploring the healing properties of Ayuverda. Jung wrote that plant motifs often recur in dreams, are often spontaneously drawn, and in alchemy, the tree is the symbol of Hermetic philosophy. His 'Tree of Life' is as intricate as mosaic - a serpent, a dog, a lizard convene among the curling black roots, which the upper branches dissolve into an ecstatic blue circle - while the muscular, patterned branches of the Philosophical Tree strain towards the heavens, illuminated by a glowing, white orb.

His paintings echo other trees of life from different locales and eras: a meticulously detailed eighteenth-century Indian version, the trunk pulsating like a body, full of veins; a nineteenth-century etching illustrating Norse mythology, in which a mountainous landscape, deer, owls and crystals are contained within its leafy world. I think of Marion Milner approvingly quoting Cézanne: 'To love a painting, one must first have drunk deeply of it in long draughts. Lose consciousness. Descend with the painter into the dim tangled roots of things, and rise again from them in colours, be steeped in the light of them.'

Immersed as I was in gardens and magic during lockdown, it was timely that I was asked to write about Hilma af Klint for her exhibition 'The Secret Paintings' at the Art Gallery of New South Wales in Sydney in 2021. Revisiting her work, varnished by a digital screen, for a show on the other side of the world in the middle of a pandemic, felt oddly apt for so cosmic an artist: I suspect that nothing would have surprised her. In 1913 and 1915, she worked on her 'Tree of Knowledge' series. In watercolour, ink, gouache and graphite, af Klint visualises the tree split in two, like cross-sections of an apple, lungs, planets, a cosmos filled with doves and swans, bleached bones and hearts, swirling roots that reach upwards and branches that spiral through the earth; the bright rays of heaven balanced by the weight of rich soil from which everything emerges. She had been influenced by a 1912 lecture given by Rudolf Steiner, in which he outlined his idea that the brain is the entrance to the cosmic tree, the leaves of which are 'the leaves of the Veda [Holy teachings of the Hindus] book, which put together, yield the Veda knowledge'.

A line by af Klint - tender, enigmatic, questioning - leaps out at me. It was found on a scrap of paper in one of her notebooks: 'The phenomenon we are trying to explain is truly bewildering. What is this phenomenon, you ask? Well, beloved, it is that which we want to call the secret growing.' In the 1920s, af Klint returned to making pictures of plants, which she envisages as the intermingling of the terrestrial and the celestial. Her 1922 series 'On the Viewing of Flowers and Trees' is much looser and more impressionistic; some of the watercolours are only rooted in the world of appearance via their titles. *Plant world etc. completed in Sweden*, for example, is awash with green, indigo, red and purple stains; *Produced while thinking of the oat grain* is a swift, loose image comprised of two cloudy halves in red and yellow; *On observing the rose hip* comprises sunny tendrils in a pink sea.

In an unauthored note from 1903 found inside one of af Klint's notebooks, the writer sees a connection between the plant and spiritual worlds: 'for just as invisible hands help and tend every plant on this green Earth, so every budding sprout of goodness is tended and shaped by invisible powers and when the time comes you too will see the beautiful plant that grew in secrecy'.

Many of af Klint's pictures could be termed 'biomorphic', a term which derives from the Greek words *bios* (life) and *morphe* (shape). It's often used in reference to the work of a loose cross-section of twentieth-century artists who sought inspiration from organic forms: the spiral of a snail's shell, a pebble, the curve of a body, cells observed under a microscope, all of which are employed to various ends - literal, symbolic, metaphorical. From sculptures by Barbara Hepworth, which rise like ancient stones from the earth, to the paintings of Wilhemina Barns-Graham, Sophie Taeuber-Arp and Paule Vézelay and others - that contain shapes that curve, swell, balloon or appear to float - a cosmic balance is evoked: the sense of timelessness humming in the midst of modernity's impatience.

What links these works - notwithstanding their often very different motivations - is the suggestion that time itself is nothing more than a footnote: an old tree is as expressive of multitudes as the hard lines of a modernist building. 'In a flower,' wrote Sophie Taeuber-Arp, 'in a beetle, every line, every form, every colour has arisen from a deep necessity.'

In Amorgos in the summer of 2021, time became jumbled; the deep past merged with the recent present. Thinking about art and its role at a time of crisis, I kept returning to a prescient exhibition I visited in Palermo, Sicily, in 2018. Although it was dryly titled 'The Planetary Garden. Cultivating Co-existence', the experience of seeing the exhibition was anything but: groupings of art - not only paintings and films but lemon trees and vegetable gardens, sand, clay and pots - wove in and around Palermo's Baroque palaces, streets, gardens and housing estates. The show took the garden as a symbol of growth, cross-pollination and hope. In their mission statement, the curators cited the French botanist Gilles Clément who, in 1997, described Earth as a 'planetary garden' with humanity as its gardener. They asked big, complicated questions, such as: 'But how to tend to a world that is moved by invisible informational networks, transnational private interests, algorithmic intelligence, environmental processes and ever-increasing inequalities?' The many possible answers were inconclusive. Given the speed at which the planet is changing, this seems apt.

At the heart of Palermo is the *Orto Botanico*: an oasis amid the city's heat and dust that was founded in 1789. To enter its gates is to time travel; the light dims, the temperature drops, and strange and wonderful things emerge from the gloom. A multitude of plants - medicinal, decorative, useful - are gathered from around the globe: enormous fleshy ficus trees that loom over narrow paths like surreal elephants; giant ferns that reach for the sky, tiny flowers as delicate as rain. There are around 391,000 species of plants on Earth and 94 per cent of them can flower (oh, happy fact!). And the numbers keep growing: in 2020, 156 plant and fungal species were named as 'new to science' - some of which have the potential to be developed into a future food or medicine. Wandering along the narrow paths, I found it reassuring that we are still making discoveries about this place we call home - especially regarding the

natural world, which, despite the violence we inflict upon it, somehow soldiers on. That said, gardens, for all the joy they impart, can
be elegiac: two in five plants face extinction. Weaving through the
garden questions hummed about the role of nature in planetary
healing. How to respond not only to the physical challenges our
home faces, but to its spiritual crisis, too? It's a question that more
and more artists are asking.

Looking back over the many artists I interviewed while I was at
frieze, one of the most inspiring was the Palestinian artist and activist Vivien Sansour, who I met in 2019. She works with farmers to
bring back threatened heritage seeds - to the fields, to the market
and to the table. When, in previous centuries, an artist might paint
a plant, now, for many of them, the plant itself has become the
artwork and the act of growing, harvesting and cooking it, a ritualistic - and practical - performance. Vivien has a small, portable
wooden kitchen that was designed by an artist friend, Ayed Arafah.
She travels with it across the West Bank, setting it up in village
squares to cook local produce, an open invitation to anyone who is
hungry or who just wants to talk.

I asked Vivien why the seeds are so important to her. She replied
that plants are not simply about food but about who people are -
recipes entwine with memories; they tell stories about a country
and its people, its land, its history, its rhythms. Cultural nourishment is central to well-being and a sense of belonging. When these
communal ways are lost, something deeper is lost, too. 'Plants,' she
says, 'create opportunities to talk about cultural diversity and bio-
diversity - and the fact that life is so magical.'

Vivien's work - the intersection of art, healing and plants - has
precedents stretching back millennia. I keep coming across references - in exhibitions and essays, on classical radio stations and
wellness sites, in yoga classes - to the twelfth-century German
nun, artist, herbalist and composer, Hildegard of Bingen. During

the pandemic, I often played her music; its remote, celestial calm could make almost anything bearable. For women, in particular, so much begins with this medieval mystic, who was canonised in 2012: she raised her voice and owned her power when everything conspired to silence both. Her concept of *Viriditas* – the greening of the Earth, the spreading of seeds and the beauty of plants as symbolic of God's abundance – infuses every aspect of her work. Many of her visions came to her via a 'lux vivens' (living light) which she described in a letter as 'far, far brighter than a cloud which carries the sun'. She kept her gifts secret for decades: regardless of her eventual fame, she may well have been frightened of being condemned as a witch. Silence and humility were deemed the appropriate behaviour for a woman, especially a nun. Hildegard was financially and emotionally dependent on the Church; to be evicted from it would have meant destitution. She finally received permission to express her mystical powers in her forty-third year: God told her to say and write what she saw and what she heard. What followed her revelation resulted in a new life; her visions became public knowledge and, after being investigated for heresy and then cleared by agents of the Pope, she was appointed pro-Abbess at Disibodenberg.

Hildegard's life was filled with creativity and industry. She built a new, larger convent in Bingen and wrote music for her nuns to sing – even though she had never studied notation. For her, song was a 'sacred sound' – the aural embodiment of the fabric of the cosmos. Her morality play, *Ordo Virtutum* (The Play of the Virtues; c.1150), includes eighty-two compositions and seventy-seven poems set to music.

In 1141, Hildegard began the ten years it would take her to compile her celebrated work, *Scivias* or 'Know the Way', a three-part account of creation, redemption and salvation, that comprises twenty-six visions. In 1158, now known as a mystic and a prophetess and nicknamed 'The Sibyl of the Rhine', she toured Germany spreading the word, which was highly unusual for a woman at the time - Benedictine nuns couldn't leave their cloisters without male permission and, in the normal state of affairs, only priests were allowed to preach. Within a few years, she was advising religious and political leaders across Europe. From 1175 to 1180, an illustrated edition of *Scivia* was produced. Although it was lost in the bombing of Dresden in the Second World War, and only black-and-white photographs remain, an illuminated copy was made from the original at the Hildegard Abbey, Eibingen, from 1927 to 1933.

It's unknown whether Hildegard painted her visions herself or directed others to do so. Whatever the answer, the result is all hers: images full of powerful women, their arms outstretched, flames erupting from their heads. They float in a golden circle; a Mother Church has a monster for genitals; the sky is filled with burning lights and tumbling stars; the sun is an eye above a boiling Earth. Perspective is skewed, naturalism is sacrificed for metaphor. Hildegard's mystical vision of the universe contains infinite riches: it's a cosmic egg formed of layers - of the land, the celestial canopy, meaning.

Physica and *Causae et Curae* - together known as the *Book of the Subtleties of the Diverse Nature of Creatures* (1151-8) - is Hildegard's study of natural medicine and healing: the original manuscript is lost. *Physica* comprises nine books and includes descriptions of a thousand plants and animals - some, such as the unicorn, are mythical - as well as the various properties and powers of trees, herbs, stones, metals and the elements. *Causae et Curae* is a holistic study of the causes and cures of illnesses. Hildegard believed - in a way that chimes today - that the health of the body reflected the health of the soul and mind. She considered the whole person in her analysis: their gender, sex lives, and moral well-being. Some of her remedies are still current - such as cutting back on salt or using spearmint to aid digestion - while others, such as curing jaundice by tying an unconscious bat to your loins until it dies, are, perhaps, less useful.

Like Hilma af Klint centuries later, Hildegard expressed herself in a secret language and alphabet - her 'lingua ignota' (Unknown Language, 1150-60). It is unclear if she shared it with anyone. One-third of the 900 invented words relate to botany and medicine; most refer to the liturgy.

Despite her genius, it took more than five hundred years for Hildegard to be recognised for the polymath she was. Although she's the earliest named composer in history, her name is not mentioned in the 1927 *Grove Dictionary of Music and Musicians*, the *New Oxford History of Music Vol. 2* (1954) - the standard reference work on medieval music - or the 1971 *Larousse Encyclopedia of Music*. Everything changed in 1981, when Hyperion Records released Christopher Page's Gothic Voices album of Hildegard of Bingen's music starring the voice of the sublime English soprano Emma Kirkby. Titled *A Feather on the Breath of God* - after a line from *Scivias* - the engineer remarked 'lovely music, shame no one will buy it'. How wrong he was: it is still the label's bestselling recording. The album helped generate not only a revival of interest in medieval music but an outpouring of interest in Hildegard's life and work - she's become something of a cult figure not only for her music and art but to feminist, New Age, artist and ecological groups. In 2017, Sarah Shin and Ben Vickers founded a publishing venture in London named Ignota, which 'publishes at the intersection of technology, mythmaking and magic' (and sells a tote bag, emblazoned with the advice 'leave husband, practice witchcraft'). It was named after Hildegard's Lingua Ignota.

When I began at art school in Canberra, my mother bought me a CD of *A Feather on the Breath of God*. As I painted, I played it in the studio, again and again. I knew nothing about Hildegard, but her music spoke to an art student on the other side of the planet, eight hundred years after it was written. I'm listening to it as I write this. Although I don't understand Latin, it's deeply consoling; austere, hypnotic, pure. The singers' magnificent voices have the sharp clarity of blue sky on a cold winter's day. Everything superfluous has been stripped back; only a delicate purity remains. Is it possible to hear compassion in music? If so, it's here. The beauty is unearthly, even though Hildegard's inspiration grew from the very real world she inhabited.

Many of the female artists in the nineteenth and early twentieth centuries who channelled spirits drew or painted plants, flowers, trees and landscapes. Although they were considered respectable subjects for women, some of them created pictures that were more complex than at first they may have appeared. Anna Mary Howitt's ecstatic spirit drawings, such as *The Lady (Sensitive Plant)* of 1855, look like bouquets formed of heavenly flames and in 1860 the New York medium Mrs E.J. French drew a picture of a white rose from which a hand emerges holding a 200-word excerpt from the Bible, which she claimed took her only eleven seconds to produce. The English artist Madge Gill (1882-1961) believed herself possessed by a spirit called Myrninerest (my inner rest), under whose power she drew flowers, petals and spider's webs, a girl's face or figure surrounded by swirling lines and abstract patterns. In a trance-like state, she often created up to a hundred black-and-white ink drawings in one sitting. She once stated: 'If I were a man, I would have gone abroad and studied botany.' In Switzerland, the medium and artist Hélène Smith – who died in 1929 and who the Surrealists considered the 'muse of Automatic Writing' – alleged she could communicate with, among others, Martians, Victor Hugo and the eighteenth-century occultist Count Cagliostro; she sang 'exotic melodies, played with an imaginary monkey'. Before she devoted herself exclusively to Christian imagery, she painted elaborate Martian landscapes – a barren Earth full of flaming stones and hybrid flowers and plants, inhabited by quasi-humans and 'dog-like creatures with heads that looked like cabbages that not only fetched objects for their masters, but also took dictation'. Later in the twentieth century, the German author and artist Unica Zürn also practised automatic writing, weaving her autobiography from anagrams and conjuring fantastical drawings of chimerical beasts, psychedelic plants, and all-seeing eyes. In the United States, Minnie Evans, who was born in 1892, painted and drew kaleidoscopic faces that emerge from a tangle of flowers in trippy gardens. Describing her process, she declared: 'I have no imagination. I never plan a drawing, they just happen. In a dream it was shown to me what I have to do, of paintings. The whole entire horizon all the way across the whole earth was out together like this with pictures. All over my yard, up all the sides of trees and everywhere were pictures.'

Luke, Sylvia and I are lying on hot rocks by the sea, reading in between swims. Sylvia keeps laughing. She's absorbed in the novel *Drive Your Plow Over the Bones of the Dead* by the Nobel Prize-winner Olga Tokarczuk. I had assumed it to be a dark and difficult novel, but she can't put it down. When she finishes it, she gives it to me, saying it will be useful in my research. She's right. I'm entranced by it – and I, too, constantly laugh, even as I'm deeply moved. Tokarczuk has written a page-turner that reflects the complications of our time. Her novel is a feminist mystery narrated by a former bridge-engineer and retired teacher, Janina Duszejko, who discusses her connections with animals, her thoughts on growing old, her fury at human cruelty, the wisdom of the stars and more. She declares: 'I have been practising Astrology for many years, and I have extensive experience. Everything is connected with everything else, and we are all caught in a net of correspondences of every kind. They should teach you that at police training college. It's a solid, old tradition. From Swedenborg.'

The title of the novel is a quote from Blake's *Proverbs of Hell*: 'In seed time learn, in harvest teach, in winter enjoy. Drive your cart and your plow over the bones of the dead.' At one point, Janina proclaims that:

> Reality has grown old and gone senile; after all, it is definitely sub-
> ject to the same laws as every living organism - it ages. Just like
> the cells of the body, its tiniest components - the senses, succumb
> to apoptosis. Apoptosis is a natural death, brought about by the
> tiredness and exhaustion of matter. In Greek this word means 'the
> dropping of petals'. The world has dropped its petals.

It doesn't surprise me to discover that Tokarczuk was influenced by the elderly, vegetarian, unreliable narrator of Leonora Carrington's novel *The Hearing Trumpet*, and Sigmund Freud's *Beyond the Pleasure Principle*, which she read as a young girl. She writes: 'it helped me to understand that there are thousands of possible ways to interpret our experience, that everything has a meaning, and that interpretation is the key to reality. This was the first step to becoming a writer.'

I want to ask her: What are we to do when reality finally ups and dies? Or is it immortal?

I go for a long walk with Luke over rocky fields that look like Mars to a small church that can only be reached on foot. Along the way, the earth changes colour: from a soft, dusty lilac to a rich ochre that recalls the deserts of Australia; in the distance, the sea swells, dissolves, reappears; distant islands shimmer like mirages, shrouded in a heat mist.

Traversing this rocky landscape, its harshness softened by spiky, geometric flowers and bushes, I am, once again, astounded at my ignorance about the meanings contained in the Earth I inhabit, the air I'm breathing, and the history that pulsates from every rock. But I suddenly understand the concept of 'sacred geometry' - forms which organically recur in various incarnations across the planet. The idea that it might grant insight into the mysteries of existence

A geometric flower in Amorgos

has endured across centuries and cultures and influenced myriad artworks and architecture.

Small piles of stones have been arranged at handy intervals: functional sculptures that tell us we are on the right track. We reach a tiny, whitewashed stone Greek Orthodox church, battered and beautiful on a wild promontory. The door is unlocked: two young people are sitting in silence; they turn and smile a welcome. The walls of the church are lined with icons: Mary, tenderly holding her son, her halo a golden ray; St Jerome in the desert, gesturing to a crow; Jesus, with enormous wings, ascending to heaven like an eagle. A painting of Jesus in a chariot pulled by two white horses, driven by an angel, is placed on a plinth, adorned with an embroidered yellow cloth: a crucifix decorated with vivid pink flowers and green leaves. A pile of slim beeswax candles and a box of matches are ready for anyone who needs them. The young people have lit two candles; he smiles at me, shrugs and says: it can't hurt, can it? It's more a statement of fact than a question. I nod my assent. I'm not a believer, in the paid-up Christian sense, but this modest, unlocked place of refuge, with its paintings of mysterious happenings, its encouragement of private ritual and respect for the worlds we each carry within us, is moving. The young couple leave, and

I light a candle to my father, who died six years ago. He was never happier than when he was by the sea. He would have loved this place. We light one, too, for our faraway friend whose mother is dying. It can't hurt.

Later, I tell Sylvia about our walk. 'You know,' she says, 'that the churches on the islands were built on the places of ancient sacrifice? It's simply one belief system replacing another.' This makes sense. The site of the church is powerful, at the axis of sea and sky and earth. Even without believing in, or knowing about, the gods, there is something god-like here - if you understand, that is, the word 'god' to mean a power beyond human comprehension.

The Active Imagination

'Nature-mystical movements are experiencing a revival, invoking the unity of humankind and the natural world. The question of whether and how art can heal no longer arises only in the context of art therapy but also . . . at a societal level.'

Yasmin Afschar, 'Emma Kunz, A Visionary in Dialogue with Contemporary Art' (2021)

Despite having been immersed in thinking about art for the past four decades, I'm constantly surprised by what I don't know. How is it possible that I hadn't come across the astonishing paintings of the Dutch artist and theosophist Olga Fröbe-Kapteyn?

Olga Fröbe-Kapteyn

I recently came across them at James Brett's wonderful Gallery of Everything in London: hard-edged, high-key compositions that pulsate with life but were guided by the various permutations of the mind and soul. Between 1926 and 1934, she created around two hundred hypnotic, meticulously patterned images that echo the sleek modernism of Art Deco, the lines of a pyramid and occult references to the third eye, sacred geometry, the golden ratio and a slew of encoded symbols. Some of her images were inspired by Ludwig Derleth, a poet and mystic associated with the short-lived Munich Cosmic Circle, who believed that humanity could be reanimated through a study of its pagan origins. From 1934, her work became more personal: these works she called her 'Visions'. Fröbe-Kapteyn's titles are telling: *The Portal of Initiation* (1930), *Yoga and Meditation in East and West* (1933), *The Gestalt and Cult of the Great Mother* (1938), *The Hermetic Principle in Mythology, Gnosis, and Alchemy* (1942), *The Mysteries* (1944), *Spirit and Nature* (1946) and *Man and Time* (1951).

Perhaps I hadn't come across her work before because it emerged from a therapeutic framework. As is very clear, traditional art history likes nothing more than a pigeonhole, and Fröbe-Kapteyn's work didn't fit into the one ascribed to so-called High Art. Like her friend Carl Jung, she believed in 'the active imagination' - the idea that creating art opened a window into the psyche. Immersed in spirituality, studying Indian philosophy, meditation and Theosophy, in 1928, as she was drawing, a vision came to her: a lecture hall on the shores of a lake deep in the heart of the Swiss countryside, a 'place of encounter and experience and a free space for the spirit, where Eastern and Western thought could meet'. She was wealthy, and so could act on her vision and make it a reality. To honour the nourishment of her endeavour, she called it 'The Eranos Foundation': 'eranos' is Ancient Greek for a banquet where everyone pays their way.

As with so many artists who explored spiritual realms, tragedy shaped Fröbe-Kapteyn's formative years. Born in London in 1881, her father, Albertus, was a Dutch engineer and photographer, and her mother, Truus Muysken, a social reformer and feminist. In 1900, she moved to Zurich, where she studied design and art history. In 1909, she married a Croatian-Austrian flautist and conductor, Iwan Fröbe, but in 1915 he died in a plane crash, only months after Fröbe-Kapteyn had given birth to their daughter. Grieving, the artist retreated to Monte Verità, or Mountain of Truth, in the Swiss village of Ascona, the hotbed of anarchism, vegetarianism and nudism where both Sophie Taeuber-Arp and Mary Wigman had, at various points, stayed. Her father bought a nearby farmhouse, the Casa Gabriella on the banks of Lake Maggiore at Ascona-Moscia, where Fröbe-Kapteyn lived for the rest of her life.

During the early days of the Eranos Foundation, the English Theosophist, writer and artist Alice Bailey – possibly the first person to use the term 'New Age' – assisted Fröbe-Kapteyn. The inaugural symposium took place in 1933: the theme was 'Yoga and Meditation in the East and the West' and Jung spoke about 'The Psychological Process of Individuation'. It was while visiting Eranos in 1956 that he decided to write his autobiography, *Memories, Dreams, Reflections*. Published in German in 1962 and in English in 1963, it has never been out of print.

In 1934, Jung commissioned Fröbe-Kapteyn to help research his study of alchemy and archetypes. The artist rose to the challenge and travelled to libraries throughout Europe and the United States: the archive of more than 6,000 symbols that she assembled is now part of the Warburg Institute in London – and the Eranos Foundation is still going strong. The 2020 lectures were themed around the subject: 'Hope and Crisis of the Future: Individual, Community and Environment Facing the Disillusionment with Progress'.

It's curious that Fröbe-Kapteyn didn't meet the healer and artist Emma Kunz. They were close contemporaries and both ran healing centres in Switzerland that pivoted around the curative possibilities of art, science and spirituality. Perhaps it's because Kunz never

considered herself an artist; rather, she thought of herself as a researcher. Her 'energy field' pencil drawings on graph paper, which
she created with the aid of a technique called 'radiesthesia' - the use
of a pendulum to direct the lines - were never publicly displayed
in her lifetime. Untitled and undated, they're mesmerising: more
than five hundred softly coloured, detailed mandalas, stars within
stars, squares dissected by ragged green lines, circles floating in a
dusty blue expanse that seem to spin and pulsate. Often created in
forty-eight-hour marathons, her pictures were the physical manifestation of her research, what she described as: 'Shape and form
expressed as measurement, rhythm, symbol and transformation of
figure and principle.' Kunz thought of them as holograms, spaces
to enter, answers to questions - be they physical, political, spiritual
or philosophical. You don't need to know anything about either art
or mysticism to appreciate their beauty.

How apt that Emma Kunz was born into a family of weavers.
Like Hildegard of Bingen, she worked on a cosmic loom: mysticism and medicine, art and botany were her materials. Born in
1892 in Brittnau, in the German-speaking region of Switzerland,
from a young age she developed telepathy and healing powers;
she felt a close affinity to plants. When she was eighteen, she
began to use her powers to help people in need. Her treatments
were often successful - she claimed to have cured a boy of polio
- but she saw herself as a conduit who activated the powers that
lie dormant in everyone. She never went to art school and only
began making her pictures when she was forty, exploring the idea
of sacred geometry - the balance inherent in plants, that reveal a
vegetal intelligence - in order to heal her patients of physical and
spiritual malaises. Unlike Hilma af Klint, whose spirit guides had
names, Kunz channelled the forces of the universe. She would ask
the pendulum a question - anything from the health of a patient
to politics - and in response her hand would be guided to make an
image. She trusted her instincts while nurturing her objectivity;

she knew positive powers lie dormant in both the earth and the mind. She also used her pendulum to 'polarise marigolds in her garden to produce multiple flower heads' and documented the process with photography. Her images expand the possibilities of what images can do. She knew that drawing was the inscription of knowledge, and that knowledge can assume different shapes.

In 1942, she discovered a mineral called AION A - 'aion' is Greek for 'without limits' - in a Roman quarry in Würenlos which, she felt, could cure myriad ills, in particular rheumatism and inflammation. The Swiss curator Hans Ulrich Obrist, who orchestrated an exhibition of Emma Kunz's work at the Serpentine Gallery in London in 2019, says that Kunz's design for AION A - which is widely available in Swiss pharmacies - was one of his earliest encounters with art, as his mother used to buy it and the family used it 'for a range of health benefits'.

The legendary Swiss curator Harald Szeemann, who came across Kunz's pictures in the 1970s, was an admirer. Unusually for the time, he didn't dismiss her work as therapy or nonsense:

> Her gift was an awareness of connections that contradicted both normal experience and scientific interpretations of the laws of Nature and art. This was a supernatural event, a miracle that, in revealing divine truths conveyed a secret impulse on a par with that of cosmic creation. Emma Kunz's drawings are attempts to find a universal connection. They are the records of her concentration on the question of the Whole.

Emma Kunz died in 1963; the centre dedicated to her opened in Würenlos in 1986 to continue the extraction of AION A and to operate as a meeting place for healing. The quarry where she discovered the mineral is known as the Emma Kunz Grotto and is open to visitors who need to recharge their batteries. In recent years, her drawings have been shown in major museums across

Europe and the United States. For the 2019 exhibition of her work at the Serpentine Gallery, the Cypriot artist Christodoulos Panayiotou designed a series of simple stone benches made from AION A that were placed in front of Kunz's drawings. I have a bottle of AION A which I rub on sore muscles. It seems to help.

Emma Kunz at her working table, Waldstatt, 1958

A photograph of Emma Kunz was taken in 1958. She's sixty-six, in a clinical white dress. She's gazing intently at a geometric drawing on the table in front of her: the walls around her are covered in her pictures. There's something of a 1950s sci-fi movie about the scene: a respectable middle-aged woman in what could be a lab coat amid a cosmic experiment taking place in the bucolic Swiss countryside.

Emma Kunz once said that she designed her drawings for the twenty-first century. In this, she was prophetic. Her drawings hum, spin and glow across the decades, their energy unabated. In March 2021, an exhibition opened in Aargaus in Switzerland. Titled 'Emma Kunz Cosmos: A Visionary in Dialogue with Contemporary Art', it comprised a display of Kunz's work alongside that of fourteen artists inspired by her. Goshka Macuga created two rubber moulds of Madame Blavatsky and Kunz's heads, filled with flowers. Rezaire Tabita explored stories of West African divination and mathematics, which she displayed on an iPad in an amethyst geode. Mathilde Rosier's paintings mined the affinity between humans, plants and animals. Lauryn Youden performed a ritual of healing in the Emma Kunz Grotto with a set of singing bowls. Martina Lussi constructed an 'open space for physical and subconscious resonances'. Julie Semoroz attempted 'a utopian spatialisation of cross-species communication'. I wanted to visit the show but couldn't because of the pandemic. The curator Yasmin Afschar gave me a tour via Zoom. Like astral bodies, we connected across Europe, communicating via a small, shining screen. We wandered through the galleries talking, looking, discussing the extraordinary range of responses to Emma Kunz that bloomed, like a field of wildflowers, from a single, bright seed.

Weaving Their Way

'We use materials to satisfy our practical needs and our spiritual ones, as well. We have useful things and beautiful things - equipment and works of art. In earlier civilizations there was no clear separation of this sort.'

Anni Albers, 'Work with Material', 1938

Anni Albers at the loom

So many of the patterns in the plants we see on our walks across Amorgos are echoed in science and art across cultures and centuries - from the cosmological drawings of Hildegard of Bingen, to the desert paintings of First Nations Australians, to Indian Tantric art. They also turn up repeatedly in weavings made by women.

I read that in Sanskrit *tantra* means 'loom', 'weave' and 'treatise', and that 'textile' and 'text' are derived from the Latin *texere*, or 'to weave'. I read Madeline Miller and Charlotte Higgins about the women weaving their stories, watched over by Athena, the goddess of wisdom and war and the inventor of the loom. Higgins introduces her book on the Greek myths with a declaration: 'My women are not telling the stories. They have, rather, woven their tales on to elaborate textiles. The book, in large part, consists of my descriptions of these imagined tapestries.' In Miller's novel, the witch Circe weaves on a loom designed by Daedalus, the master designer and symbol of Wisdom; Penelope weaves to put off her suitors, hoping for Odysseus's return from Troy; Minerva (Athena), 'the goddess of a thousand crafts', teaches mortals wool-working and weaving, and the fourth book of Ovid's *Metamorphoses* is devoted to stories spun by three sister goddesses, confined to their looms. Known as 'The Three Fates', the women - who are variously depicted in white robes as maidens or crones - personify destiny: Clotho weaves the threads of fate, at the beginning of life; Lachesis measures them, determining how long a life will be; and when Atropos cuts them, life is over. In central Australia, *tjanpi*, which means 'desert grass' in the Pitjantjatjara language, refers to the woven grass sculptures and baskets made by women, which they embellish with wool, raffia, emu feathers and seeds, but it's also related to *Tjukurpa*, or ancestral law. To weave is to learn about your land, your ancestors, your community. Across the world, from culture to culture, century to century, weaving was - is - both a practical and a spiritual, as well as a creative, activity.

From the United States to Russia, Australia and elsewhere, in the twentieth century, women employed weaving to create works of strange and transcendent beauty. Many of them were masters of their craft, but the objects they made - while in thrall to centuries-old traditions - frequently employed the kinds of languages we associate more with modernist painters: they expanded the possibilities of the medium via colour, form and texture; mood, atmosphere and feeling were conveyed via warp and weft. In 1938, the German Jewish artist and master weaver Anni Albers declared: 'Today life is very bewildering . . . It is no accident that nervous breakdowns occur more often in our civilization than in those where creative power had a natural outlet in daily activities. And this fact leads to a suggestion: we must come down to earth from the clouds where we live in vagueness and experience the most real thing there is: material.'

Albers trained as a weaver at the Bauhaus because - ironically, despite its radicalism - it restricted the entrance of women into most departments; she had initially wanted to study glass. But she flourished: it's said that before her, weaving was a craft and then it became an art. Touch, to Albers, was primary: a way of grounding oneself. She believed that the useful should be beautiful and she freed weaving from the assumptions that swirled around it: that it was 'simply' a craft, a means to a practical end. Her aim was 'to let threads be articulate again and find form for themselves to no other end than their own orchestration, not to be sat on, walked on, only to be looked at'. When she and her husband, the artist Josef Albers, fled Nazi Germany for the United States in 1933, she taught at the private radical art and design school, Black Mountain College in North Carolina, where she urged her students to incorporate 'the stuff the world is made of' - grass, corn kernels, twigs - into their work.

Her designs are at once robust and refined, startling and or-dered. Influenced by pre-Hispanic weavers of Peru, pre-Columbian pottery and sculpture and the possibilities of Modernism, they look forward and back in time; in this, her designs embody the idea of change - temporal, actual, metaphorical. Albers also crafted geometric jewellery from everyday household objects: necklaces from drain strainers, wine corks and paper clips, metal seals and bobby pins, aluminium washers and ribbons. She believed that replacing the material value of objects with that of 'surprise and inventiveness' created a new value: a spiritual one. By 'spiritual' I think she meant that exploring the creative potential of an ordinary material allowed for a revitalisation of wonder in daily life.

Albers's ideas surely chimed with Maya Deren, whose 1946 film *Ritual in Transfigured Time* reconfigures the Greek myth of the three Sisters of Fate to contemporary New York. Deren is seen, in dreamy fragments, smilingly stretching a skein of wool between her two hands. A young woman, played by the Trinidadian-born dancer Rita Christiani, assists her, but gradually the room they are in is filled by a high wind. Everything slows down; the effects of nature, the wool, her body, all come together in a strange ritualistic dance. The third woman, a stern Anaïs Nin, observes them from the doorway; in the blink of an eye, we're in a wild party, men and women laughing, drinking, dancing. Deren is at once artist and archetype: the woman who weaves meaning from the world in which she finds herself.

When setting out to make a work of art, most artists and designers prefer not to predict the result; the thrill of creation lies in the possibility of what might be unearthed, both in the maker and in the materials. Accidents are not always life-threatening; sometimes they birth something new. Art is functional, in the same way that beauty can be useful; it can calm the mind, soothe the senses, and crack open new ways of seeing and - through seeing - encourage a deeper knowledge of the ebb and flow of the world around us.

Sheila Hicks weaving at her home in Taxco el Viejo,
Mexico, c.1961–2

In 2015, I caught the Eurostar train to Paris to interview the artist Sheila Hicks, who was taught colour theory by Josef Albers at Yale in the 1940s. Formidable in her eighties, Hicks's fibre sculptures and weavings still have the power to startle and move; meaning, for her, arrives via a profound engagement with material. She creates enormous installations from skeins of wildly colourful fibre that spills from the ceiling like waterfalls or piles up against walls like lumps of trippy lava and sculptures from found objects, such as sticks or feathers, that she weaves together. For more than fifty years, Hicks has also made a series of exquisite abstract weavings she calls 'minimes' on a hand-loom. These small works contain multitudes: vast landscapes and microscopic details. Each line of weaving is, in a way, a line of enquiry as unique as a sentence in a diary: a restless form of remembering, of sensual recording, evidence of the intertwining of thinking and making. Each one could be the beginning of a short story: *Twill (Mexico)* (1956–7); *Fleming Maps* (1957–8); *Zapallar Domingo* (1957); *Twenty Years is Nothing* (1958), *Self-Portrait on a Blue Day* (1977); *An Acre of Rain Forest* (1989),

among others. Some of the minimes comprise quiet, monochromatic designs, whereas others are more exuberant: structurally
complex and high key. While ostensibly abstract, these intense and
intimate artworks are portraits, of sorts: the remnant of a state of
mind or a moment in time. Each one suggests a narrative, however oblique. In *Itaka* (2012), for example, delicate quills, trapped
like daggers in the thick fibre, appear to bleed onto a dense brown
composition created from alpaca wool. In *The Wandering Lady*
(2016), lines of pink, green and ochre fibres meander like the route
of an Underground train map or the plaits of a girl blowing in the
wind. Against a background of pale thread, robust tendrils seem to
strain towards the light. Petrified wood, silk, paper, animal hair,
clam shells, pieces of copper - all have found their way into the
weavings.

When I sat down with Hicks in her Paris studio to drink coffee
and eat bananas she asked me about the provenance of my clothes
- she makes most of her own herself. Did I know who made mine?
Where the materials came from? I did not. She told me about meeting Anni Albers and how they shared an interest in pre-Columbian
design and had, in fact, both taken the same book out of the Yale
University library. Later, she wrote: 'If Josef had awakened me to
the world of colour and ways of using colour in his teaching at
the school, I believe that, in the six or seven brief meetings I had
with Anni, she helped me to think about structure.' In our conversation, again and again, she returned to the tactile aspects of her
work. I asked her 'What does touching materials add?' She replied:
'The hand connected to the eyes and the brain. Hands, eyes, brain:
it's the magic triangulation. It comes from passion, heart and intellect inseparably cemented to your times and to your emotional
experiences.' I mentioned George Kubler's 1962 book, *The Shape
of Time: Remarks on the History of Things*, and she lit up. Hicks had
studied under him at Yale in the early 1950s, and in his class 'The
Art of Latin America', she discovered pre-Columbian art and was

immediately entranced. She agreed with Kubler's theory that the art of different periods is linked by different versions of the same action, which he described as 'the transmission of some kind of energy'. For him, the idea of contemporary art was intertwined with the art of the past. He wrote: 'However fragmentary its condition, any work of art is actually a portion of arrested happening, or an emanation of past time. It is a graph of an activity now stilled, but a graph made visible like an astronomical body, by a light that originated with the activity.'

When Hicks discovered in Kubler's class that ancient tribes in the Andes had communicated with textiles, it 'blew her mind' and she taught herself how to weave. She believes that pre-Incaic textile language is 'the most complex of any textile culture in history'. For years, she travelled through Latin and South America, where textiles have for so long been central to cultural expression, researching, talking and experimenting with the possibilities of weaving; after setting up her own workshop in Mexico, she moved permanently to Paris. Her belief in the importance of fibre is near-mystical: she speaks of it having its own memory and how it reacts to tension and to the environment in different ways. At a time when most clothes are mass-produced, easily disposed of, and one of the largest polluters in the world, Hicks's attention to the symbolic potential of garments is timely. I asked her if she found weaving therapeutic. She replied: 'People are desperate for a grounding and what could be better than to sit and weave and think, and then not to think, to just interlace yarns and amass networks of threads?'

When she first started exhibiting, some critics dismissed Hicks's creations – along with many of the other women who work with fibre – as 'craft', which was considered somehow lesser than 'art'. I asked her what she thought of this. Unsurprisingly, she was bored with the question. 'I care less and less,' she said, 'about what definitions people give to my work, whether it's art or not. I keep probing ideas and fumble to give them form. Everyone has a relationship to material. The interesting question is: how sensitive are they to it?' She paused and said: 'I tend to compose fables with coloured and textured lines and work out *en route* what to do with them or how to interpret them. Fibre is my alphabet and helpmeet.'

A few months after I met Sheila Hicks, I travelled to India for the first time. In New Delhi, at the National Gallery of Modern Art, I visited an astonishing retrospective of another artist to whom fibre was central to self-expression: Mrinalini Mukherjee, who was born in 1949 in Mumbai. Best-known for her enormous, hand-dyed, knotted hemp and sisal sculptures, she had begun working in near isolation in the early 1970s; she died days before her exhibition opened. Her sculptures look like something dreamed up by a sci-fi writer or dug up in an archaeological site. Her monumental knotted, twisted and plaited creations swing from ceilings or slump on the floor, full of references to plants, gods, sex and transmutation. They evoke armour and armature; skeletons, flesh, outer space; warriors and pangolins. Humans and animals intertwine to become one: biomorphic creatures stilled at the moment of metamorphosis. In the 1980s, Mukherjee said that she wanted to arouse 'the feeling of awe [you get] when you walk into the small sanctum of a temple and look up to be held by an iconic presence'. But while many of her titles allude to Hindu deities, she was clear that she was a modernist, even as she referenced Indian craft traditions. Her idea of the sacred was intuitive and idiosyncratic; what she called 'parallel invocations in the realm of art'.

In late 2021, it was hard leaving Greece. London felt monochrome, cold, choked, and I felt untethered. The pandemic was a constant reminder of the fragility of our bodies; touching something might infect you, the air might kill you. On a bleak day in early winter, the airwaves filled with alarm about the rising numbers of people struck down by new strains of the virus, I visited an exhibition at the Alison Jacques gallery by the late American artist, Lenore Tawney. Born four decades before Mukherjee, she, too, expanded the expressive possibilities of fibre. Throughout her life Tawney practised meditation; she was fascinated with Carl Jung and Zen Buddhism and was a follower of the Indian guru, Swami Shree Muktananda, and his successor, the spiritual head of Siddha Yoga, Swami Gurumayi. She said: 'I sometimes think of my work as breath.' In an undated page in her journal, she transcribed an excerpt from Max Beckmann's *On My Painting* (1938): 'I am seeking for the bridge which leads from the visible to the invisible.'

In the midst of the sheer awfulness of everything, her show was a joyful reminder of the transcendent power of simple materials: weavings made from rough-hewn fibre twisted into squares and diamonds, patterns that wobble at their edges; sacred geometry rendered with a human touch. They hung from the ceilings and clung to the walls, like cryptic totems or abstract flags, their earthy colours animated by the occasional flash of burnt red or vivid ochre. One weaving especially leapt out, a burst of colour in a harsh landscape: *Waterfall* from 1974, a hot orange arrangement of meandering lines that tumble down the wall, an ode to movement frozen in time. As I left the gallery, I felt lighter.

Tawney's career as a full-time artist didn't begin in earnest until she was fifty. Born in 1907 in Lorain, Ohio, and raised on the shores of Lake Erie, 'without a touch of art in her life', she moved to Chicago, worked as a proof-reader and studied art at evening classes at the Art Institute. The sudden death of her husband George in 1943, after only two years of marriage, made her an artist, because, she said, she had to go down deep in herself to survive his loss. She travelled to Mexico and Paris and returned to Chicago, where she studied at the Institute of Design: sculpture with Alexander Archipenko, drawing with László Moholy-Nagy and weaving with Marli Ehrman, who had studied at the Bauhaus. Later, Tawney met the modernist Finnish tapestry designer, Martta Taipale, who opened her mind to the expressive possibilities of materials that were more commonly associated with everyday objects. Tawney discovered what she described as 'the potential of woven cloth to be a filter of light but also a natural and organic process where threads could be loosely built up as a surface in a sedimentary way'. In 1957, at the age of fifty, she and her cat Pansy moved from Chicago to New York in search of 'a barer life, closer to reality, without all the things that clutter and fill our lives'. She moved to Coenties Slip, the old seaport at the lower tip of Manhattan with a view of the Brooklyn Bridge, an inspiring and supportive place that attracted artists, filmmakers and writers, many of them queer, including her close friend and possibly lover, the artist Agnes Martin. The two women delved into mysticism and meditation, Zen Buddhism and Siddha Yoga. On the edge of the sea, many of the artists incorporated water as a symbolic element into their work; a reference not only to the view from their windows but to the new fluidity they were exploring in every aspect of their lives. Tawney's weavings became pared back, monochromatic: whites, beiges and blacks dominated; she made sculptures from linen, wild cotton, wool. She had a technical breakthrough, manipulating her loom so that warp threads could diverge from parallel lines and flow diagonally; she likened the result to breathing or the movement of water. Despite the radicality of what she was creating, the fact that she worked in weaving rendered it of minor importance in the grand scheme of modern art.

One morning in 1958, the 'idea of weaving in volume' floated into her consciousness. She spent the next fifty years exploring what this might mean. Her weavings leapt off the loom in her exploration of the symbolic possibilities of fire, water, light; her frequent motif was a bird. Like Sheila Hicks, Tawney incorporated feathers, bones, paper, birds' eggs, skeletons, feathers, shells, pebbles, corks and sticks with handmade or woven shapes in her work. Her titles attest to her spiritual concerns: *Secret Path*, *Spirit River, Dark River*. Some weavings are as much as 8.5 metres high: 'I was searching for the source of myself, that's why they got so tall.'

In the early 1960s, Tawney allowed her 'woven forms' to breathe, leaving areas bare or transparent. In 1961, Agnes Martin - whose paintings and drawings, as tough and as delicate as spider webs, employ the grid as a symbol of infinity - wrote about Tawney's work: 'To see new and original expression in a very old medium, and not just one new form but a complete new form in each piece of work, is wholly unlooked for, and is a wonderful and gratifying experience.'

Martin titled some of her friend's works - the only time she ever did so: *The King, The Queen, The Bride, The River, The Foundation, The Veil, The Arc*. There's a small room at Tate Modern devoted to Agnes Martin and Lenore Tawney: *The Queen* rises resplendent sixty years after it was created: a four-metre hanging sculpture, made from oaty woven and knotted linen, suspended from bamboo rods. Its shape is like an abstracted version of a Cycladic woman: a swelling body, a small head, the sense of royalty evoked through the power of her body. Nearby is Martin's *Morning* (1965), a grid in dark graphite and red lines on a white acrylic base: an image so faint it almost disappears. The artist explained: 'I was painting about happiness and bliss and they are very simple states of mind I guess. Morning is a wonderful dawn, soft and fresh.' In the midst of the crowds, the work of the two friends - which, at first glance, appears modest, restrained, monochromatic - emanates a quiet power, a joy, even. It's a room to retreat to, and to emerge from refreshed.

Tawney preferred her works to hang in space rather than on a wall. In her dreamlike 'Cloud Series' of the 1970s and 1980s, thousands of threads appear to float down from the ceiling in a minimal cascade: air is as much a material as thread. Her use of repetition here is meditative, the result, exalted. She worked either in silence, or to a recording of a sacred chant or mantra. 'I want to be under the leaf,' she said, 'to be quiet until I find my true self.'

In 1998, the writer Lee Lawrence visited Tawney's whitewashed loft on the lower West Side of Manhattan. The artist was ninety-one; she still had another nine years to live. The writer evokes how the air was fragrant with irises and essential oils; a large black weaving dominated the space, which Tawney told Lawrence was inspired by the Greek letter 'tau'. In ancient times, it was a symbol for life and resurrection but in Greek it became 'theta': a symbol of death. Tawney was, however, far from maudlin. She recounts how she had just visited her brother and they stayed up all night dancing to Benny Goodman. Towards the end of the interview, she tells Lawrence of a dream she had of coming across a beautifully made wooden canoe on a riverbank. She realises that it's her transport to the other side but it has no paddles: she understands that it's up to her to make them. 'It's a beautiful dream,' she said. 'It's nice to know I have a beautiful canoe.'

Temenos

'Look . . . I am the Medusa
Look and be turned to stone
I'm the Image of She
The Dancing Lady
The Lady of a Thousand Guiles'

Liliane Lijn, 'Woman of War', 1986

The heat of the islands feels like years ago but it's only been a couple of months. On a cold night in December 2021, I visit a new public sculpture created by my friend, the artist Liliane Lijn, for Granary Square, in London's King's Cross. A new strain of the virus has just been announced, something that everyone takes in their stride with an exhausted acceptance. That said, something has shifted; what was familiar has been rendered strange. Two years of global illness and quarantine has affected people's sense of their place. Conversations revolve around the possibility of change - physical, mental, spiritual, geographical.

Liliane was invited to create a sculpture to celebrate the end of this terrible year and the advent of Christmas. She decided on *Temenos* - an Ancient Greek word that translates as a sacred grove or a sanctuary, which she describes as 'a magic circle, a space believed to contain a protective energy'. She first came across the concept in the 1980s while reading Joseph Campbell's *The Masks of God*, one of his four books on myth and religions that made him famous.

Temenos is an enormous open structure made of nineteen poles; the highest one supports the whole. At once seemingly very old and very modern, the inside of each pole is lined with an LED strip, which creates lines of light that move dreamily through the colour spectrum, shifting tone and intensity every second. From a distance, it looks like a Christmas tree from outer space; as you get closer to it, it recalls a wing, unfurling. Liliane sees it as an 'embracing angel', and 'a metaphor for the dependency that all living beings, from humans to the simplest algae have between each other'; the embodiment of mutual support.

The sculpture first took flight as a drawing Liliane made when she was nineteen, of an empty triangle floating in a circle full of creatures; it grew from her work with prisms and study of Crystallography and spectra that began in the 1960s. Before deciding upon a final shape, she played with proportions and relations between the forms, using numerical dimensions that create energy or vibrations. 'The Pythagoreans,' she tells me, 'may have been the first to relate certain numbers to increased energy or power; similar theories are expounded in the Kabbalah and in Tantric Buddhism.'

Liliane, who has been an artist in residence at both NASA and the European Gravitational Observatory, has the sharp mind of a scientist and a lifelong interest in geometry 'and the ways in which it reflects and relates to nature and the chemistry of life'. But she is also a lifelong student of archetypes, myths and feminism. Her investigations are manifested in sculptures, wall-works, books; cones that spin with poems, jewellery made from lava and fossils, and carpets in which patterns and words are interwoven, their meaning dependent on the direction from which they were seen and read. In the 1960s, she decided to challenge what she describes as 'the false claim' of men over women's bodies and minds through an immersion in a study of female archetypes, mythology and new spiritual paths. I ask her what she thinks of the rekindling of interest in other realms. She applauds it. 'The Spirit world,' she tells me, 'has been pooh-poohed as feminine and therefore not of interest for far too long.'

When I was at *frieze* I commissioned Liliane to write about her influences. Her first line is riveting: 'I am alive because my grandfather bought a Cuban passport in 1923.' Her life has been, and continues to be, remarkable. She was born in 1939 in New York, where her Jewish family had arrived after fleeing Nazi Germany. She had a Cuban nanny, so her first words were Spanish, and she grew up speaking six languages. 'My father and mother spoke German, especially when they quarrelled. My mother and my grandmother (her mother) spoke Polish with each other. My father spoke Yiddish to his father, who also lived with us, and Russian to my mother's mother. My uncles and aunts spoke French and everyone tried to speak English to my brother and me.' She moved to Paris in the 1950s to become an artist and discovered Indian and Japanese Zen Buddhism, Marx, Engels and Trotsky, the Surrealist manifesto and William Blake, Baudelaire, Rimbaud and Antonin Artaud. Liliane quotes Artaud in the introduction to her book, *Crossing Map* (1983): 'Become conscious of opposite forces in life because if you are not aware of this, you are dead.' His words awoke in her 'a belief in the urgent necessity for awareness, that has remained a central aspect of both my art and my life'. She became fascinated by Southeast Asian art and believes that the carvings at the temples of Angkor Wat 'indicate a prescience that natural abundance will overcome human control and the irrational will swallow the rational'. In 1959, she visited an exhibition of Chinese horizontal scroll paintings of landscapes at the Musée Cernuschi in Paris, observed that people are only a small part of the natural world, and 'realized that these were cosmic paintings'. She became an avid reader of *Scientific American* magazine and felt that the science of light and matter was 'pure poetry'. She attended lectures by the American-British physicist, David Bohm, who was interested in Buddhism and who described matter as 'frozen light'. She writes: 'In ancient Greek, *Endios* is one of the earliest epithets for god and it means "in the light". Light is a symbol for a higher state of consciousness in most spiritual quests. Light is also the most common appearance of energy, the light of the sun, lightning, fire.'

Liliane Lijn by Pablo Volta, 1963, Paris

In the 1960s, Liliane moved to Greece with the sculptor Takis, and they built a house on the Attic plain. They imagined a 'pure place, a centre for artists and poets, a cosmic observatory'. She visited the Parthenon, sat against a marble pillar of the great temple, listened to the hum of the wind in the tubes of scaffolding that surrounded it and felt she heard ancient murmurings. She read Greek classics and the eleventh-century Tibetan Buddhist texts *The Life of Jetsun Milarepa* and *The Hundred Thousand Songs of Milarepa*, so many times that she 'almost knew them by heart'. When she left Greece in 1967, she sensed that her 'body and mind were imbued with a luminosity that would remain with me. I had spent three years thinking and meditating on what was most important to me.'

In 1983, she published the loosely autobiographical *Crossing Map*, a fragmented narrative formed of images, poems and songs that is presented in sixteen sections and which, in Liliane's words, 'explores the idea that the human mind is disposed of a vast supply of untapped energy'. It traces the spiritual journey of a woman artist who questions the meaning of time and journeys to a place where 'she meets the last man and is witness to the death of her society'. It describes her relationship with a man with whom she builds a 'house of light' on a hill and her move to a city where she eventually achieves artistic success with works that explore light and reflection. Turn the pages and it explodes with patterns of colour, above which words float, like thoughts transmitted onto a kaleidoscopic sky. Meaning emerges not through linear logic but via snatches of thoughts, glimpses of possibility, association:

> The net had been thrown
> It was pulling tight around me and I had to get busy and look for
> a hole
> Spatial shift and more variety of others
> Greater possibility for random selection
> And a feeling inside me that I would find another whom I could
> become . . .

For six decades or so, Liliane's sense of communion with old knowledge has inflected everything she makes – but, like so many of the nineteenth-century artists who were interested in Spiritualism, she's captivated by new technologies, the behaviour of different materials and how they interact with one another. She describes her recent series *Catastrophic Encounters* and *Cosmic Sea*, for example, as 'traces of a collision between an ancient material, glass, and a new composite material, Vapourshield . . . Under extreme conditions, materials seem to mimic macrocosmic events.'

In the early 1980s, Liliane began exploring female archetypes, fusing references to mythological beings with images from nature and industry. Her sculpture from 1983, *Lady of the Wild Things* - a portrait of sorts of a nymph goddess from her 'Cosmic Dramas' series - is over two metres tall, and created from painted steel, glass prism, aluminium mesh, synthetic fibres, LEDs, and an electronic sound-to-light system. A towering figure with wings that appear bright green and red from the front and black from the back, Liliane describes her as a 'lunar archetype': she has light and dark sides, she's at once threatening and embracing. The sculpture's title is taken from Robert Graves, who mentions the supreme nymph goddess in his *Greek Myths*: 'As "Lady of Wild Things", or patroness of all the totem clans, Artemis had been annually offered a living holocaust of totem beasts, birds, and plants, and this sacrifice survived in Classical time at Patrae, a Calydonian city; she was there called Artemis Laphria.'

Many years before she made the sculpture, Liliane had a vision. She was nineteen, and in the midst of painting, she stepped onto her balcony in Paris to watch a sunset. She tells me that she distinctly saw a female figure in the clouds, who was so real to her that she can recall her details sixty years on. 'She stayed inside me,' she says. Liliane describes her as a 'prismatic bird goddess, but kind of frightening'. Years later, her vision became the sculpture *Woman of War*.

In 1984, Liliane was walking across the Place de la Bastille and a song came to her, complete with words and melody: she felt as if the 'earth was singing through her'. She told me that 'it took a while for me to understand that this song described a sculpture (or in ancient Greece and India – an Ikon) that I had to make. Once the work was made, I gave her my voice. When the Woman of War sings, the Lady of the Wild Things transforms her voice into light across her red and green wings':

> My eye is a laser beam
> My mind the prism through which you take your aim
> My breath is the fire of Death
> And my voice is a siren of alarm
>
> I'm a Woman of War
> A Woman of War
> I'm your Image of Woman
> A Woman of War

In many ways, *Woman of War* is an alarming work: like an enormous bird or avenging angel enveloped in smoke, she looms in the dark, with black and yellow wings, her head a computer that spits red helium laser beams.

Woman of War and *Lady of the Wild Things* are always displayed together, under the title, *Conjunction of Opposites*. The two sculptures face each other like abstracted mechanical birds or avenging angels. They're at once ominous and strangely uplifting as they perform a six-minute drama, moving, flashing, smoking: sound and song transformed into light, into energy.

In 2001, Liliane made *Lilith*, a 'self-portrait with fire', from patinated bronze, phlogopite mica, gas, brass and stainless-steel fittings. Lilith was a pre-Eve woman who refused to be dominated by a man and is considered a demon by both Christians and Jews. Her story begins 5,000 years ago in Ancient Sumer where she invaded the cultural tree of the goddess Inanna and was sent into the wilderness by the hero Gilgamesh. Liliane believes that Lilith inhabits every woman. Her sculpture is a cast of the artist's torso and head which was, in the process of its making, consumed by flames. Lilith/Liliane's charred, cracked body still upright, still robust, continues to burst into flames every twenty minutes. Nothing can destroy her.

I want to know more about Liliane's long relationship to spirituality, and so I visit her at her home in Camden and we talk over a pot of nettle tea and toasted stollen. I ask her what goddesses could possibly offer to contemporary women. Liliane stresses that 'it isn't so easy to articulate, which is why I make art', but she creates big, powerful, female figures in order to engender a sense of empowered spirituality. The spiritual side of women, she believes, was, for too long appropriated by men. Liliane shakes her head in exasperation. 'Take the Virgin Mary. The most popular saint in the Catholic Church is a figure whose sexual power is denied her - which is to deny her innate power. Women's minds have been stamped on and oppressed and locked up for far too long. There's so much female masochism, so much self-torture and guilt - women go through such misery, attempting to live up to impossible ideals.' Liliane often returns to the story of Inanna, the Sumerian goddess of love, sensuality, justice, fertility and war, who she sees as a far more powerful symbol than Mary: she is impetuous and adventurous, has lovers, wreaks revenge. For the Akkadians and Assyrians, she became the goddess Ishtar, for the Greeks, Aphrodite, and for the Romans, Venus, the brightest star of the morning and evening. Inanna's High Priestess, Enheduanna, who lived in Mesopotamia around 2300 BCE, is the earliest named poet in history; aside from her forty-two poems, her most famous work is 'The Exaltation of Inanna', a wild exhortation to female power: 'My lady, you are the guardian of the great divine powers! You have taken up the divine powers, you have hung the divine powers from your hand. You have gathered up the divine powers, you have clasped the divine powers to your breast.'

Like Persephone of the Greek myths, Inanna descended into the Underworld. Her journey, however, is not at the behest of a man, but because she is avid for knowledge: the Underworld was ruled by her sister Ereshkigal, who has her killed, but Inanna is resurrected and sends her lover in her place. 'Erotic, funny and tragic,' says Liliane, 'the story of Inanna has all the characteristics of great drama.'

I ask Liliane what the word 'spirituality' means to her. She thinks for a moment and shakes her head. 'Although the ultimate goal is to be enlightened, I don't think you can pin it down. It's different for everyone. It's just a path and you never reach the end of it because you want to keep going.'

Into the Ether

I'm seated next to a gallery director at dinner. She asks me what I am writing, and I tell her about this book. She frowns, and says: 'But surely the old superstitions are what women have needed to shake off? It was the old ways of thinking that kept them in their place.' It's a fair question. I take a moment to answer her.

I think of the women painters who conjured their visions with a creative freedom they were denied beyond the walls of their rooms.

I think of the different types of knowledge explored by women, many of which were deemed lunatic, unserious or illogical by patriarchal structures.

I think of the permission that Spiritualism, in myriad forms, gave them to be themselves, whoever that might be; to make the marks or inscribe the words that sprang to their hearts or minds.

I think about the late American artist Susan Hiller, who spent much of her life using art to explore dreams and ghost sightings, automatic writing, UFOs, ESP, angels, halos and fairy rings. She said that: 'I'm interested in things that are outside or beneath recognition . . . I see this as an archaeological investigation.'

I think of the Turner Prize-winning artist, Lubaina Himid, who was part of the British Black Arts Movement in the 1980s. In paintings and installations, she digs into the legacies of racist histories in part via a reimagining of myth and ritual from the perspective of the disempowered - she makes clear that individual lives are not grand narratives but formed of delicate connections and intimate, often secret, languages.

I think about the African American artist Betye Saar, to whom time is cyclical and whose repurposing of daily materials has influenced Lubaina's work. Over the past seven decades, in her exploration of death and rebirth - of ancestors, ideas, politics, feelings - Saar has combined a personal cosmology with 'materials that have power' and says she has a 'sort of psychic intuition'. In 1989, she said: 'I can no longer separate the work by saying this deals with the occult and this deals with shamanism or this deals with so and so . . . It's all together and it's just my work.'

I think about how, in Athens, on my way back to London from the islands, I came across a film of a woman burying herself in the earth as a form of rebirth. It was by the Cuban American artist Ana Mendieta, who died in 1985 at the age of thirty-six after falling from the window of her 34th floor apartment following an argument with her husband, the artist Carl Andre. Her work, which is shot through with premonition, explored ritual, violence against women, our connection to the earth; new ways of forging fresh paths that were sustained by the old ones. 'My art,' she said, 'is grounded on the belief in one universal energy which runs through everything - from insect to man, from man to spectre, from spectre to plant, from plant to galaxy.' She wanted her images to have magical qualities - and she believed that magic stems from the source of life: Mother Nature.

I think about the intriguing works on paper by the British artist, Suzanne Treister, that I came across in the same exhibition as Ana Mendieta: they look like visions by Hilma af Klint filtered through futuristic cartoons. I read that Treister is interested in exploring the existence of 'covert, unseen forces at work in the world, whether corporate, military or paranormal'. Her works have titles like *Kabbalistic Futurism* and *Technoshamanic Systems*. She says she wants people looking at her pictures to 'make a hallucinatory jump in order to enter a disembodied viewing state'.

I think about being back in London and talking to a painter friend, Sophie von Hellermann, who invited me to an exhibition of her new work in Margate: large murals that she created alongside sculptures by another artist, Anne Ryan. Their show is in an airy gallery overlooking the sea: it's titled 'Sirens' and draws on various mythologies and fables. Sophie has painted a giant woman on a yellow beach, somehow both beneath and above the water, on the walls of the gallery. She holds two skulls.

I think about watching a Zoom talk with the artist Portia Zvavahera in her studio in Zimbabwe. She paints symbolic, bird-like creatures and trippy, colourful figures that blossom in landscapes. Her latest show is titled *Ndakaoneswa murima* which, translated from the Shona, means 'I was made to see the dark side'. She talks about her grandmother discussing her dreams every morning, and how her dreams would often come true. 'When I'm painting,' she says, 'I don't know where it comes from. The energy of the dream brings out the colours of the pictures.'

I think about how, out of the blue, a friend who is involved with ocean ecology sends me a text: 'When we emphasise the magic, humans change into crops.'

I think about my friend the artist Adam Chodzko, who invites me to his latest performance: a science-fiction audio walk through Northfleet in Kent, guided by the collective souls, ghosts and spirits of millions-of-years-old phytoplankton. His recent video melds Hildegard of Bingen's *lingua ignotae* and image-recognition algorithms. I ask him: 'Why Hildegard?' He replies: 'The simple answer is every path seems to head towards her. She is very much in the present.'

I think about the artist Emma Talbot, who won the Max Mara Art Prize for Women in 2020. She's spent time in Rome and writes on Instagram that she's trying to 'rethink the body and being in the world, through the lens of ancient imagery – where myth is a stand-in for the wishful dynamics of control and desire'.

I think about the New Zealand biodynamic gardener and artist Sarah Smuts-Kennedy, whose practice 'is focused on a research-based investigation into fields of energy as they engage with conceptual thinking' and whose hand is often guided by a pendulum.

I think about the British-Kenyan artist Grace Ndiritu who, since 2012, has been working on a project titled 'Healing the Museum' and who sees 'shamanism as a way to re-activate the dying art space as a space for sharing, participation and ethics'.

I think about the many talks I've attended in which artists try to explain that they are grappling with the past in order to move into the future. How, they ask, can art help heal this planet and uncover new, better ways of living in it?

I think of the consolation of Hildegard of Bingen's music, the strange fury of her pictures.

I think about Circe and Scylla and Erato and Nausicaa.

I think about the Seven Sisters weaving their way across the central deserts of Australia, escaping into the vast sky.

I think about Hilma af Klint, Ithell Colquhoun, Olga Fröbe-Kapteyn, Georgiana Houghton, Anna Mary Howitt, Emma Kunz and Agnes Pelton.

I think about the outliers.

I turn to the gallery director and say: 'It's more complicated than that.'

Notes

Prologue

5   'the strange things among us': Vivienne Roberts, London's College of Psychic Studies, 'Strange Things Among Us', 5 June-6 August 2021, https://tinyurl.com/2p962udb

8   'One cannot grasp . . .': Charlene Spretnak, *Spiritual Dynamic in Modern Art: Art History Reconsidered, 1800 to the Present* (New York: Palgrave Macmillan, 2014), p. 2.

8   'we are learning something . . .': Waldemar Januszczak, 'The Woman Who Changes Everything', *Sunday Times*, 26 June 2016.

8   Hilma af Klint exhibition: Since then, a documentary on af Klint's life, *Beyond the Visible*, directed by Halina Dyrschka, has been released, exhibitions of her paintings tour internationally, and a new biopic, *Hilma*, is directed by Lasse Hallström.

9   'a vogue that . . .': Ben Davis, 'Agnes Pelton Went to the Desert in Search of Solace . . .', 13 March 2020, Artnet, https://tinyurl.com/y6xzskba

9   'something magical': Jori Finkel, 'Gender Alchemy is Transforming Art for the 21st Century', *New York Times*, 21 September 2021, https://tinyurl.com/2safmzu8

9   'Supernatural America': 12 June-5 September 2021: Toledo Museum of Art; 7 October 2021-2 January 2022: Speed Art Museum; 19 February-15 May 2022: Minneapolis Institute of Art.

9   'Instead of treating . . .': Katherine C. Luber, Director's Foreword, catalogue to *Supernatural America: The Paranormal in American Art* (Minneapolis Institute of Art, in association with The University of Chicago Press, 2021), p. 7.

10 'The Milk of Dreams': I wrote an essay for the 59th Venice Biennale catalogue, titled 'Body Language'.

10 'How is the definition . . .': Cecilia Alemani, curator of the 59th Venice Biennale, statement, https://www.labiennale.org/en/art/2022/statement-cecilia-alemani

10　'Surrealism and Magic': Organised with the Museum Barberini, curated by Gražina Subelyte and Daniel Zamani.

10　'During a time . . .': Gražina Subelyte, 'Metaphors of Change: Surrealism, Magic, and World War II', *Surrealism and Magic: Enchanted
Modernity* (New York: Prestel, 2022), p. 47.

11　'a third of Americans . . .': Casey Cep, 'Why Did So Many Victorians Try to Speak with the Dead?', *New Yorker*, 31 May 2021, https://
tinyurl.com/5bfpj5w9

11　'I would call myself . . .': Radheyan Simonpillai, 'Maybe Death Isn't
the End: Can a TV Series Prove the Existence of an Afterlife?', *Guardian*, 7 January 2021, https://tinyurl.com/5cjdks2e

11　Spiritualist churches: Cep, 'Why Did So Many Victorians Try to
Speak with the Dead?'

11　'been variously recognized . . .': Tomás Prower, 'Why is Queer Magic
so Powerful?', Llewellyn, 4 June 2018, https://www.llewellyn.com/
journal/article/2696

11　'What would it mean . . .': Jamie Sutcliffe, *Magic* (Documents of Contemporary Art), (MIT Press, 2021), Kindle Edition, p. 13.

A Season in the Life of a Thought

15　'To see a World . . .': William Blake, 'Auguries of Innocence', 1863,
accessed online https://www.poetryfoundation.org/poems/43650/
auguries-of-innocence

16　Blake visions: John Higgs, *William Blake Now: Why He Matters More
Than Ever* (London: Weidenfeld & Nicolson, 2019), Kindle Edition,
p. 7.

17　'mysterious and secret': Wassily Kandinsky, *Concerning the Spiritual
in Art and Painting in Particular*, trans. W.T.H. Sadler (Barakaldo
Books, 2020), Kindle Edition.

17　'In music a light . . .': Ibid.

17　'Colour is the keyboard . . .': Ibid.

18　'The earth will be . . .': Ibid.

21　1914 Baltic Exhibition: Julia Voss, *Hilma af Klint: A Biography* (trans.
Anne Posten) (Chicago, IL, and London: University of Chicago
Press, 2022), p. 194.

21　'Indeed, it's the world's . . .': Julia Voss, 'The First Abstract Artist?
(And it's not Kandinsky)', *Tate Etc*, 25 June 2019, https://tinyurl.com/
yck664kd

23　'. . . the impact of motherhood . . .': Hettie Judah, 'Full, Messy and

Beautiful', Representation of Female Artists in Britain during 2019, Freelands Foundation, p. 14.

23   Female artists in galleries: Liam Kelly, 'Works by Women Make Up Just 7% of Art in Top Galleries', *Sunday Times*, 10 April 2022. A 2022 report by the Murray Edwards College, Cambridge - which has the largest collection of work by modern and contemporary women artists in Europe - discovered that of the National Gallery's collection of 2,391 artworks, only 1% are by women; at the National Galleries of Scotland, the figure is 2.8%, at the National Portrait Gallery, 11.1%, and at Tate's four galleries it's 13.1%; https://tinyurl.com/ma8rrrsp

Enter the Fairies

33   'forbearance, courtesy, consideration . . .': Charles Dickens, 'Frauds on the Fairies', *Household Words: A Weekly Journal*. Conducted by Charles Dickens, no. 184, vol. VIII, pp. 97-100. Sourced online: https://victorianweb.org/authors/dickens/pva/pva239.html

33   On fairy tales: Stella Beddoe, 'Fairy Writing and Writers', in *Victorian Fairy Painting*, ed. Jane Martineau (Royal Academy of Arts, London; The University of Iowa Museum of Art, Iowa; The Art Gallery of Ontario, Toronto, Merrell Holberton Publishers, London, 1997), p. 30.

34   Queen Victoria and laudanum: 'Did This Beloved Queen of Britain Use Drugs?', Tracey Borman, Chief Curator, Historic Royal Palaces interview with Dr Rosemary Leonard, video, *Smithsonian Magazine*, https://tinyurl.com/4pevr247

34   On laudanum: See Vivienne Roberts, 'A History of Vicky's Ticker', *Light: A Review of Psychic and Spiritual Knowledge and Research*, vol. 138, Winter 2017.

Islands in the Mist

37   'Tell us this story . . .': Homer, *The Odyssey*, trans. E.V. Rieu, revised trans. D.C.H. Rieu (London: Penguin Classics, Penguin Books Ltd), Kindle Edition, p. 67.

41   Fairies and photography: Jennifer Higgie, 'Seeing is Believing: How Photography Killed Victorian Fairy Painting', *frieze*, issue 40, May 1998.

Mysterious Knockers

44   'mysterious knocker': Emily Midorikawa, *Out of the Shadows: Six*

Visionary Victorian Women in Search of a Voice (Berkeley, CA: Counterpoint, 2021), Kindle Edition, p. 36.

44   'What hath God wrought!': Ibid, p. 17.

45   'heavenly beings, the dead . . .': Peter Ackroyd, *Introducing Swedenborg* (London: The Swedenborg Society, 2021), p. 25.

45   'It is a truth . . .': Karen Abbott, 'The Fox Sisters and the Rap on Spiritualism', *The Smithsonian Magazine*, 30 October 2012, https://tinyurl.com/3m6sbs8k

45   'About daylight this morning . . .': Ibid.

46   Americans and Spiritualism: Lars Bang Larsen, 'Infinite Redress', *Not Without My Ghosts: The Artist as Medium* (London: Hayward Gallery Publishing), p. 79.

46   'The professional medium . . .': Laurence R. Moore, 'Spiritualism and Science: Reflections on the First Decade of the Spirit Rappings', *American Quarterly*, vol. 24, no. 4, 1972, p. 476, https://doi.org/10.2307/2711685

46   Spiritualist publications: Casey Cep, 'Why Did So Many Victorians Try to Speak with the Dead?', *New Yorker*, 31 May 2021, https://tinyurl.com/5bfpj5w9

46   'spiritualism will work . . .': Ada Calhoun, 'The Sisters Who Spoke to Spirits', Narratively.com., 9 February 2015, https://tinyurl.com/ycxy9wp9

47   'she was under . . .': Gloria T. Hull, 'Rebecca Cox Jackson and the Uses of Power', *Tulsa Studies in Women's Literature*, vol. 1, no. 2, University of Tulsa, 1982, pp. 203–9, https://doi.org/10.2307/464081

47   'the eloquent and earnest . . .': Cep, 'Why Did So Many Victorians Try to Speak with the Dead?'

47   'I am a woman's rights . . .': The speech is commonly known as 'Ain't I a Woman' but this is based on erroneous reporting. See https://www.thesojournertruthproject.com/compare-the-speeches   The first published report of the speech, which I quote, was written by Sojourner Truth's friend, Marius Robinson; it is documented that Truth approved his version of events. *Anti-slavery bugle*, June 21, 1851, p. 160, https://tinyurl.com/ysddud3u

47   Kate Fox being particularly engrossed: Calhoun, 'The Sisters Who Spoke to Spirits'.

47   'I do this because . . .': Signed Confession of Margaret Fox Kane, October 1888, ParanormalEncylopedia.com
https://www.paranormal-encyclopedia.com/f/fox-sisters/confession.html

48   'Spiritualism is a fraud . . .': Cep, 'Why Did So Many Victorians Try to Speak with the Dead?'

48   'false in every particular': Midorikawa, *Out of the Shadows*, p. 252.

49   'There is no death.': Calhoun, 'The Sisters Who Spoke to Spirits'.

The Cracked People

49   'Cries are heard . . .': Barbara Leigh Smith Bodichon, *Women and Work*, 1857, https://www.bl.uk/collection-items/women-and-work

50   Female visibility and universal suffrage: Lars Bang Larsen, 'Infinite Redress', *Not Without My Ghosts: The Artist as Medium* (London: Hayward Gallery Publishing), p. 80.

50   Cornelius Vanderbilt: Emily Midorikawa, *Out of the Shadows*: Six Visionary Victorian Women in Search of a Voice (Berkeley, CA: Counterpoint, 2021), Kindle Edition, p. 141.

50   'The witch of Washington Avenue': Ibid, p. 127.

50   First female presidential candidate: Ibid, pp. 256-7.

50   'They cannot roll back . . .': 'Victoria for President – in 1872', https://www.theattic.space/home-page-blogs/woodhull

51   'minorities, as well as majorities . . .': Midorikawa, *Out of the Shadows*, p. 167.

51   'a disease': Simon Grant, 'Spiritualist Sisters in Art', *Not Without My Ghosts: The Artist as Medium* (Hayward Gallery Publishing), p. 21.

51   'devoted to the History . . .': Midorikawa, *Out of the Shadows*, p. 174.

54   'What schemes of life . . .': Anna Mary Howitt, *An Art-Student in Munich*, vols. 1-2 (London: Longman, Brown, Green), and Longmans (Miami, FL: Hard Press, 2017), Kindle Edition, location 1361.

54   'There is a fascination . . .': *New York Times*, 11 May 1854, accessed online: https://tinyurl.com/37yudj6h

54   'like stepping out of . . .': Ibid.

55   'the present industrial employments . . .': Alexandra Wettlaufer, 'The Politics and Poetics of Sisterhood', in Anna Mary Howitt's 'The Sisters in Art', *Victorian Review*, 36(1), 2010, http://www.jstor.org/stable/41039112, p. 32.

55   'one of the cracked . . .': Dinah Birch, 'One of the Cracked', *London Review of Books*, vol. 20, no. 19, 1 October 1998.

56   'What is this but . . .': Alexandra Wettlaufer, 'The Politics and Poetics of Sisterhood': Anna Mary Howitt's *The Sisters in Art*, *Victorian Review*, 36(1), http://www.jstor.org/stable/41039112, p. 141.

56   'the woman's intellect . . .': Ruskin, John, *Works of John Ruskin*,

Library Edition, vol. XVIII (1905), p. 122, cited in Katy Hessel, *The Story of Art Without Men* (London: Penguin, 2022), p. 86.

56   'What do you know . . .': Wettlaufer, 'The Politics and Poetics of Sisterhood', p. 142.

56   'king among critics . . .': Susan Tallman, 'Seeing Things: Anna Mary Howitt in Art History', in Paul Coldwell and Ruth M. Morgan, eds, *Picturing the Invisible: Exploring Interdisciplinary Synergies from the Arts and the Sciences* (London: UCL Press, 2022), p. 164.

56   'If only the spirits . . .': *The Diary of M.W. Rossetti, 1870-73* (Oxford: Clarendon Press, 1977), p. 35.

56   'Have you heard . . .': Tallman, 'Seeing Things', p. 164.

56   'spiritual drawings': Anna Mary Howitt, writing as 'Comfort', in Mrs Newton Crosland, *Light in the Valley: My Experiences of Spiritualism* (London: Kessing Publishing, 1857, reprint, 2010), p. 129.

57   'jargon of silliness . . .': Unauthored review in *The Spectator*, 25 July 1857.

A Dagger in Her Hair

59   'Everybody is talking about . . .': Georgiana Houghton, *Evenings at Home in Spiritual Séance [annotated]: Second Series, Victorian Secrets*, Kindle edition, p. 98.

60   The photograph Houghton chose to represent herself: Georgiana Houghton (1814-1884), photograph used as the frontispiece to her *Evenings at Home in Spiritual Séance, Prefaced and Welded Together by a Species of Autobiography*, 2nd series (London: E.W. Allen, 1882).

62   'Holy Symbolist': Georgiana Houghton, *Evenings at Home in Spiritual Séance*, Kindle edition, p. 12.

62   'the essence of a person's . . .': Ernst Vegelin Van Claerbergen and Barnaby Wright, Introduction, *Georgiana Houghton: Spirit Drawings* (London: Courtauld Institute, 2016), p. 36.

63   Using colours for states: For a full record of the symbolic meaning of Georgiana Houghton's colours, see http://georgianahoughton.com/drawings

63   'a type of the Love . . .': Houghton, *Evenings at Home in Spiritual Séance*, Kindle edition, pp. 68-9.

64   'would be out of place . . .': All descriptions of the evolution of the exhibition: ibid, pp. 46-7.

64   'Miss Houghton has taken . . .': Ibid, p. 80.

64   'tangled threads . . .': *Daily News*, 27 May 1871, quoted in Simon

Grant and Marco Pasi, 'Works of Art Without Parallel in the World: *Georgiana Houghton's Spirit Drawings*', Georgiana Houghton Spirit Drawings (London: Courtauld Gallery, 2016), p. 19.

65   'the brilliancy and harmony . . .': Houghton, *Evenings at Home in Spiritual Séance*, Kindle edition, p. 85.

65   'The water-colour drawings . . .': Ibid, p. 88.

65   'revelled in the glories . . .': Ibid, p. 96.

65   'all artists well know . . .': Ibid, p. 98.

65   'And about my Gallery! . . .': Ibid, p. 115.

66   The Courtauld Institute of Art staging an exhibition: The curatorial team was Simon Grant, Lars Bang Larsen, and Marco Pasi.

66   'To look at these . . .': Ella Cory-Wright, 'Georgiana Houghton: Spirit Drawings, Courtauld Gallery', https://www.culturewhisper.com/r/visual_arts/preview/6383

66   'The time was approaching . . .': Houghton, *Evenings at Home in Spiritual Séance*, Kindle edition, p. 6.

66   'My dear sister Zilla . . .': http://www.costumecocktail.com/2016/12/19/georgiana-houghtons-spirit- photographs-1872-76

66   'I send them forth . . .': Georgiana Houghton, *Chronicles of the Photographs of Spiritual Beings and Phenomena Invisible to the Material Eye* (London: E.W. Allen, 1882), https://tinyurl.com/ymk8pjr8

67   'a neat and curious . . .': Madame Blavatsky, review of Georgiana Houghton's *Chronicles of the Photographs of Spiritual Beings and Phenomena Invisible to the Material Eye*, in *The Theosophist*, vol. III, no. 7 (April 1882), pp. 179–80. Cited in *Evenings at Home in Spiritual Séance*, Kindle edition, p. 337.

67   'fresh marvels': Houghton, *Evenings at Home in Spiritual Séance*, Kindle edition, p. 100.

67   'My face is pressed . . .': Ibid, p. 335.

68   'Hudson, who obtained . . .': Sir Arthur Conan Doyle, *The History of Spiritualism*, two vols. (London, New York, Toronto and Melbourne: Cassell, 1926), vol. II, p. 129.

68   'While to our eyes . . .': Simon Grant, 'Spiritualist Sisters in Art', *Not Without My Ghosts: The Artist as Medium* (London: Hayward Gallery Publishing), p. 26.

68   'On the 6th . . .': Houghton, *Evenings at Home in Spiritual Séance*, Kindle edition, p. 6.

68   'Cast thy burden . . .': Ibid, p. 23.

68   'instructive message': Ibid, p. 24.

69   'Neapolitan tortoise-shell . . .': Ibid, p. 32.

70   'I had the pleasure . . .': Ibid, p. 110.

Oceanic States

71   'I had often felt . . .': Marion Milner, *On Not Being Able to Paint* (New York: Taylor and Francis, 1956), Kindle Edition, p. 156.

73   Painted sculptures: 'Early Cycladic Art and Culture', The Metropolitan Museum of Art, New York https://www.metmuseum.org/toah/hd/ecyc/hd_ecyc.htm

73   'a sense of eternity . . .': Shelley Klein, 'Marion Milner: A Kind of Uncommon Sense', unpublished paper, 2021.

74   Grace Pailthorpe: Alberto Stefana, 'Revisiting Marion Milner's Work on Creativity and Art', *The International Journal of Psychoanalysis*, 100:1, 2019, 128–47.

74   'emptiness, formlessness . . .': Marion Milner, 'Winnicott and Overlapping Circles' (1977) in *The Suppressed Madness of Sane Men* (Tavistock Publications Ltd, London, 1987), p. 285, quoted in Shelley Klein, 'Marion Milner: A Kind of Uncommon Sense', unpublished paper, 2021.

The Benefits of Not Knowing

81   *Löwenmensch*: Jill Cook, 'The Lion Man, an Ice Age Masterpiece', British Museum Blog, 10 October 2017, https://blog.britishmuseum.org/the-lion-man-an-ice-age-masterpiece

81   Hahn and Schmid theories: Matthias Schulz, 'Solving the Mystery of a 35,000-Year-Old Statue', *Spiegel International*, 9 December 2011, https://tinyurl.com/yckwkmxn

81   'icon of the women's movement': Ibid.

81   'We cannot know . . .': 'The Lion Man', Museum Ulm http://www.loewenmensch.de/lion_man.html

82   'Irreconcilabilities . . .': Paul Chan, 'Can Metaphysic Help Us Heal the World?', *frieze*, 5 June 2020, https://www.frieze.com/article/can-metaphysics-help-us-heal-world

82   Venus of Hohle Fels: M. Stannard and M. Langley, (2021), 'The 40,000-Year-Old Female Figurine of Hohle Fels: Previous Assumptions and New Perspectives', *Cambridge Archaeological Journal*, 31(1), pp. 21–33. doi:10.1017/S0959774320000207

83   Goddess worship: Charlene Spretnak, introduction to *The Politics of Women's Spirituality: Essays on the Rise of Spiritual Power within the*

Feminist Movement (New York: Anchor Books, 1982), p. xii.

84 'an attempt to peel . . .': Helen Langdon, *Salvator Rosa, Paint and Performance* (London: Reaktion Books, 2022), pp. 155-61.

84 'great magician': Ibid, p. 155.

85 'is difficult and still uncertain': https://www.visituffizi.org/ artworks/la-primavera-allegory-of-spring-by-sandro-botticelli

85 'wholly the instrument . . .': Sixten Ringbom, 'Art in "The Epoch of the Great Spiritual": Occult Elements in the Early Theory of Abstract Painting', *Journal of the Warburg and Courtauld Institutes*, vol. 29, 1966, p. 412, https://doi.org/10.2307/750725

86 'striking voices I couldn't . . .': Jerry Salz, 'The Best of the Basement', 6 December 2012, *New York Magazine*, https://nymag.com/arts/art/ reviews/saltz-trisha-donnelly-2012-12

86 'So much art today . . .': Martin Herbert and Trisha Donnelly, *Art Review*, 12 January 2015, https://tinyurl.com/2p87hscf

86 'I like late . . .': https://www.serpentinegalleries.org/whats-on/ trisha-donnelly

87 'unexplored country . . .': Angela Carter, *American Ghosts and Old World Wonders* (London: Random House, 1993), Kindle Edition, p. 123.

87 Not knowing for learning: Marion Milner, *A Life of One's Own* (London and New York, Routledge, Taylor & Francis Group, 1934). Shelley Klein makes this clear in her essay 'Marion Milner: A Kind of Uncommon Sense', unpublished paper, 2021.

87 'We make Idols . . .': Klein, 'Marion Milner: A Kind of Uncommon Sense'.

88 'the worst thing . . .': Bridget Riley, 'Painting Now', 1996, in *The Eye's Mind: Bridget Riley, Collected writings 1965-1999*, ed. Robert Kudielka (London: Thames & Hudson, 1999), p. 201.

88 'Vision can be arrested . . .': Bridget Riley, 'The Pleasures of Sight', 1984, in ibid, p. 33.

88 'learn to listen . . .': Riley, 'Painting Now', p. 211.

88 'Everyone has two bodies . . .': Jan Gordon, *A Step Ladder to Painting*, pp. 206-7, quoted by Milner, *On Not Being Able to Paint*, p. 42.

88 'psychic creativity': Alberto Stefana, 'Revisiting Marion Milner's Work on Creativity and Art', The International Journal of Psychoanalysis, 100:1, 2019, pp. 128-47

Between Mortals and Beings

91 'The Mind is the great . . .': Helena Blavatsky, 'Fragment 1: The Voice of the Silence', *Helena Blavatsky, Premium Collection: Isis Unveiled, The Secret Doctrine, The Key to Theosophy, The Voice of the Silence, in Studies in Occultism, Nightmare Tales* (Illustrated) e-artnow, Kindle Edition, p. 4,341.

91 Goshka Macuga's portrait: Mario Mainette, ed., *Before the Beginning and After the End, Goshka Macuga* (Milan: Fondazione Prada, 2016), pp. 113-15.

91 'extend beyond the visible . . .': Ibid.

93 Princess Helena Pavlovna Dolgorukov: Gary Lachman, *Madame Blavatsky* (London: Penguin, 2012), Kindle Edition, p. 21.

94 Childhood home: Ibid, p. 26.

94 *Solomon's Wisdom* Marion Meade, *Madame Blavatsky: The Woman Behind the Myth* (New York: Open Road Media, 2014), Kindle Edition, p. 26.

94 Baranig Bouyak: Ibid, p. 276.

94 'All the devilries . . .': Lachman, *Madame Blavatsky*, p. 27.

94 Aversion to dancing: Meade, *Madame Blavatsky*, p. 37.

94 'There is nothing . . .': Ibid.

94 'heard the voices . . .': Ibid, p. 32.

94 'the powers of nature . . .': Ibid, p. 38. (H.P.B. to Alexander Dondoukoff-Korsakoff, 1 March 1882, *HPBSP*, vol. 2, p. 61.)

95 In England: Ibid, p. 48.

95 Tibet: Lachman, *Madame Blavatsky*, p. 49.

95 'flapdoodle': Ibid, p. 132.

96 'From seventeen to forty . . .': Ibid, p. 11.

96 'after a number of . . .': Meade, *Madame Blavatsky*, p. 49.

96 Ancient knowledge: Lachman, *Madame Blavatsky*, p. 63.

97 Seven years in Tibet: Ibid, p. 73.

97 Metrovich death on ship: Meade, *Madame Blavatsky*, p. 66.

97 Metrovich death in Ramleh: Lachman, *Madame Blavatsky*, p. 43.

97 'a mediator between . . .': Meade, *Madame Blavatsky*, p. 56.

97 'our acquaintance began . . .': Ibid, p. 81.

97 'loyal to a fault . . .': Ibid, p. 77.

98 'to purify the new . . .': Ibid, p. 96.

98 Mahatmas as real men: Ibid, p. 8.

98 'the strength of theosophy . . .': Lachman, *Madame Blavatsky*, p. 118.

99 'We believe in no Magic . . .': Helena Blavatsky, *The Essential Works of*

Helena Blavatsky: Isis Unveiled, The Secret Doctrine, The Key to Theoso-phy, The Voice of the Silence, Studies in Occultism, Nightmare Tales (New York: Musaicum Books), Kindle Edition, p. 7.

99 Newspaper reviews: Meade, *Madame Blavatsky*, pp. 122–3.
99 'Somebody comes and envelopes . . .': Ibid, p. 110.
100 'There is no religion . . .': Ibid, p. 153.
100 Albert Einstein and theosophy: Lachman, *Madame Blavatsky*, p. 9.
101 Claimed to be a virgin: Meade, *Madame Blavatsky*, p. 7.
101 Howling critics: Ibid, p. 317.
101 Inevitability of attacks: Ibid, p. 328.
101 Relationship with nature: Blavatsky, *The Essential Works of Helena Blavatsky*, p. 7.
102 'As he believes . . .': Julie Kane, 'Varieties of Mystical Experience in the Writings of Virginia Woolf', *Twentieth Century Literature*, Winter 1995, vol. 41, no. 4, p. 343.
103 'our eyes, as they range . . .': Ibid, p. 335.

Thought-Forms

105 'Every thought gives rise . . .': Annie Besant and C.W. Leadbeater, *Thought-Forms*, facsimile (Brooklyn, New York: Sacred Bones Books, 2020), p. 18.
105 'auras, vortices, etheric matter . . .': Mitch Horowitz, 'Visions from Somewhere: The Occult Background of Thought Forms', in *Thought-Forms*, p. xi.
106 'To paint in earth's dull . . .': Ibid, no page number.
106 'As knowledge increases . . .': Besant and Leadbeater, *Thought-Forms*, p. 11.
108 'I went out . . .': Annie Wood Besant, *An Autobiography*, 1893, Kindle Edition.
109 'the over-mastering sway . . .': Ibid.
109 'against war, against capital . . .': Ibid.
109 'the over-exploited . . .': Meade, *Madame Blavatsky*, p. 301.
109 'mystical and imaginative . . .': Besant, *An Autobiography*, no page number.
109 '. . . there had been slowly . . .': Ibid.
110 W.T. Stead: Thanks to Vivienne Roberts for alerting me to this. Email to the author, 6 November 2021.
110 'the study of the book . . .': Meade, *Madame Blavatsky*, p. 302.
111 'Dearly Beloved One . . .': Ibid.

112 'a belief in bacteria . . .': Besant, *An Autobiography*, no page number.

112 'and ask themselves . . .': Ibid.

113 'the most unique . . .': Meade, *Madame Blavatsky*, pp. 326-7.

113 Margaret Watts Hughes: Telephone conversation between the author and Vivienne Roberts, 5 November 2021.

114 'I have heard articulate . . .': Letter from Alexander Graham Bell to Alexander Melville Bell, 1880, quoted in Rob Mullender-Ross, 'Picturing a Voice: Margaret Watts Hughes and the Eidophone', *The Public Domain Review*, 27 November 2019, https://tinyurl.com/2hj5enxk

114 Watts Hughes and Royal Society: Teal Martz, 'Women of the Conversazioni', 8 March 2013, The Royal Society blog, https://royalsociety.org/blog/2013/03/women-of-the-conversazioni/

114 'scattering promiscuously . . .': Margaret Watts Hughes quoted in Mullender-Ross, ibid.

114 'singing into shape . . .': Michael Lavorgna, 'The Voice Made Visible: Margaret Watts Hughes and Her Eidophone', Twittering Machines, 24 August 2020, https://tinyurl.com/2c6ks48a

114 'voice flowers': Ibid.

115 '. . . are more like, perhaps . . .': Rob Mullender, 'Divine Agency: Bringing to Light the Voice Figures of Margaret Watts-Hughes', *Sound Effects*, vol. 8, no. 1, 2019, p. 133.

115 'revelation of yet another . . .': Rob Mullender-Ross, 'Picturing a Voice: Margaret Watts Hughes and the Eidophone', *The Public Domain Review*, 27 November 2019, https://tinyurl.com/2hj5enxk

115 Henry Olcott article: Email from Vivienne Roberts to the author, 6 November 2021.

115 'The voice-forms so admirably . . .': Besant and Leadbeater, *Thought-Forms*, p. 28.

115 Watts Hughes' discovery unrecognised: Mullender, 'Divine Agency', p. 132.

116 'A number of drawings . . .': '14th Istanbul Biennial: SALTWATER: A Theory of Thought Forms', https://tinyurl.com/24ffeht2

Magnetic Fields

117 'Where war has torn . . .': Hilma af Klint quoted by Julia Voss, 'Hilma af Klint, Painter and Revolutionary Mystic', *Hilma af Klint: The Secret Paintings*, ed. Sue Cramer with Nicholas Chambers (Sydney: Art Gallery of New South Wales; Wellington: City Gallery, Te Whare Toi Te Ngākau Civic Square; in association with the Heide Museum of Modern Art, 2021), p. 48.

119 'the energy field . . .': Email from Donna Huddleston to the author, 13 June 2021.

119 'the various receptors': Email from Frank Hannon to the author, 9 December 2021.

120 Pauli and Jung: Read more about the friendship in Arthur I. Miller, *Deciphering the Cosmic Number: The Strange Friendship of Wolfgang Pauli and Carl Jung* (New York: W.W. Norton, 2009).

121 *tankeformer*: Voss, 'Hilma af Klint, Painter and Revolutionary Mystic', p. 43.

122 De Fem: Ibid, p. 41.

122 Room in which De Fem met: The image can be seen in the Guggenheim online resources: Johan af Klint and Hedvig Ersman, 'Inspiration and Influence: The Spiritual Journey of Artist Hilma af Klint', https://tinyurl.com/49z7k632

123 Deepening concentration: Sue Cramer, 'Hilma af Klint, The Secret Growing', in *Hilma af Klint: The Secret Paintings*, ed. Cramer with Chambers, p. 25.

123 'astral paintings': Quoted by Cramer, 'Hilma af Klint', in ibid, p. 24.

123 'you cannot imagine . . .': Voss, *Hilma af Klint*, p. 112.

123 'slow looking, communal exchange . . .': Aaron Lister, 'receiver/received', in *Hilma af Klint*, ed. Cramer with Chambers, p. 79.

123 'the one great task . . .': Hilma af Klint Notebooks, 1 January 1906, quoted in Gertrud Sandqvist, 'The Great Affirmation', in Kurt Almqvist and Louise Belfrage, eds, *Hilma af Klint: The Art of Seeing the Invisible* (Stockholm: Axel and Margaret Ax:son Johnson Foundation, 2015), p. 255.

123 'The pictures were painted . . .': Hilma af Klint Notebooks, 14 May 1907, p. 274, quoted in Iris Müller-Westermann, *Hilma af Klint: A Pioneer of Abstraction* (Ostfildern: Hatje Cantz, 2013), p. 38.

124 Process of exchange: Voss, 'Hilma af Klint, Painter and Revolutionary Mystic', p. 43.

124 Alter egos: Thanks to Julia Voss for this information.

124 'give the world a glimpse . . .': Hilma af Klint, notebook entry 27 September 1907, quoted in Cramer, 'Hilma af Klint, The Secret Growing', in *Hilma af Klint*, ed. Cramer with Chambers, pp. 29-30.

124 Oneness: Kurt Almqvist and Daniel Birnbaum, Foreword, *Hilma af Klint Catalogue Raisonée*, 'The Paintings for the Temple, 1906-1915', vol. 2 (Stockholm: Bokförlaget Stolpe, 2020), p. 10.

125 Universal harmony and equality: Cramer, 'Hilma af Klint, The Secret Growing', p. 29.

125 'You've now completed . . .': Voss, *Hilma af Klint*, p. 144.

125 Violence and 'The Swan': Voss, 'Hilma af Klint, Painter and Revolutionary Mystic', p. 39.

126 'was not just the animal . . .': Voss, *Hilma af Klint*, p. 198.

126 'according to the divine . . .': Sixten Ringbom, 'Art in "The Epoch of the Great Spiritual": Occult Elements in the Early Theory of Abstract Painting'. *Journal of the Warburg and Courtauld Institutes*, vol. 29, 1966, p. 390, https://doi.org/10.2307/750725

126 https://anthroposophy.org.uk/rudolf-steiner

127 'belongs to the astral world': Voss, *Hilma af Klint*, p. 234.

127 'Should the paintings . . .': Ibid, p. 238.

127 'Steiner has not warned . . .': With thanks to Kurt Almqvist and the Hilma af Klint Foundation for supplying this citation, which I also used in my essay 'Becoming One Again: The Role of Gender in the Creation and Reception of Hilma af Klint's Art', *Hilma af Klint*, ed. Cramer with Chambers, p. 73.

127 Devoted disciple: Almqvist and Birnbaum, Foreword, *Hilma af Klint Catalogue Raisonée, 'Late Watercolours, 1922–41'*, p. 7.

128 Those sympathetic to Spiritualism: Conversation between the author and Kurt Almqvist, co-editor of the *Hilma af Klint Catalogue Raisonée*, 17 November 2021.

128 Anthroposophic display: Voss, *Hilma af Klint*, pp. 296–8.

129 'Studies in Spiritual Life': Daniel Birnbaum and Emma Enderby, 'Painting the Unseen', in Daniel Birnbaum et al., eds, *Hilma af Klint: Painting the Unseen* (London: Serpentine Gallery, 2016), p. 10. Julia Voss also discusses the colour codes in her biography.

129 'Many who fight . . .': Voss, *Hilma af Klint*, p. 212.

129 Works marked +x: Voss, 'Hilma af Klint, Painter and Revolutionary Mystic', p. 52.

129 'Paintings for the Temple': Voss, Hilma af Klint, p. 264.

129 'The experiments I have . . .': Quoted by Sue Cramer, 'Hilma af Klint, The Secret Growing', p. 22.

130 'You have service . . .': Voss, 'Hilma af Klint, Painter and Revolutionary Mystic', p. 53.

130 Klint's ashes: Voss, *Hilma af Klint*, p. 303.

130 'the most important exhibition . . .': Museum of Modern Art, New York, press release, 20 February 1931, https://tinyurl.com/sj8tukt8

131 'The land is full . . .': S. Elizabeth, *The Art of the Occult* (London: Frances Lincoln), Kindle Edition, p. 163.

132 'The witch, like Af Klint . . .': Anya Ventura, 'Secret Séances and High Masters: The Making of Mystic Painter Hilma af Klint', *frieze*, 11 October 2018, https://tinyurl.com/2aspxb68

133 'Non-Objectivity will be . . .': Hilla Rebay quoted, https://www.guggenheim.org/history/hilla-rebay

133 'an esoteric, occult place . . .': https://www.guggenheim.org/history/hilla-rebay

133 'a lover of space . . .': Caitlin Dover, 'The Makers of the Guggenheim', 6 February 2017, https://www.guggenheim.org/blogs/checklist/the-makers-of-the-guggenheim

She Danced a Goldfish

135 '. . . in the early 20th century . . .': Philip Hoare, 'This Dis-Remembered Land', essay in the catalogue of *The Dark Monarch: Magic and Modernity in British Art* (London: Tate Publishing, 2009), p. 85. © Tate 2009. Reproduced by permission of the Tate Trustees.

137 'Wisdom made him old . . .': Robert Graves, 'Babylon', Fairies and Fusiliers, 1918, accessed https://tinyurl.com/y4psf3bv

138 'Yesterday in Oxford Street . . .': Rose Fyleman, 'Yesterday in Oxford Street', *Fairies and Chimneys* (New York: George H. Doran Company, 1920), accessed https://tinyurl.com/2p922wrs

138 Australian casualties: 'The Battle of Fromelles', Australian War Memorial, https://tinyurl.com/2p8dfd6k

141 'I should not have done . . .': Oliver J. Lodge, *Raymond, or Life and Death* (London: Methuen, 1916), pp. vii–viii.

142 'the family scepticism . . .': Ibid, pp. 81–4.

142 Spiritualism's popularity: David Nash, 'The Rise of Spiritualism after World War 1', History Extra, *BBC History Magazine*, 3 May 2020, https://tinyurl.com/mux3b2mf

143 'mark an epoch . . .': Arthur Conan Doyle, *The Coming of the Fairies* (London: Hodder & Stoughton Ltd., 1922), sourced online: Chapter 2, 'The First Published Account', https://www.arthur-conan-doyle.com/index.php/The_Coming_of_the_Fairies#Preface

143 Venues for séances: J. Hazelgrove, 'Spiritualism After the Great War', in *Twentieth Century British History*, vol. 10, issue 4, 1999.

144 Republication of Bond: David Nash, 'The Rise of Spiritualism after World War 1'.

144 Cover of *The Vital Message*: Sir Arthur Conan Doyle, *The Vital Message*, 1919, accessed online, https://tinyurl.com/23ub2rkp

145 Parts of this section on Sophie Taeuber-Arp are developed from my essay 'Colour, Geometry and Pure Radiance', *Tate Etc*, 1 June 2021, https://tinyurl.com/2pezmujm

146 'She danced a goldfish . . .': Hans Arp quoted in Carolyn Lanchner, *Sophie Taeuber Arp* (New York: The Museum of Modern Art, 1981), p. 18.

147 'a strayed Bohemian . . .': Jessica Dismorr, 'June Night', *BLAST*, issue 2 (London: John Lane, the Bodley Head, 1915), p,68

147 'TO SUFFRAGETTES . . .': *BLAST*, issue 1, 1914, http://writing.upenn.edu/library/Blast/Blast1-1_To-Suffragettes.pdf

New Worlds

150 'the more adventurous . . .': For an in-depth discussion of modernist art-history's negation of Spiritualism, see Spretnak, *Spiritual Dynamic in Modern Art*, p. 5.

150 'The artist must have . . .': Kandinsky, *Concerning the Spiritual in Art and Painting in Particular*.

151 'concerned with the development . . .': Harold Porcher, 'An Introduction to the Transcendental Painting Group', 12 June 2020, https://tinyurl.com/2p8ktpzt

152 'a clear sign . . .': Michael Zakian, 'Agnes Pelton, Transcendental Symbolist', in *Agnes Pelton, Desert Transcendentalist, Phoenix Art Museum* (Munich: Hirmer Verlag, 2019), p. 44.

152 'a mystical house . . .': Elizabeth Armstrong, 'Agnes in the Desert', in *Agnes Pelton, Desert Transcendentalist*, p. 58.

153 'The two mountains . . .': Ibid, p. 60.

153 Deepening abstractions: Erika Doss, 'Agnes Pelton's Spiritual Modernism', in *Agnes Pelton, Desert Transcendentalist*, p. 37.

153 Images in reverie: Michael Zakian, 'Agnes Pelton, Transcendental Symbolist', p. 41.

153 Quotes in notebooks: Ibid, p. 47.

154 'especial light message . . .': Erika Doss, 'Agnes Pelton's Spiritual Modernism', p. 35.

154 'little windows, opening . . .': Pelton quoted by Michael Zakian, 'Agnes Pelton, Transcendental Symbolist', p. 41.

154 'magical, inherently musical . . .': Roberta Smith, 'Agnes of the Desert Joins Modernism's Pantheon', *New York Times*, 12 March 2020.

155 'modern art began . . .': Spretnak, *Spiritual Dynamic in Modern Art*, p. 3.

155 'indescribably embarrassing . . .': Rosalind Krauss, 'Grids', *October*, vol. 9 (Summer 1979), pp. 50–64.

155 'to use the word "spiritual" . . .': Maurice Tuchman, 'Hidden Meanings in Abstract Art', *The Spiritual in Art: Abstract Painting 1890–1985*, Los Angeles County Museum of Art (New York: Abbeville Publishers, 1986), p. 18.

155 Janet Sobel: I first came across Janet Sobel when James Brett of the Museum of Everything in London commissioned me to write a piece on her for his gallery in October 2021. This section is an amended version of it: Jennifer Higgie, 'I Paint What I Feel: The Radical Inventions of Janet Sobel', *The Gallery of Everything*, London, October 2021.

157 'I only paint what I feel': Gallery label for Janet Sobel's Milky Way, 1945, Museum of Modern Art, New York. https://www.moma.org/collection/works/80636

157 'In 1942, I'm a tot . . .': Ashley Shapiro, email to James Brett, September 2021.

157 'I don't think that . . .': Gail Levin, 'Janet Sobel: Primitivist, Surrealist, and Abstract Expressionist', *Woman's Art Journal*, vol. 26, no. 1, Spring–Summer 2005, p. 12.

157 'impression of the music . . .': Ibid, p. 8.

159 'Janet Sobell will probably . . .': Maya Blackstone, 'Overlooked No More: Janet Sobel, Whose Art Influenced Jackson Pollock', *New York Times*, 30 July 2021.

159 'the best woman painter . . .': Eleanor Nairne, 'Janet Sobel', *Women in Abstraction* (Paris: Centre Georges Pompidou Service Commercial, 2021), p. 154.

159 'Back in 1944 . . .': Clement Greenberg, 'American-Type Painting', *Art and Culture* (London: Thames and Hudson, 1973), p. 218.

160 'had to create art . . .': Ashley Shapiro, email to James Brett, September 2021.

160 'perhaps the most important . . .': Brian Patterson, 'Art Stop: Janet Sobel', San Diego Museum of Art, 29 March 2012, https://www.youtube.com/watch?v=Isk6sWXzKtE

160 'a magical human being . . .': Ashley Shapiro, email to James Brett, September 2021.

160 'bursting with a flow . . .': Quoted by Maya Blackstone, 'Overlooked No More: Janet Sobel, Whose Art Influenced Jackson Pollock', *New York Times*, 30 July 2021.

The Vibrations of Different Souls

161 'Cinema consists of . . .': Maya Deren, 'Magic is New', *Essential Deren: Collected Writings on Film* (Kingston, New York: Documentext, 2019), p. 206.

161 'I was interested . . .': Marcel Duchamp quoted in 'Eleven Europeans in America', James Johnson Sweeney, ed., *The Museum of Modern Art Bulletin*, New York, vol. 13, no. 4/5, 1946, p. 20.

161 'To all appearances . . .': Marcel Duchamp, 'The Creative Act', Lecture at the Museum of Modern Art, New York, October 19, 1961, accessed online: http://www.fiammascura.com/Duchamp.pdf 1957.

161 Duchamp's interests: Maurice Tuchman, 'Hidden Meanings in Abstract Art', *The Spiritual in Art: Abstract Painting 1890–1985*, Los Angeles County Museum of Art (New York: Abbeville Publishers, 1986), p. 47.

162 'make the world dance': Wieland Rambke, 'Divine Horsemen: Maya Deren and Haitian Vodou', undated, https://magazine.artland.com/maya-deren-and-haitian-vodou

162 'wickedest man in the world': Ithell Colquhoun, *The Living Stones* (London: Peter Owen), Kindle Edition, location 2384.

164 On unfinished art: Graham Williamson, 'Witch's Cradle', Letterboxd, 25 May 2015, https://letterboxd.com/gdw/film/witchs-cradle

165 Frederick Kiesler: Rodrigo Ortiz Monasterio, 'The Witch's Cradle', *Teremoto*, 13 April 2015, https://tinyurl.com/58nnfkxs

165 Paintings hung from ropes: James J. Conway, 'Witch's Cradle', 13 October 2011, *Strange Flowers*, https://tinyurl.com/b3sjtxt3

166 'cabalistic symbols . . .': Maya Deren, 'Programme Note for Witch's Cradle', New York, author's collection, undated, cited in Judith Noble, 'Maya Deren: The Magical Woman as Filmmaker', *Frames Cinema Journal*, undated, https://tinyurl.com/mrx52nah

167 'To understand the misunderstood . . .': Emma Anquinet, 'Suzanne Duchamp: Art Reflecting on a Modern Life', *Woman's Art Journal*, vol. 38, no. 2, Old City Publishing, Inc., Woman's Art Inc., 2017, www.jstor.org/stable/26430758, p. 18.

168 'the unknowable and invisible': Ibid, p. 20.

Demeter in Paris

169 Brief biography of Ithell Colquhoun: Amy Hale, 'The Magic Surrealism of Ithell Colquhoun', 17 June 2020, https://tinyurl.com/yc58pjky

170 A modern Demeter: Ithell Colquhoun's choice of wheat as a reference to Demeter is mentioned in Richard Shillitoe's talk

'Ithell Colquhoun's Islands', 17 December 2018, https://tinyurl.com/3ewe6t4a

172   'The myth belongs . . .': T.S. Eliot, 'Scylla and Charybdis', Lecture in Nice, 29 March 1952, published in *Agenda*, ed. William Cookson and Peter Dale, vol. 23: nos. 1–2 (1985), p. 6.

172   'It was suggested by . . .': Matthew Gale, Catalogue entry for Ithell Colquhoun, T02140 Scylla 1938, Tate Britain, October 1997, https://tinyurl.com/2p8rab4r

172   'For an animist . . .': Ithell Colquhoun, *The Living Stones* (London: Peter Owen (2016), Kindle Edition, location 193.

173   'In the compendia . . .': Charlotte Higgins, *Greek Myths* (London: Random House, 2021), Kindle Edition, pp. 6–7.

173   'When I was born . . .': Madeline Miller, *Circe* (London: Bloomsbury, 2018), p. 1.

173   Circe in the Renaissance: Catherine McCormack, *Women in the Picture* (London: Icon Books, 2021), p. 207.

175   'There is bookishness . . .': Alun Rowlands, 'Notes from the Luminous and the Numinous', essay in the catalogue *The Dark Monarch: Magic and Modernity in British Art* (London: Tate Publishing, 2009), p. xxviii.

176   'Valley of streams . . .': Colquhoun, *The Living Stones*, location 193.

177   'I have always been . . .': André Breton, 'Surrealist Manifesto', in *100 Artists' Manifestos*, ed. Alex Danchev (London: Penguin Modern Classics, Penguin Books), Kindle Edition, location 4425.

179   'relaxed and other-worldly . . .': Colquhoun, *The Living Stones*, location 300.

179   'an attraction for . . .': Ibid, location 1705.

179   'earth energy': Ibid, location 2317.

179   '. . . in 1971, I made . . .': Ithell Colquhoun, foreword to 'Grimoire of the Entangled Thicket', quoted in *The Botanical Mind*, ed. Gina Buenfeld and Martin Clark, Camden Arts Centre, London, 2020, p. 136.

180   Unconventional: Amy Hale, *Ithell Colquhoun: Genius of the Fern Loved Gully* (London: Strange Attractor Press, 2020), p. 20.

180   Website by Richard Shillitoe: http://www.ithellcolquhoun.co.uk

180   'Woman is the magician . . .': Ibid.

181   'Her idea of what . . .': Hale, *Ithell Colquhoun*, p. 271.

181   'transcendent': Zoom conversation between Amy Hale and Jennifer Higgie, 21 July 2022.

181 'Does not all . . .': Ithell Colquhoun, 'Children of the Mantic Stain', essay in the catalogue *The Dark Monarch: Magic and Modernity in British Art* (London: Tate Publishing, 2009), p. 105.

181 'details the full range . . .': Notes sent by Linder to the author via email, 2 June 2021.

182 'He's the only composer . . .': Ibid.

182 'wanted to extend . . .': Telephone conversation between the author and Linder, 9 June 2021.

182 'Where Ithell Colquhoun leads . . .': Notes sent by Linder to the author via email, 2 June 2021.

183 'anxieties, trauma and instability . . .': Martin Clark and Mark Osterfield, Foreword to the catalogue *The Dark Monarch*, p. i.

183 'When the war . . .': Colquhoun, *The Living Stones*, location 200.

185 'There's such a wealth . . .': Telephone conversation between the author and Linder, 9 June 2021.

In the Cards

187 'taro': Telephone conversation with Richard Shillitoe, who explained this on 3 December 2021.

187 'This design for . . .': Ithell Colquhoun, 'The Taro as Colour', 1977, in Steve Nichols, *The Magical Writings of Ithell Colquhoun*, Kindle Edition, p. 161.

188 'portals for contemplation': Zoom conversation between Amy Hale and Jennifer Higgie, 21 July 2022.

188 'After I had completed . . .': Colquhoun, 'The Taro as Colour', p. 161.

189 Tarot around the world: Sharmista Ray, 'Reviving a Forgotten Artist of the Occult', *Hyperallergic*, 23 March 2019, https://hyperallergic.com/490918/pamela-colman-smith-pratt-institute-libraries

189 'These are psychological . . .': *Visions: Notes of the Seminar given in 1930-1934 by C.G. Jung*, edited by Claire Douglas. Vol. 2. (Princeton NJ, Princeton University Press, Bollingen Series XCIX, 1997), p. 923.

189 Tarot's origins: Jessica Hundley, 'The Sacred and the Arcane: A Brief History of Tarot', *Tarot* (Cologne: Taschen, 2021), pp. 12-13.

189 'Like all esoteric . . .': Ibid.

190 'a most imaginative . . .': S. Elizabeth, *The Art of the Occult* (London: Frances Lincoln), Kindle Edition, p. 213.

192 Parts of this section on Pamela Colman Smith were published in my essay 'Pamela Colman Smith: The Queen of Tarot' for *Engelsberg Ideas*, 25 April 2022, https://tinyurl.com/yc8djcjj

192 'Pamela Colman Smith is a young . . .': Dawn Robinson, *Pamela Colman Smith, Tarot Artist: The Pious Pixie* (Stroud: Fonthill Media), Kindle Edition, p. 121.

192 'curious and fascinating': Ibid, pp. 122-3.

192 'What I wish . . .': Sharmista Ray, 'Reviving a Forgotten Artist of the Occult', *Hyperallergic*, 23 March 2019, https://hyperallergic.com/490918/pamela-colman-smith-pratt-institute-libraries

193 'Learn from everything . . .': Colleen Lynch and Melissa Staiger, *Pamela Colman Smith - Life and Work: Exhibition at Pratt Institute Libraries, Brooklyn Campus, curated by Colleen Lynch and Melissa Staiger*, Kindle Edition, 2019, p. 12.

193 Unlikely to have met Colquhoun: Thank you to Richard Shillitoe for clarifying this for me in an email on 6 December 2021.

193 'introduced a gender balance . . .': See: http://www.ithellcolquhoun.co.uk/taro_pack.htm

194 'opportunity to explore . . .': Penny Slinger, 'The Alchemy of Self', *Tarot* (Cologne: Taschen, 2021), p. 6.

195 Unless otherwise mentioned, all Niki de Saint Phalle quotes, http://ilgiardinodeitarocchi.it/en

196 'I'm not a person . . .': Niki de Saint Phalle speaking in the video, *Niki de Saint Phalle, Spirit, 2021 San Diego County Women's Hall of Fame*, Women's Museum of California, https://www.youtube.com/watch?v=SD0_l7kiCcw

Witch Dance

199 'What is magic . . .': Rebecca Tamás, 'Interrogation (1)', WITCH (London: Penned in the Margins, 2019), p. xx.

199 All Donna Huddleston quotes, conversations with the author, early 2021.

200 'visualization of the incomprehensible': Dianne S. Howe, 'The Notion of Mysticism in the Philosophy and Choreography of Mary Wigman 1914-1931', *Dance Research Journal*, vol. 19, no. 1, Congress on Research in Dance, 1987, p. 20.

201 'Dance is unity . . .': Ibid.

201 'I am the dance . . .': Ted Fisher, 'The Choreographer as a Witch in Contemporary Dance Documentaries', *Frame Cinema Journal*, undated, https://tinyurl.com/y8wzb94b

201 'The mystic dance . . .': Howe, 'The Notion of Mysticism in the Philosophy and Choreography of Mary Wigman 1914-1931', p. 20.

202 'Miss Mary Wigman suddenly . . .': 'Mary Wigman, Dance Innova-
tor, Dies', *New York Times*, 20 September 1973, p. 50.

202 'The Nazis were not . . .': Starhawk, 'Witchcraft as Goddess Reli-
gion', 1979, *The Politics of Women's Spirituality: Essays on the Rise of
Spiritual Power within the Feminist Movement*, ed. Charlene Spretnak
(New York: Anchor Books, 1982), p. 56.

203 'fascinatio': Brian Copenhaver, *The Book of Magic* (London: Penguin
Classics), Kindle Edition, p. xv.

205 'to release the truth . . .': J.G. Ballard, 'What I Believe', *Interzone*, #8,
Summer 1984, https://www.jgballard.ca/uncollected_work/what_i_
believe.html

Trees of Knowledge

207 'Though lowly, the plant . . .': Gina Buenfeld, 'The Ur Plant', in *The
Botanical Mind*, ed. Gina Buenfeld and Martin Clark, Camden Arts
Centre, London, 2020, pp. 28, 12-13.

207 Global warming: 'What Caused Australia's Disastrous Wildfires? It's
Complicated', *Physics Today*, 20 March 2020,
https://physicstoday.scitation.org/doi/10.1063/PT.3.4428

207 Climate sceptics: Amy Remeikis and Josh Taylor, 'There Is No Link:
The Climate Doubters Within Scott Morrison's Government', *Guardian*, 15 January 2020, https://tinyurl.com/ys82zkwz

210 'My garden's boundaries . . .': Derek Jarman, *Modern Nature (The
Journals of Derek Jarman)* (London: Random House), Kindle Edition,
p. 19

210 'Songlines: Tracking the Seven Sisters': Part of this section is developed from a piece I wrote for *frieze*: 'Stories from Indigenous
Australia', 30 November 2021, https://www.frieze.com/article/
songlines-review-2021

210 'You mob gotta . . .': Margo Neale, 'Alive with the Dreaming', essay in
the catalogue *Songlines: Tracking the Seven Sisters* (Canberra: National
Museum of Australia Press, 2017), p. 14.

211 'It's a tale of tragedy . . .': Margo Neale, 'The Seven Sisters Songline',
in *Songlines: The Power and the Promise* (First Knowledges) (Melbourne: Thames & Hudson, Australia, 2020), Kindle Edition, p. vii.

212 'The tree which moves . . .': Maria Popova, 'William Blake's Most
Beautiful Letter: A Searing Defense of the Imagination and the Creative Spirit', *The Marginalia*, no date, https://tinyurl.com/yy3d356d

213 'Each plant as . . .': Kate Lebo, 'A Secret, Symbolic History of

Pomegranates', 9 April 2012, https://tinyurl.com/3fhxkbfr

213 'I never eat meat . . .': Leonora Carrington, *The Hearing Trumpet* (London: Penguin Books, 2005), pp. 1-2.

214 'as in cook-ing': Chloe Aridjis, 'Tea and Creatures with Leonora Carrington', *frieze masters*, issue 6, 2017, p. 76.

214 'imbued with a *Fantasia* . . .': Ibid.

214 'I've always had access . . .': Museum of Modern Art, New York, Leonora Carrington, https://www.moma.org/audio/playlist/309/3989

215 'the inner sanctum': Joanna Moorhead, *The Surreal Life of Leonora Carrington*: (New York: Little, Brown), Kindle Edition, p. 12.

216 'never to abandon . . .': Carl Jung, *Memories, Dreams, Reflections: An Autobiography* (London: William Collins, 2019), Kindle Edition, p. 166.

216 'I knew that I would . . .': Ibid.

217 'observe my psychic . . .': Ibid, p. 211.

217 'My mandalas were . . .': Ibid, p. 212.

217 'it is ironical that . . .': Ibid, p. 204.

218 'The Botanical Mind: Art, Mysticism and the Cosmic Tree': organised by Gina Buenfeld and Martin Clark, Camden Arts Centre, London, 2020, https://www.botanicalmind.online/about

218 'During this period . . .': Ibid.

218 Plant motifs: Carl Jung, 'Psychology and Alchemy', quoted in *The Botanical Mind*, ed. Gina Buenfeld and Martin Clark, Camden Arts Centre, London, 2020, p. 28.

219 'To love a painting . . .': Milner, *On Not Being Able to Paint*, p. 29.

219 'the leaves of the Veda . . .': Voss, *Hilma af Klint*, p. 189.

219 'The phenomenon we are . . .': '1 Handwritten note dated 16 Sep 1903, found inside The Five notebook HaK1522, 1904', quoted by Sue Cramer, 'Hilma af Klint, The Secret Growing', in *Hilma af Klint*, ed. Cramer with Chambers, p. 21.

220 'for just as invisible . . .': Cramer with Chambers, 'Hilma af Klint', ibid.

220 'In a flower . . .': Sophie Taeuber quoted in Roswitha Mair, *Sophie Taeuber-Arp and the Avant-Garde*, trans. Damion Searls (Chicago, IL: University of Chicago Press, 2018), p. 48.

221 'But how to tend . . .': http://m12.manifesta.org/planetary-garden/index.html

222 Two in five plants facing extinction: 'The Top Ten Species New to Science', Royal Botanic Gardens, Kew, 17 December 2020 https://www.kew.org/read-and-watch/top-10-species-named-2020

222 'Plants create opportunities . . .': Unless otherwise mentioned, all
    Vivien Sansour quotes are from 'Jennifer Higgie Interviews Vivien
    Sansour on Food, Farming, Heritage and Healing', *frieze*, issue 205,
    accessed online https://tinyurl.com/4tsparjt

223 'far, far brighter . . .': Hildegard von Bingen letter to Guibert of Gem-
    bloux in 1175, *Hildegard of Bingen: Selected Writings* (London: Penguin
    Classics, Penguin Books, 2001), Kindle Edition, location 296.

223 'sacred sound': Mark Atherton, introduction to Hildegard of Bingen:
    Selected Writings, ibid, location 113.

224 On health: Fiona Maddocks, *Hildegard of Bingen: The Woman of Her
    Age* (London: Faber & Faber, 2013), Kindle Edition, p. 151.

225 Lingua ignota: Ibid, p. 124.

225 Not mentioned in music dictionaries: Ibid, p. 188.

225 'lovely music, shame . . .': Ibid, p. 189.

226 Anna Mary Howitt and E.J. French: S. Elizabeth, *The Art of the Occult*
    (London: Frances Lincoln, 2020), Kindle Edition, p. 205.

226 'If I were a man . . .': https://the-line.org/artist/madge-gill-3

226 'exotic melodies . . .': Kate Cherrell and Hélène Smith, 'The
    Medium Who Spoke to Martians', 17 May 2019, Burials and Beyond,
    https://burialsandbeyond.com/2019/05/17/helene-smith-the-
    medium-who-spoke-to-martians

226 'dog-like creatures . . .': Ibid.

227 'I have no imagination . . .': Minnie Evans quoted in Nina Howell
    Starr, 'The Lost World of Minnie Evans', *The Bennington Review*,
    vol. 111, no. 2 (Summer 1969), p. 41. Accessed https://americanart.
    si.edu/artist/minnie-evans-1466

228 'Reality has grown old . . .': Olga Tokarczuk, *Drive Your Plow Over the
    Bones of the Dead* (London: Fitzcarraldo Editions, 2018), p. 65.

228 'it helped me . . .': Olga Tokarczuk, 'Books That Made Me', *Guardian*,
    24 August 2018, https://tinyurl.com/2pat38vz

The Active Imagination

231 'Nature-mystical movements . . .': Yasmin Afschar, 'A Visionary in
    Dialogue with Contemporary Art', *Emma Kunz Cosmos: A Visionary
    in Dialogue with Contemporary Art* (Stockholm: Scheidegger & Spiess,
    2021, in collaboration with the Aargauer Kunsthaus, Aarau), p. 17.

232 'place of encounter . . .': Eranos Foundation: http://www.eranos-
    foundation.org/page.php?page=4&pagename=history

234 'Shape and form . . .': https://www.emma-kunz.com/en/emma-kunz

234 Treatment powers: Ibid.

235 'for a range of health benefits': Hans Ulrich Obrist and Emma Kunz, *Purple magazine, The Cosmos Issue* 32, 2019, https://tinyurl.com/2p8npkmb

235 'Her gift was . . .': 'Emma Kunz, Visionary Drawings', Serpentine Gallery, London, 23 March-19 May 2019, https://tinyurl.com/5n8tw4sr

Weaving Their Way

240 'My women are not . . .': Charlotte Higgins, *Greek Myths* (London: Random House, 2021), Kindle Edition, p. 9.

240 'the goddess of . . .': Ibid, p. 270.

241 'Today life is very . . .': Anni Albers, 'Work with Material', 1938, https://tinyurl.com/mryntxhz

241 Weaving as craft then art: Laura Snoad, 'The 20th-Century Textile Artists You Should Know', Crafts Council UK, https://tinyurl.com/3wt7jmr8

241 'to let threads be . . .': Anni Albers quoted in the exhibition guide to Tate Modern's 'Anni Albers' (2018-19), https://tinyurl.com/bdcns86b

242 'surprise and inventiveness': Anni Albers, 'On Jewelry', 1942, https://tinyurl.com/59p59vzc

243 Minimes: Extract adapted from an essay I wrote on Sheila Hicks's 'minimes' for the catalogue published on the occasion of 'Sheila Hicks: Off Grid' at Hepworth Wakefield, 2022.

244 'If Josef had awakened . . .': Sheila Hicks, 'My Encounters with Anni Albers', *Tate Etc*, 10 October 2018, accessed online: https://tinyurl.com/54sny6j3

244 'What does touching . . .': Jennifer Higgie interviews Sheila Hicks, 'Fibre Is My Alphabet', *frieze* magazine, January 2015.

245 'the transmission of some . . .': George Kubler, *The Shape of Time: Remarks on the History of Things* (New Haven, CT, and London: Yale University Press, 1962), p. 9.

245 'However fragmentary . . .': Ibid, p. 19.

245 'blew her mind': All quotes in this paragraph, Jennifer Higgie interview with Sheila Hicks, 'Fibre Is My Alphabet', *frieze*, 169, March 2015, p. 130.

245 'I care less . . .': Ibid.

246 'the feeling of awe . . .': Guide to the exhibition 'Phenomenal Nature: Mrinalini Mukherjee', The Met Breuer, 4 June-29 September 2019.

247 Lenore Tawney exhibition: 'Lenore Tawney: Part One', Alison

Jacques Gallery, 12 October–6 November 2021.

247 Tawney biography: For details of Lenore Tawney's life and work, see Lenore G. Tawney Foundation, https://lenoretawney.org

247 'I sometimes think . . .': Text for Lenore Tawney artist page, Alison Jacques Gallery, London, https://tinyurl.com/2rrdxktfy

247 'I am seeking . . .': Ibid.

247 'without a touch . . .': Remark by Kathleen Nugent Mangan (executive director, Lenore G. Tawney Foundation), as part of a Zoom discussion organised by Alison Jacques Gallery, London, in response to the exhibition 'Lenore Tawney: Part One'. The panel also included Glenn Adamson, Mark Godfrey and Harry Thorne, 11 October 2021, https://tinyurl.com/23mstdut

247 Death of husband: Lawrence Lee, 'Artist of the Eternal Moment', *American Style*, Spring 1998, p. 58.

248 'the potential of woven . . .': Warren Seelig, 'Thinking Lenore Tawney', in Kathleen Nugent Mangan, Sid Sachs, Warrant Seelig and T'ai Smith, *Lenore Tawney: Wholly Unlooked For* (Baltimore, MD: Maryland Institute College of Art, 2013), p. 19.

249 'I was searching . . .': Lee, 'Artist of the Eternal Moment', p. 58.

249 'To see new . . .': Art Institute of Chicago, page on Lenore Tawney, https://tinyurl.com/mw6nn5aj

250 'I want to be . . .': Lenore Tawney, Alison Jacques Gallery, London, https://tinyurl.com/4f9tystm

250 Lee Lawrence visit: Lee, 'Artist of the Eternal Moment', p. 56.

250 'It's a beautiful dream': Ibid, p. 61.

Temenos

251 'a magic circle . . .': Liliane Lijn, notes on Temenos, sent to the author, 31 October 2021.

252 'embracing angel': Ibid.

252 'The Pythagoreans . . .': Ibid.

252 'and the ways in which . . .': Ibid.

253 'I am alive . . .': Unless otherwise mentioned, all quotes in this passage are from 'Liliane Lijn: My Influences', *frieze*, issue 164, May 2014.

253 'realized that these . . .': Unless otherwise mentioned, the following quotes are from conversations between the author and Liliane Lijn, 17 November 2021

255 'almost knew them . . .': Email from Liliane Lijn to the author, 12 July 2022.

255 'The net had been . . .': Liliane Lijn, *Crossing Map* (London: Thames and Hudson, 1983), p. 29.

256 'traces of a collision . . .': http://www.lilianelijn.com/portfolio-item/catastrophic-encounters-1-2019

256 'As "Lady of Wild Things" . . .': Robert Graves, *The Greek Myths* (London: Penguin Books, 1958), Kindle Edition, p. 86.

256 'earth was singing . . .': Email from Liliane Lijn to the author, 11 July 2022

258 Author visits Liliane: Unless otherwise mentioned, all following quotes are from a conversation between the author and Liliane Lijn, 17 November 2021.

258 'My lady, you are . . .': Jeremy A. Black, *The Literature of Ancient Sumer* (Oxford: Oxford University Press, 2006), p. 316.

Into the Ether

261 'I'm interested in things . . .': Figgy Guyver, 'Artists: The New Paranormal Investigator', *ArtReview*, 7 October 2020.

262 'materials that have power': Betye Saar, 'Influences', *frieze*, issue 182, (27 September 2016), https://tinyurl.com/3f8rmybm

262 'I can no longer . . .': Betye Saar and Beryl Wright, eds, *The Appropriate Object* (Buffalo, NY: Albright-Knox Art Gallery, 1989), p. 54, quoted by the Museum of Modern Art, New York, https://www.moma.org/artists/5102#fn:1

262 'My art is grounded . . .': https://alisonjacques.com/artists/ana-mendieta#top

263 'When I'm painting . . .': Zoom discussion between Portia Zvavahera and Helen Molesworth, David Zwirner Gallery, New York, 5 November 2021.

264 'is focused on . . .': Zoom conversation between Sarah Smuts-Kennedy and Jennifer Higgie, 21 July 2022.

264 'shamanism as a way . . .': Grace Ndiritu, 'Healing the Museum', *Gropius Bau Journal*, 2021, https://tinyurl.com/bdey7ub2

Select Bibliography

Aberth, Susan, Simon Grant, and Lars Bang Larsen, *Not Without My Ghosts: The Artist as Medium*, London: Hayward Gallery Publishing, 2020

Ades, Dawn, and Michael Richardson, eds, with Krzysztof Fijalkowski, *The Surrealism Reader: An Anthology of Ideas*, London: Tate Publishing, 2015

af Klint, Hilma, *Notes and Methods*, University of Chicago Press, annotated edition, 2018

Afschar, Yasmin, ed., *Emma Kunz Cosmos: A Visionary in Dialogue with Contemporary Art*, Aargauer Kunsthaus, Switzerland: Scheidegger & Spiess, 2021

Alemani, Cecilia, *Biennale Arte Venice 2022 – The Milk of Dreams*, Milan: Silvana Editoriale, 2022

Almqvist, Kurt, and Louise Belfrage, eds, *Hilma af Klint: The Art of Seeing the Invisible*, Stockholm: Axel and Margaret Ax:son Johnson Foundation, 2015

Almqvist, Kurt, and Daniel Birnbaum, eds, *Hilma af Klint Catalogue Raisonée* (seven volumes), Stockholm: Bokförlaget Stolpe, 2022

Althaus, Karin, Matthias Mühling, and Sebastian Schneider, eds, *World Receivers: Georgiana Houghton, Hilma af Klint, Emma Kunz*, Munich: Hirmer, 2019

Bashkoff, Tracey, *Hilma af Klint: Paintings for the Future*, New York: Guggenheim Museum Publications, 2018

Bauduin, Tessel M., *Surrealism and the Occult: Occultism and Western Esotericism in the Work and Movement of André Breton*, Amsterdam:

Amsterdam University Press, 2014

Besant, Annie Wood, *An Autobiography*, Kindle Edition, 1893

Besant, Annie, and C.W. Leadbeater, *Thought-Forms*, Brooklyn, NY: Sacred Bones Books, 2020

Bingen, Hildegard of, *Selected Writings*, London: Penguin Classics, 2001

Birnbaum, Daniel, Hans Ulrich Obrist et al., *Hilma af Klint: Painting the Unseen*, Verlag der Buchhandlung Walther Konig, 2016

Blanchflower, Melissa, ed., *Emma Kunz*, Verlag der Buchhandlung Walther Konig, 2019

Blavatsky, Helena, *The Essential Works of Helena Blavatsky: Isis Unveiled, The Secret Doctrine, The Key to Theosophy, The Voice of the Silence, Studies in Occultism, Nightmare Tales*, New York: Musaicum Books, Kindle Edition

Bracewell, Michael, Martin Clark, and Alun Rowlands, eds, *The Dark Monarch: Magic and Modernity in British Art*, London: Tate Publishing, 2009

Bramble, John, *Modernism and the Occult*, London: Palgrave Macmillan, 2015

Braude, Annie, *Radical Spirits and Women's Rights in Nineteenth-Century America*, Bloomington: Indiana University Press, 2020

Buenfeld, Gina, and Martin Clark, eds, *The Botanical Mind: Art, Mysticism and the Cosmic Tree*, London: Camden Arts Centre, 2020

Butcher, Carmen Acevedo, *Hildegard of Bingen: A Spiritual Reader*, Orleans: Paraclete Press, 2009

Calvino, Italo, *The Castle of Crossed Destinies*, London: Vintage Classics, 1998

Carrington, Leonora, *The Milk of Dreams*, New York: The New York Review Children's Collection, 2013

Chadwick, *Whitney, Women Artists and the Surrealist Movement*, London: Thames and Hudson, (revised edition), 2021

Choucha, Nadia, *Surrealism & the Occult*, Oxford: Mandrake of Oxford, 1991

Colquhoun, Ithell, *The Goose of Hermogenes*, London: Peter Owen, 1961

Colquhoun, Ithell, *The Crying of the Wind: Ireland*, London: Peter Owen, 2016

Colquhoun, Ithell, *The Living Stones: Cornwall*, London: Peter Owen, 2016, Kindle edition

Conan Doyle, Sir Arthur, *The History of Spiritualism*, two vols., London, New York, Toronto, and Melbourne: Cassell, 1926

Conan Doyle, Sir Arthur, *The Vital Message*, London: The Psychic Press and Bookshop, 1925

Conan Doyle, Sir Arthur, *Pheneas Speaks*, London: The Psychic Press and Bookshop, 1927

Copenhaver, Brian, *The Book of Magic: From Antiquity to the Enlightenment*, London: Penguin Classics, 2015

Cozzolino, Robert, ed., *Supernatural America: The Paranormal in American Art*, Minneapolis Institute of Art, in association with The University of Chicago Press, 2021

Cramer, Sue, ed., with Nicholas Chambers, *Hilma af Klint: The Secret Paintings*, Sydney: Art Gallery of New South Wales; Wellington: City Gallery, Te Whare Toi Te Ngākau Civic Square; in association with the Heide Museum of Modern Art, 2021

Danto, Arthur C., Joan Simon, and Nina Stritzler-Levin, *Sheila Hicks: Weaving as Metaphor*, New Haven and London: Yale University Press, 2018

de Martino, Ernesto, *Magic, A Theory from the South*, Translated and Annotated by Dorothy Louise Zinn, Chicago, IL: Hau Books, 2001

Deren, Maya, *Essential Deren: Collected Writings on Film*, Documentext, New York: Kingston, 2019

Dore, Jessica, *Tarot for Change*, London: Hay House, 2021

Duchamp, Marcel, *The Writings of Marcel Duchamp*, Boston, MA: Da Capo Press, 1989

Elizabeth, S., *The Art of the Occult*, London: Frances Lincoln, Kindle

Edition, White Lion Publishing, 2020

Elkins, James, *On the Strange Place of Religion in Contemporary Art*, London: Routledge, 2004

Federici, Silvia, *Witches, Witch-Hunting and Women*, Oakland, CA: PM Press, 2018

Federici, Silvia, *Caliban and the Witch*, London: Penguin Modern Classics, 2021

Fer, Briony, *On Abstract Art*, New Haven and London: Yale University Press, 1997

Gamwell, Lynn, *Exploring the Visible: Art, Science and the Spiritual*, Princeton, NJ: Princeton University Press, 2002

Gipson, Ferren *Women's Work: From Feminine Arts to Feminist Art*, London: Frances Lincoln, 2022

Grant, Simon, Lars Bang Larsen, and Marco Pasi, *Georgiana Houghton, Spirit Drawings*, London: The Courtauld Gallery, organised in collaboration with Monash University Museum of Art, 2016

Graves, Robert, *The Greek Myths*, London: Penguin Books, 1958

Hale, Amy, *Ithell Colquhoun: Genius of the Fern Loved Gully*, London: Strange Attractor Press, 2020

Hale, Amy, *Essays on Women in Western Esotericism: Beyond Seeresses and Sea Priestesses*, London: Palgrave Macmillan, 2022

Hessel, Katy, *The Story of Art Without Men*, Huchinson Heinemann, 2022

Higgins, Charlotte, *The Greek Myths*, London: Vintage, 2021

Homer, *The Odyssey*, London: Penguin Classics, 2003

Houghton, Georgiana, *Evenings at Home in Spiritual Séance*, Hardpress, Kindle Edition, 2018

Houghton, Georgiana, *Catalogue of the Spirit Drawings in Water Colours, Exhibited at the New British Gallery, Old Bond Street. By Miss Houghton, through Whose Mediumship They Have Been Executed*, London: W. Corby, 1871

Howitt, Anna Mary, 'Sisters in Art', *The Illustrated Exhibitor and*

Magazine of Art, vol. II, John Cassell, La Belle Sauvage Yard, Ludgate Hill, London, 1852

Howitt, Anna Mary, *An Art Student in Munich*, Miami: Hardpress, 2017

Hundley, Jessica, *Tarot: The Library of Esoterica*, Cologne: Taschen, 2021

Jarman, Derek, *Modern Nature*, London: Vintage Classics, 2018

Jung, Carl, *Memories, Dreams, Reflections: An Autobiography*, London: Fontana Press, 1995

Jung, Carl, *The Red Book*, New York: Philemon Foundation and W.W. Norton, 2009

Kandinsky, Wassily, *Concerning the Spiritual in Art and Painting in Particular*, trans. W.T.H. Sadler, Barakaldo Books, 2020

Kaplan, Stuart R., *Pamela Colman Smith: The Untold Story*, Stamford: U.S. Games Systems Inc.; illustrated edition, 2018

Klee, Paul, *Creative Confession and Other Writings*, London: Tate Publishing, 2013

Kubler, George, *The Shape of Time: Remarks on the History of Things*, New Haven and London: Yale University Press, 1962

Lachman, Gary, *Madame Blavatsky*, London: Penguin, 2012

Langdon, Helen, *Salvator Rosa, Paint and Performance*, London: Reaktion Books, 2022

Le Guin, Ursula K., *The Carrier Bag of Fiction*, London: Ignota, 2019

Lijn, Lilian, *Crossing Map*, London: Thames and Hudson, 1983

Lodge, Oliver J., *Raymond, or Life and Death*, London: Methuen, 1916

Lynch, Colleen, and Melissa Staiger, eds, *Pamela Colman Smith, Life and Work*, Brooklyn: Stuber Publishing, 2020

Macel, Christine, and Laure Chauvelot, eds, *Women in Abstraction*, Paris: Centre Georges Pompidou Service Commercial, 2021

Maddocks, Fiona, *Hildegard of Bingen: The Woman of Her Age*, London: Faber & Faber, 2003

Martineau, Jane, ed., *Victorian Fairy Painting*, London: Royal Academy of Arts; Iowa: The University of Iowa Museum of Art; The

Art Gallery of Ontario, Toronto; London: Merrell Holberton Publishers, 1997

McDermott, Robert, ed., *The New Essential Rudolf Steiner: An Introduction to Rudolf Steiner for the Twenty-First Century*, Hudson: Lindisfarne Books, 2010

Meade, Marian, *Madame Blavatsky: The Woman Behind the Myth*, New York: Open Road Media, 2014

Midorikawa, Emily, *Out of the Shadows: Six Visionary Victorian Women in Search of a Voice*, Berkeley, CA: Counterpoint, 2021

Miller, Madeline, *Circe*, London: Bloomsbury Publishing, 2018

Miller, Madeline, *The Song of Achilles*, London: Bloomsbury Publishing, 2011

Milner, Marion, *On Not Being Able to Paint*, New York: Taylor and Francis, 1956

Moorehead, Joanna, *The Surreal Life of Leonora Carrington*, London: Virago, 2019

Neale, Margo, ed., *Songlines: Tracking the Seven Sisters*, Canberra: National Museum of Australia Press, 2017

Neale, Margo, and Lynne Kelly, *Songlines: The Power and the Promise* (First Knowledges), Melbourne: Thames and Hudson (Australia), 2020

Nugent Mangan, Kathleen, Sid Sachs, Warrant Seelig, and T'ai Smith, *Lenore Tawney: Wholly Unlooked For*, Baltimore, MD: Maryland Institute College of Art, 2013

Owen, Alex, *The Darkened Room: Women, Power, and Spiritualism in Late Victorian England*, Chicago, IL: University of Chicago Press, 1989

Parker, Rozsika, and Griselda, Pollock, *Old Mistresses: Women, Art and Ideology*, London: Bloomsbury Academic, 2020

Patterson, Karen, *Lenore Tawney: Mirror of the Universe*, Chicago, IL: University of Chicago Press, 2019

Rabinovitch, Celia, *Surrealism and the Sacred: Power, Eros and the Occult in Modern Art*, New York: Basic Books, 2002

Robinson, Dawn, *Pamela Colman Smith, Tarot Artist: The Pious Pixie*, Stroud: Fonthill Media, 2020

Rudick, Nicole, *What Is Now Known Was Once Only Imagined: An (Auto)biography of Niki de Saint Phalle*, New York: Siglio, 2022

Shillitoe, Richard, *Ithell Colquhoun: Magician Born of Nature*, lulu.com, 2010

Shin, Sarah, and Rebecca Tamás, eds, *Spells: Twenty-First Century Occult Poetry*, London: Ignota, 2019

Shin, Sarah, and Ben Vickers, eds, *Altered States*, London: Ignota, 2021

Simon, Joan, and Whitney Chadwick, *Sheila Hicks: Fifty Years*, Andover, MA: Addison Gallery of American Art, 2010

Spretnak, Charlene, *The Spiritual Dynamic in Modern Art: Art History Reconsidered, 1800 to the Present*, New York: Palgrave Macmillan, 2014

Spretnak, Charlene, ed., *The Politics of Women's Spirituality: Essays on the Rise of Spiritual Power within the Feminist Movement*, New York: Anchor Books, 1982

Subelyte, Gražina, and Daniel Zamani, eds, *Surrealism and Magic: Enchanted Modernity*, Munich, London, and New York: Prestel, 2022

Sutcliffe, Jamie, ed., *Magic*, Cambridge, MA: MIT Press, Whitechapel Documents of Contemporary Art, 2021

Tamás, Rebecca, *WITCH*, London: Penned in the Margins, 2019

Thorne, Sam, and Rachel Thomas, eds, *As Above, So Below: Portals, Visions, Spirits and Mystics*, Dublin: IMMA Publishing, 2017

Tokarczuk, Olga, *Drive Your Plow Over the Bones of the Dead*, London: Fitzcarraldo Editions, 2018

Tompkins, Calvin, *Duchamp: A Biography*, New York: The Museum of Modern Art, 2014

Tuchman, Maurice, ed., *The Spiritual in Art: Abstract Painting 1890–1985*, Los Angeles, CA: Los Angeles County Museum of Art; New York: Abbeville Publishers, 1986

Vicario, Gilbert, *Agnes Pelton, Desert Transcendentalist*, Phoenix Art Museum; Munich: Hirmer Verlag, 2019

Voss, Julia, *Hilma af Klint: A Biography* (trans. Anne Posten), Chicago, IL, and London: University of Chicago Press, 2022

Warner, Marina, *Phantasmagoria*, Oxford: Oxford University Press, 2006

Wohlleben, Peter (transl. Jane Billinghurst), *The Hidden Life of Trees*, London: Harper Collins, 2017

Zegher, Catherine de, ed., *3x an Abstraction: New Methods of Drawing by Hilma Af Klint, Emma Kunz and Agnes Martin*, New Haven, CT, and London: Yale University Press, 2005

Acknowledgements

I am eternally grateful to my publisher Jenny Lord and my agent, David Godwin, for their wisdom, support and enthusiasm. A huge thank you to the brilliant team at Orion: Elizabeth Allen, Eleni Caulcott, Hannah Cox, Cait Davies, Natalie Dawkins, Richard Mason, Kate Moreton, Leanne Oliver, Clarissa Sutherland, Emily Taylor and Liam Wheatley.

Thank you to Donna Huddleston for her generosity in granting permission to use her extraordinary drawing for the cover; also to Dominic Eichler, Jennifer Kabat and Shelley Klein, who read early versions of this manuscript and whose suggestions were invaluable. An edited section of this book was the subject of a five-part BBC Radio 3 essay that was broadcast at the beginning of 2022: many thanks to the commissioner, Matthew Dodd, Joby Waldman of Reduced Listening and my editor Chris Elcombe. Huge thanks to Vivienne Roberts at the College of Psychic Studies, who has taught me so much about nineteenth-century women, art and spirituality, and Amy Hale, Victoria Jenkins, Richard Shillitoe and Linder for so generously sharing their vast knowledge of Ithell Colquhoun. Thank you to Daniel Birnbaum, Sue Cramer and Julia Voss for their deep insights and tireless research into the life and work of Hilma af Klint, and Margo Neale for teaching me so much about First Nations Australian art and culture. I'm so grateful to Luke Milne for his beautiful Amorgian hospitality, Toby Follett in Syros and Sylvia Kouvali in Athens. This book is the result of too many conversations to mention but in particular I would like to thank Yasmin Afschar, Chloe Aridjis, Michael Bracewell, James Brett, Lisa Brice, Judith Clark, Simon Grant, Frank Hannon, Sheila Hicks, Liliane Lijn, Caroline Marciniak, Martine Murray, Barbara Novak, David Noonan, Felicity Packard and Renee So. Thank you, too, to everyone who so generously allowed images to be reproduced and words to be quoted. I am indebted to every author and artist cited in my bibliography and endnotes. An endless thank you to my beloved family, near and far, in particular my brother Andrew Higgie and my mother, Jean Higgie, for her unwavering support. I dedicate this book to the kindest and most musical of sisters, Suzie Higgie.

Illustration Credits

p. 163 Public domain sourced / Access rights from Archive PL / Alamy Stock Photo.

p. 169 Artwork © Man Ray 2015 Trust / DACS, London. Photo © Guy Carrard - Centre Pompidou, MNAM-CCI / Dist. RMN-GP.

p. 174 *Circe*, photo Julia Margaret Cameron (1815-79). © Victoria and Albert Museum, London.

p. 191 Wikimedia Commons.

p. 200 Jerome Robbins Dance Division, The New York Public Library. 'Mary Wigman in Hexentanz'. Photographer Dursthoff, Hans.

p. 214 Chloe Aridjis.

p. 231 Ciourtest of Eranos Foundation.

p. 236 Staatsarchiv Appenzell Ausserrhoden. Photographer: Werner Schoch.

p. 239 Anni Albers © Western Regional Archives.

p. 243 Photo by Ferdinand Boesch. Courtesy American Craft Council Library & Archive.

p. 254 Courtesy of Lilian Lijn. Photo by Pablo Volta.

Illustrations in the plates

1. Hildegard von Bingen, illumination from *Liber Scivias*, c.1151. Public domain sourced / Access rights from The History Collection / Alamy Stock Photo.

2. Richard Dadd, *The Fairy Feller's Master Stroke*, 1855-64. Artwork © Richard Dadd 1817-1886. Photo © Vidimages / Alamy Stock Photo.

3. Georgiana Houghton, *The Spiritual Crown of Mrs Oliphant*, 1867. Georgiana Houghton / College of Psychic Studies.

4. Georgiana Houghton, *The Spiritual Crown of Annie Mary Howitt Watts*, 24 April 1867. © Public domain.

5. Margaret Watts Hughes, *Voice Figure*, late nineteenth century. © Public domain.

6. 'Astral Plane', plate from *Thought Forms*, 1905: Charles Walker Collection / Alamy.

7. Hilma af Klint, 'Adulthood', from *The Ten Largest*, 1907. Photo by Historic Images / Alamy Stock Photo.

8. Wassily Kandinsky, *Composition V*, 1911. The Artchives / Alamy Stock Photo.

9. Estella Canziani, *The Piper of Dreams*, 1915. Medici / Mary Evans.

10. Suzanne Duchamp, *Broken and Restored Multiplication*, 1918. Artwork © Suzanne Duchamp / ADAGP, Paris and DACS, London 2022. Photo © Art Institute of Chicago / Bridgeman Images.

11. Carl Jung, 'Tree of Life', image from *The Red Book*, 1922. © 2009 Foundation of the Works of C.G. Jung. First published by W.W. Norton & Co.

12. Ithell Colquhoun, *Scylla*, 1938. Artwork © Samaritans, © Noise Abatement Society & © Spire Healthcare. Photo © Tate Images.

13. Janet Sobel, *The Milky Way*, 1945. Digital image, The Museum of Modern Art, New York / Scala, Florence.

14. Madge Gill, *untitled*, 1954. Photo © The Museum of Everything.

15. Unica Zürn, *untitled*, 1955. Photo © The Museum of Everything.

16. Lenore Tawney, 1959, portrait by Yousuf Karsh. Photographer: Yousuf Karsh / Camera Press

17. Minnie Evans, *untitled*, 1968. Photo © The Museum of Everything. Artwork © Minnie Evans Estate.

18. Liliane Lijn, *Conjunction of Opposites: Lady of the Wild Things and Woman of War*, 1986. © Liliane Lijn. All Rights Reserved, DACS 2022.

19. Niki de Saint Phalle, *The Empress*, The Tarot Garden, 1998. Photo by Alex Ramsay / Alamy Stock Photo. Artwork ©

Niki de Saint Phalle Charitable Art Foundation / ADAGP, Paris and DACS, London 2022.

20. Goshka Macuga, *Madame Blavatsky*, 2007. © Goshka Macuga. All rights reserved, DACS / Artimage 2022.

21. Ngamaru Bidu, Yikartu Bumba, Kumpaya Girgirba, Thelma Judson, Yuwali Janice Nixon, Reena Rogers, Karnu Nancy Taylor, Ngalangka Nola Taylor, *Yarrkalpa (Hunting Ground)*, Parnngurr Area, 2013.

22. Linder, *Children of the Mantic Stain*, 2016. Northern Ballet, Leeds, 2015. Choreography: Kenneth Tindall. Venue: The Clore Ballroom at Royal Festival Hall, London. Photographer: Justin Slee. Courtesy of the artist, Modern Art, London; Northern Ballet, 2015; and Dovecot Studios Ltd.

23. Sheila Hicks, *Escalade Beyond Chromatic Lands*, installation at the Venice Biennale, 2016-17. © Sheila Hicks. Courtesy: Alison Jacques, London. Photo: Michael Brzezinski.

24. Donna Huddleston, *Brighter*, 2021. Courtesy of the artist and Simon Lee Gallery.

Index

Page numbers in *italic* refer to the illustrations